Sex in Christianity and Psychoanalysis

William Graham Cole

Sex in Christianity and Psychoanalysis

New York

Oxford University Press

1955

Printed in the United States of America

To Doris

CONTENTS

INTRODUCTION

Sex is one of the most fundamental facts of human life. We pass through its portals into life and in turn usher our own progeny between its gates; it is the organic link, binding us to past and future. Our sexuality unites us to all forms of animal life and to most forms of the plant kingdom. Asexual reproduction is limited to a very small portion of the phenomenon we call life.

Yet man alone has interpretations of sex. Man alone exercises a degree of self-conscious control over his sexual behavior. The animal creates no codes of sexual morality. Non-human life couples and begets in accordance with timeless laws of instinct. While monogamy and certain analogues to human love are to be found among birds and other mammals, there is no evidence that this represents deliberate choice, the suppression of certain tendencies and desires for others which are regarded as greater goods. In the animal world, each individual within a species duplicates in his own life the history of every other member of that species. Only man seems to possess a certain freedom with regard to his sexual activity. In personal love, he rises to heights unknown to the lower forms of life, and in perversions of the sexual drive, he sinks to depths likewise unknown among the animals.

This freedom evidently gives rise to a measure of anxiety about sex, for every society, however primitive, has its sexual taboos. No such anxiety and no such taboos are to be found among animals.

Deviations from the 'norm,' for example, homosexual relations between two male dogs or two male monkeys do not, so far as can be seen, produce any sense of guilt or shame, nor do they give rise to any disapproval in other members of the species. Sexual norms seem to be an exclusively human creation. Yet it would be difficult to find any specific norm which is universally valid for all ages and all cultures. Sexual standards vary widely from society to society and from group to group. Fifth-century Athens held love between men in high esteem, and the ancient Hittites freely practiced incest. But regardless of the content of the laws and taboos governing sexual behavior, there seem always to be such laws. Nowhere do we find human beings living in utter abandon, indulging their sexual drives in whatever fashion strikes their fancy, regarding the method of release from sexual tension and the object of sexual desire as matters of indifference. There is no society which looks upon sexual activity as purely 'natural,' requiring no governance and no control. Always certain types of sexual activity are forbidden; always there seems to be a fear of the power of the libido if left completely unbridled and uninhibited.

In our own western civilization, the sexual *mores* have been determined for centuries by the Judao-Christian tradition. This is not to say that there have not been deviations from the norms established by that tradition, but these have been the exceptions. On the whole, society has obeyed the dicta of the Old Testament and the Christian Church, and even the deviants have been profoundly influenced by those dicta. Underlying the codes of morality, the specific items of command and taboo, there is an attitude, an interpretation of sex which has been well-nigh universal in the western world, and this has been the interpretation of the Church. In recent decades, there has been what is regarded by many as a kind of sexual revolution. Sigmund Freud and the whole school of psychoanalysis have profoundly challenged the accepted standards of our society, and on the basis of an impressive mass of clinical data, they offer an alternative interpretation of sex. Without indicating that there is any necessary relationship of cause and effect, we may suggest that the revolution has extended to behavior as well as to thought. Whatever one may think of the work of Dr. Kinsey, there are many signs that the sexual practices of both men and women are in our time undergoing significant changes. The 'accepted standards' of our society are being subjected to a scrutiny and a questioning as they have not been before. Individuals, indeed society as a whole, are beginning to wonder whether our sexual codes and *mores* are not sadly outdated and in need of thorough revision. The whole interpretation of sex, the ideological base on which these codes are built, is being given a detailed examination.

Against this background, it seems worth while to offer a study of Christian interpretations of sex side by side with the psychoanalytic interpretations. The concern of the ensuing pages is not so much with a sociological study of sexual codes and patterns of behavior as with an ideological study of the basic attitudes that produced those codes. Obviously, it is not possible within the limits of one volume to present anything like a detailed account of the development of those ideas and attitudes, either in Christianity or in the psychoanalytic traditions, and what is offered here is a synopsis, a view of the most important eras in each school. Part One deals with interpretations of sex in Christianity, beginning with Jesus and Paul, moving to Augustine as the link between the ancient and medieval worlds. The classical Catholic and Protestant ideas are examined through Thomas Aquinas and the Council of Trent on the one hand, and Martin Luther and John Calvin on the other. The section concludes with a survey of the contemporary scene in both Catholic and Protestant circles. Part Two surveys the psychoanalytic interpretations of sex first in the writings of Sigmund Freud and then in the work of some of the present-day analysts. Part Three represents an attempt at a critical reconstruction of a Christian interpretation of sex, a restatement for our own times, in view of the historical background and the psychoanalytic findings.

W. G. C.

Williamstown, Massachusetts
June 1955

ACKNOWLEDGMENTS

No AUTHOR is unto himself an island. He is more like a coral reef, constructed out of the countless bodies of ideas contributed to him by others: parents, teachers, friends, and other authors. Only the prodigious memory of a Marcel Proust could do justice to the totality of one's indebtedness to things past. The more modest memory must be content with the most vivid impressions.

To Aaron Karush, M.D., my debt extends far beyond the scope of these pages. He has served as the Socratic midwife to many important insights and ideas. Professor William A. Christian, of the Department of Religion at Yale University, a former colleague on the Faculty of Smith College, read the first draft of the manuscript and made many valuable suggestions. Professor Horace L. Friess, of Columbia University, and the late Professor David E. Roberts, of Union Theological Seminary, patiently and carefully labored with me through the entire enterprise, and from them I learned what it means to be a teacher. The untimely death of Dr. Roberts last January was not only a great personal loss but a loss to the whole field of religion and psychotherapy in which he was a pioneer. He brought to bear on the problems a double competence all too rare. Professor Paul Tillich, now of Harvard University, through his lectures, books, and personal conversations, has been of invaluable assistance, and my indebtedness to him is readily apparent in the ensuing pages. William Murphy, M.D.,

took the time for two readings of the manuscript and offered several helpful criticisms, especially of Part Two. The Class of 1900
Fund of Williams College has made possible the typing of two
drafts of the book, and grateful acknowledgment of that fact is
here recorded. The gentle warmth and sustained encouragement
of Mr. Wilbur D. Ruggles, Religious Editor of the Oxford University Press, have contributed in no small measure to the writing
of these pages.

My greatest debt is to my wife, who has not only struggled with
my illegible handwriting, typed pages without number, and played
the role of the indispensable Martha, but has also at every step
of the way offered constructive criticisms, stimulating suggestions,
and unflagging interest. Her active participation in the work
should entitle her to be listed as co-author, and to her the volume
is dedicated with affection and gratitude.

ONE

Interpretations of Sex in Christianity

JESUS AND PAUL

WESTERN CIVILIZATION is like an Oriental rug. Many hands have contributed to its weaving, and numerous threads of varied hues constitute its pattern. Greek classicism, Old Testament Hebraism, Roman law, Christianity, Teutonic tribal customs, these are but a few of the more clearly discernible strands which have been laid upon the loom of the centuries. Two of these threads are the particular concern of this book: their origins and their vicissitudes as they move in and out, back and forth across the weaving. One of them is the thread of naturalism, a term which is used here in a special sense to mean a positive and accepting attitude toward the physical, material world. The other is the thread of dualism, defined as a point of view that regards the realm of matter as illusory or evil, or both, and displays a marked preference for the 'spiritual.' Interpretations of sex in the western world have usually been characterized by one or the other of these two outlooks. Essentially naturalistic individuals or societies have accepted the sexual nature of man with gratitude and even joy. In some manifestations, there has been an exuberance almost without restraint, as in Rabelais, or Boccaccio, while in others a more dignified moderation has prevailed, as in Aristotle, or Montaigne. But even the advocates of the golden mean reveal little or no hostility to the erotic as such. They counsel moderation in all things, even in virtue! They do not, like the dualists, regard man's passion as his

3

problem but as his prize. They glory in the beauty of the naked human form, seeking to perfect it in the Olympic Games, in the sculpture of fifth-century Athens to exalt it, and in the painting of the Renaissance to sanctify it. They write odes to the goddess Eros, from the bibulous banqueteers of Plato's *Symposium*, to the flirtatious knights and ladies of Castiglione's *Courtier,* to the un-inhibited protagonists of Joyce's *Ulysses.* The scarlet thread of naturalism appears in the first pattern of the weaving, and though it seems, at times, almost to vanish, obscured by the somber and sober blue of dualism, it persists in its undulating presence.

It is from what Will Durant calls 'Our Oriental Heritage' that the second strand derives. The dualist is he who regards the body as a tomb from which the immortal soul must be released. The visible world, peopled with tangible, physical bodies, is the realm of illusion, and bondage to it means death. The *real* world is im-material and invisible, at least to the eyes of the flesh. The goal of life is to soar above the sordid demands of the body, to achieve the liberation of the spirit through contemplation of the eternal verities. And such a good can be realized only by walking the harsh and narrow path of asceticism, by sternly resisting the allur-ing but faded primroses which grow beside the road. For if the soul allows itself to become enamored and ensnared by the fad-ing beauties of mortal flesh, then it will share the ultimate destiny of all flesh, mortality and death. So gluttony and greed and espe-cially lust are to be rigidly checked, disciplined, and finally ex-tirpated. The dualists shrink from nudity, covering the genitals of the gods of Praxiteles and Phidias with fig leaves, painting modest draperies over the Venuses of the Renaissance. They sing hymns of praise to virginity and celibacy, from the sages of the Hellenistic Age to the medieval monastics. They regard their life as a pil-grimage through a strange and tempting world, from the Pythag-oreans to the Puritans. The rug becomes at times a cloth of blue.

It is one of the myths of modernity that the strands of dualism were first woven into the fabric of western civilization by Chris-tianity. The earliest squares were, so it is popularly understood, all scarlet, all naturalistic, created by the happy and healthy pagans of Hellas. Even the gods of Olympus were well versed in the arts of love from philandering Zeus to poor, lame Hephaestos mooning after the remote Aphrodite. The heroes of Homer quarreled over a prize of war feminine and fair far more fiercely than over gold. Physical perfection was a cult in which the numerous gymnasia served as temples. What contrast to the anti-feminism of the Apostle Paul, the graceless asceticism of the church fathers! The ranks of those pointing the accusing finger at Christianity have not lacked ever-fresh recruits. The mythical account of man's fall contained in Genesis has been superseded by a new one. The first parents of western man, according to this legend, were Greeks, walking naked and unashamed in the Garden of Hellas. They played together as lovely children, carefree and guiltless in their sexual freedom. Then entered the serpent, who was really the Church in disguise, and persuaded these holy innocents that their bodies were evil and disgusting, that they must cover their nakedness and control their desires. He did not succeed in persuading them to give up sex altogether. After all, he was realistic enough to admit that the race must be carried on, somehow. But he did render it exceedingly difficult, if not impossible, for anyone ever completely to enjoy sex again. Henceforth, western man was fallen, an aura of guilt destined to hang over what had previously been untrammeled and free.

It is remarkable how widespread belief in this myth has become, even among those who ought to know better. One historian has called it 'a modern literary mirage, more popular among essayists and journalists than among classical scholars.' For the fact of the matter is that the strand of dualism is contributed to western civilization and not merely contributed but laid on so heavily that it becomes the dominant pattern, not by Christianity at all but by Hellenistic culture, which begins in the fourth century before Christ. There is some truth in the assertion that classical Greek civilization was naturalistic. From Homer to Aristotle, the dominant motif of the age was summed up in the one word, *sophrosune*, moderation. Any man who refused to accept the joys of the flesh made himself an object of curiosity and pity, like Euripides' Hippolytus, who sought to lead a life of celibacy. The libertine, on the other hand, was equally censured, for he also violated the golden mean, transgressed the *via media*. Asceticism and over-indulgence were alike condemned. Sin was not sensuality but the violation of measure, the rupture of the bonds of delicate balance. Sex was to be savored and enjoyed like wine or sweet-meats, never in excess because the aftereffects corroded the experience with a sordid and painful rust. This temperate and healthy naturalism prevailed in the flourishing days of the Greek city state. But even as early as the fifth century, the Pythagoreans sounded their hymn of *soma sema,* the body is a tomb, and they clearly impressed and influenced Plato. Dualism remained in the background, however, until the devastation of the Peloponnesian wars had prepared the way for the Alexandrian Empire. Then the naturalistic spirit perished with the Athenian democracy, giving way to the so-called 'failure of nerve.' Alexander saw himself as the apostle of Hellenism, the purveyor of Greek culture to the backward and unenlightened Orient. And no doubt his mission in some measure succeeded. But the traffic was by no means one way. The twain of East and West did meet in the wake of the Macedonian conqueror. The dualism of Egypt and Mesopotamia and India flowed at full tide into Greece. The Oriental mystery cults blended with their Hellenic counterparts. It would be difficult to award the prize of cultural conquest, to declare that the West had evangelized the East or whether missioner had turned convert. Actually, neither carried off the victor's laurel wreath. The result was rather a syncretism, a blending of the two civilizations into a new creation, the culture of the Hellenistic Age. Life's goal was now summed up in one word, *ataraxia,* detachment, freedom from passion. Stoic and Epicurean alike withdrew from the world of the flesh into the citadel of the soul. Salvation, conceived as immortality of the spirit, was the goal which all men sought. At whatever point a study of Hellenistic culture begins, dualism is encountered. It was the presupposition of all thought, all writing, and it was the soil in which the pale flowers of asceticism grew. Sex was regarded as low and degrading, an act in which man descended to the level of the beast. Epicurus, the philosopher of hedonism, declared that 'nobody was ever the better for the carnal act, and a man may be thankful if he was not definitely the worse.'

The corrupting serpent in the Garden of Hellas, then, was not the Church but a far older form of life, and western man was 'fallen' long before Christianity made its appearance. Of course, the new Gospel was born in the late Hellenistic Age, and it shared the fate of every other cultural movement of the period, adopting the prevailing coloration of the environment. There was no philosophical school or religious cult in the Graeco-Roman world which was not in some respect dualistic. Even Judaism, with its naturalistic heritage from patriarch and prophet, was not unaffected in the Persian and Greek periods of Israel's history. The mystery cults of Isis and Osiris, the Persian Mithras, the Syrian Baals proffered release from bondage to the mortal flesh and multitudes responded. If Christianity had not in some measure spoken in accents to which the ear of the age was attuned, it would have remained an obscure sect within the Jewish faith. That it did so speak is clear both from the New Testament itself and from the writings of the Greek and Latin fathers of the Church. Origen castrated himself in order to escape the temptations of lust; John Chrysostom declared that 'virginity is greatly superior to marriage'; and Tertullian regarded sex even within marriage as sinful. St. Paul wrote in the *lingua franca* of his time, and he unavoidably used terms which were the common coin of the Mediterranean world. Even the Gospels were written in Greek so that the portraits of Jesus were not entirely uncolored by the prevailing view.

Yet Christianity did not surrender unconditionally to Hellenistic dualism. The Church steadfastly resisted numerous efforts to sever the new faith from its Hebrew roots, to erase all traces of naturalism. The temptation of the Gospel to accommodate itself to the spirit of the age by minimizing or omitting entirely the scandalous and offensive doctrines of creation and incarnation was strong as is evident from the numerous heresies of the early centuries, all of which were essentially Hellenistic. Gnosticism denied that creation was the work of God, that the Logos had truly become flesh. Marcion denied the Old Testament any place in Christian Scripture. Montanism went to extremes in its otherworldly asceticism. The essential aim of the heretics was, in one way or another, to cast a shadow upon the material world, to exalt the spirit at the expense of the flesh. The fact that the Church branded these attempts as heretical is testimony to the naturalism of Christianity, its steady insistence upon creation and incarnation as indispensable to the true faith. The phrase referring to God as 'maker of heaven and earth' inserted in the so-called Apostle's Creed near the beginning of the second century as well as the emphasis upon the Word made flesh in the Johannine writings, which come from the same period, are evidence of the Church's struggle against the dualism of the Gnostic movement. The early Church understood the issues well. They resolutely resisted attempts to transform Christianity into another Hellenistic mystery cult. They held fast to their Jewish heritage in affirming their faith in the essential goodness of the created world and in God's love for that world, a love so great that 'He gave His only begotten Son' to take upon himself human flesh. Any suggestion that Jesus was in any respect less than wholly human was rejected.

The victory of Hellenistic dualism over Hebrew naturalism was, then, a limited one, achieving its most dramatic triumph in the realm of sex. The vantage point of contemporary naturalism enables the modern student to recognize that the negative attitude toward the bodily aspects of life manifest in the asceticism of early Christianity is sharply inconsistent with the total outlook of the Gospel which is positive in its acceptance of the material world. Such a recognition is, however, a comparatively recent phenomenon, owing a larger debt to secular thought than is sometimes acknowledged. The statement of William Temple, late Archbishop of Canterbury, to the effect that Christianity is the most materialistic of the world's great religions is characteristically modern. It is doubtful whether any Christian theologian of former times would have made such an assertion. So pervasive was the pall of dualism in the early, medieval, and even Reformation Church that sex withered under its shadow. Only since the nineteenth century have the tools of modern scholarship and the prevailing mood of naturalism made it possible to unravel the strands in the weaving of the centuries and to see the pattern clearly.

Part One of this book attempts to do just that, demonstrating the fact that Christianity remains consistently naturalistic in most respects, yet unable to resist the lure of dualism in its historic interpretation of sex. It goes without saying that a major inconsistency is revealed herein. Oil and water do not mix. The Biblical doctrines of creation and incarnation demand a positive attitude toward the body and all of its functions. Such an historical analysis and such a theological presupposition may make some contribution to contemporary efforts to arrive at a sound ideological base for codes of sexual morality.

Jesus

Jesus was a Jew, speaking and acting out of a heritage of fifteen hundred years. His teaching in both its content, which stems from the long tradition of Hebrew prophecy, and its form, which bears striking resemblance to the Hebrew sages and wise men, is comprehensible only against the religious and cultural background of Israel. The naturalism of Jesus and the early Church owes its existence to the Jewish soil in which it had its origin. And that soil is almost totally devoid of dualism. There are some traces of dualism in the late Judaism of the Persian and Greek periods of Jewish history, but these are minor motifs. The prevailing spirit of the Old Testament was throughout naturalistic in sharp contrast to the dominant mood of Hellenistic culture. This contrast is especially discernible at three points: in the doctrine of creation, in the understanding of man, and in the interpretation of sex.

The Hebrew Scriptures begin with the account of creation, a poetic description which is punctuated by the repeated refrain, 'And God saw that it was good.' The work of the six days is completed with the observation that 'God saw *everything* that he had made, and behold, it was very good.' The physical, material world is created by God, and as his handiwork it is to be accepted and enjoyed with thanksgiving. 'The earth is the Lord's and the fulness thereof, the world and those who dwell therein.' Such an attitude is far removed from the outlook of Hellenistic culture, which regarded matter, or *hule,* as the Greek has it, as an intractable 'stuff' upon which the eternal and spiritual forms sought to work. The physical is evil and illusory; only the spiritual, the immaterial, is good. Jesus, with his references to the lilies of the field, the birds of the air, the fallen sparrow, obviously stands solidly within the naturalistic tradition of Hebrew life. There is no suggestion in his teachings of any conflict between matter and mind, no trace of dualism.

The difference in outlook between the Old Testament and the Hellenistic mind is further illuminated in their respective doctrines of man, in their anthropologies. To the Hebrew, man is a psychosomatic unity, body and soul intimately and inextricably related. The Genesis narrative does not assert that man was supplied with a soul but rather that he *became* a living soul. And the Hebrew word for soul is *nephesh,* which refers to the whole human being, not simply to some vague, spiritual entity. The Israelite use of *nephesh* is very close to what modern psychology means by the term 'personality.' It is the totality of the individual, that which marks him with his unique stamp, making him what he is. His family background, his culture, his physical appearance, his temperament, his idiosyncrasies, his hopes and fears — all of these belong to his soul. They determine his being and his action. All his acts are to be understood as springing from his soul. No item of his behavior is isolated. Every word and deed is symptomatic, revealing the true character of the total man. They derive from the vital center of his being which is his soul. 'As a man thinketh within himself, so is he.' Whenever the Hebrew thinks of salvation beyond death, it is never in terms of the immortality of the soul but always as the resurrection of the body. There is in some layers of Jewish thought the concept of Sheol, a shadowy ghostly realm where disembodied spirits dwell. But such a life was to the Jew really no life at all. It was a miserable estate, an occasion for lamentation. His only real hope lay in the future resurrection where he would be reunited with his body, a whole man. Hellenistic anthropology, in contrast, split man into two divisible parts, a mortal and evil body wherein dwelt for a time an immortal and virtuous soul. Escape from the prison house of the flesh was the eager expectation of the spirit. Here again,

Athens and Jerusalem took separate roads, and it is clear that
Jesus walked the latter way.

The third area in which Hebrew naturalism displays marked
difference from Hellenistic dualism is in the interpretation of
sex. It has already been pointed out that the latter was strongly
ascetic, regarding sex as at best a necessary evil and at worst
slavery to the lower passions. The Old Testament, on the other
hand, portrays God as commanding his creatures to be fruitful
and multiply. Nowhere in its pages is there a counsel of celibacy
or an exaltation of virginity. Jephthah's daughter mourns her
virginal estate; the patriarchs and kings of Israel practice polygamy; the newlywed male is exempted by the Law from military
service for one year so that he and his bride may enjoy the pleasures of wedded sexual life. The assumption throughout is that a
man will marry and produce offspring, even taking concubines if
necessary. The concern of the Hebrews for the continuation of
their seed is one of the stronger motivations. The Law even provides for the so-called levirate marriage, wherein the childless
widow of a man shall be bedded by his brother and the resultant
child regarded as the offspring of the deceased. The only hint of
asceticism of any kind in Israel is to be found in the Nazarites and
Rechabites, who represent a prophetic protest against the luxury
and the inequities of the commercial life of Canaan and a recall
to the hardy simplicity and equality of nomadic existence. They
are not dualists in any sense, and they represent a very minor
strain in the Old Testament. There is a stern prohibition against
adultery in the Law, but this springs from the concern for the
seed, the family line. That this is not anti-sexual is demonstrated
by the glaring absence of any ban on fornication, an omission
which embarrassed later Christians of puritanical hue (cf. John
Calvin in chapter 4, p. 126f.).

It is a popular distortion to interpret the original sin of Adam
and Eve in the Garden of Eden as the sexual act, but this represents a complete misunderstanding of the myth. None of the
Jewish rabbis, nor any of the Christian theologians, not even the
most Hellenistically oriented of them, interpreted the fall of man

in sexual terms. Clement of Alexandria came perhaps closest to
it in his assertion that the serpent signifies bodily pleasure, but he
did not maintain that it was the sexual union of Adam and Eve
which was in itself evil. Their sin lay in their undue haste, their
unwillingness to wait for God's specific command to coitus. But
Clement is almost alone in this. The preponderance of theological opinion, in both Jewish and Christian circles, has interpreted
the original sin as pride and rebellion against God. The Church's
negative attitude toward sex has misled many into the belief that
the Bible portrays man's fall as erotic in origin. Neither the Bible
itself nor the history of Christian thought substantiates such a belief. If there were any truth in it, Hebrew life would have been
dominated by asceticism, which it clearly was not. The evidence
shows that the Old Testament is throughout naturalistic and
positive in its attitudes toward sex, as in its view of the material
world and of man. It is this heritage which underlies the entire
message of Jesus. He was a Jew in all respects and moreover a
Palestinian Jew, which means that he was singularly sheltered, as
far as it was possible in that time, from the taint of Gentile contacts, and hence also, of Hellenistic dualism.

Turning from the Old Testament background to Jesus himself
and his teachings, we must admit at the outset that there is a
paucity of verses in the Gospel records in which Jesus dealt specifically with sex. On the basis of a very few sayings, it would seem
difficult if not impossible to present an interpretation of sex in
his teachings. Yet when the whole of his message is considered,
some rather definite implications for a sexual ethic do emerge.
Generally speaking, then, there are three observations about the
mission and message of Jesus which can be made. The first of these
is organically related to the Jewish anthropology noted above, the
conviction that all behavior is symptomatic, that as a man thinketh within himself, so is he. Jesus was not so much interested in
what men do as in what they are. He always looked behind an act
to its motive, to its meaning within the total framework of the
personality. His ethic is throughout directed to the inner attitude
rather than the outer acts of men. He recognized that two individuals could behave in such similar fashion that the spectator

would be unable to distinguish between their acts. But if the inner motivation is different, the acts themselves are the carriers of radically different meaning. The Pharisee and the publican both go up to the Temple to pray. Both are pious men, engaged in the worship of God. No human observer could judge between them. But the Pharisee is proud before the Lord, thankful that he is not as other men, while the publican prays for mercy as a sinner. Outwardly, the act of each is the same; within, diverse. Only God can penetrate to the inner citadel of motivation and behold the commanding soul. Men cannot and must not judge one another on their deeds. The rich with pride and ostentation drop their gold into the poor box of the Temple, while the poor widow shamefacedly and covertly slips her penny into the slot. God knows what each has given. Jesus always asked the question of the meaning of an act. He refused to content himself with the external criteria of the scribes and Pharisees. They judged men by the simple standard of conformity to the demands of the Law, and they interpreted the Law as governing all aspects of human behavior. Jesus, on the other hand, saw the Law as primarily concerned with human attitudes and motives. He knew that it was possible for men to do the right things for the wrong reasons, to cultivate outer righteousness and piety for the sake of social approval. And he said of such persons, 'They have their reward.' But they directed their efforts to the outside of the cup and the plate, polishing and cleansing with great zeal, leaving the inside sticky with grime. They covered the tomb with white and shining lime, concealing the rotting flesh and decaying bones within. Jesus sought to scour and to cleanse the soul. 'The eye is the lamp of the body. So if your eye be sound, your whole body is full of light; but if your eye is not sound, your whole body will be full of darkness. If the light in you is darkness, how great is that darkness!' Or again, 'Every good tree bears good fruit, but the bad tree bears evil fruit. A sound tree cannot bear evil fruit, nor can a bad tree bear good fruit.' It is the inner attitude which is decisive and determinative. Without integrity and wholeness, all external righteousness is as filthy rags. A man may refrain from murder or adultery from fear of the consequences while still filled with seething rage and lust. Such a schizoid state of the soul is destructive, and the sternly moralistic repression of strong inner drives accomplishes little, except to aggravate the problem. What is required is the transformation of the person so that his attitudes and appetites are changed, the warfare within himself brought to an end. 'No man can serve two masters.' He must be made whole, his eye single. It was not outer conformity to some fixed ethical code that Jesus sought, but integrity, the harmonious unity of the totality called the soul. This is the first great principle which characterized all that Jesus said and did.

The second general observation about the message of Jesus points to the central locus of the law of love. He held up the love of God as the norm by which men were to regulate their lives. He proclaimed the revolutionary fact that God loves all men alike, saint and sinner, and if there is any disparity at all in the divine concern for humans, it is the sinner who holds the higher priority, for his need is greater. This strikes at the root of all social morality, including the legalism of the Pharisees, which rewards the virtuous and punishes the wicked. Pharisaic purity called for a rigid separation from all contaminating influences, a moral quarantine. Jesus was sharply criticized for associating with those on the fringes of society. It was unthinkable that any one could share the same air with the outcast without breathing in the germs of iniquity and contracting the disease. And the Pharisees believed they acted with God in judging and condemning sinners. Jesus overturned these tables and sent the coins of legalism spinning. The Son of Man, he said, had come to seek and to save those who were lost. He came not to call the righteous, but sinners to repentance. Those who are well have no need of a physician. Harlots and publicans go into the kingdom before the Pharisees. God, said Jesus, is like the shepherd who leaves the sheep who are safe in the fold to go out into the hills searching for one lost lamb. He is like the father of a prodigal son, rejoicing over the penitent return of the wastrel. He is like the woman who turns her whole house upside down to find a lost coin. God's love is not doled out simply to those who have earned it by their good deeds; it is freely given to all. He makes his sun to shine on the good and the evil, his rain to fall on the just and the unjust alike. And because God loves, men are to love him and one another. The first and great commandment calls for absolute devotion to God, heart and soul, mind and strength. And the second is like unto it: 'Thou shalt love thy neighbor as thyself.' When Jesus was asked, 'Who is my neighbor?' he responded with the parable of the Good Samaritan, answering in effect that any man in need is one's neighbor, a point sharpened still further in the parable of the Last Judgment. (Matt. 25:31–46). The love of God for all, especially the poor and the outcast, is to be emulated by men in their relations one to another. Enemies and persecutors are to be loved and prayed for. And as Jesus taught, so he lived, moving with understanding and acceptance among whores and sensualists, accused of being a winebibber of questionable morals. He was himself the symbol of his message, that love is the law of life, that men are to love each other even as God loves them. This is the inner attitude which is to be sought, toward God, toward neighbor, toward self. 'A new commandment I give to you, that you love one another, even as I have loved you.'

The third fact about Jesus' ministry which strikes the reader of the Gospels is the therapeutic and redemptive outlook which characterized his dealings with individuals. He did not, like the Pharisees, seek to force men to conform to the universal principles of the Law. Rather, he placed the concrete welfare of human beings above the abstractions of the Law. He shocked the pious by breaking the Sabbath with his healing, answering their objections with the saying, 'The Sabbath was made for man, not man for the Sabbath.' He spoke sharply against the legalism which permitted a man to deny his parents' pleas for help on the ground that his money was pledged to God. The Pharisees insisted that an oath must be kept, but Jesus saw human need as taking precedence over any cultic or ritual requirement. The Pharisees pressed the letter of the Law; Jesus sought its spirit. The Gospels present a whole series of pictures of his encounters with men and women from various walks of life, in various kinds of need. The rich young ruler, the woman taken in adultery, Bartimaeus the blind beggar, the ten lepers, Zaccheus the tax collector, Mary Magdalen;

Jesus met each one as an individual person, speaking the word
that needed to be said. He penetrated the superficial appearances
and laid his hand upon the inner core of the problem, dealing
with it in the specific terms of the specific situation. He did not
intend that his words should freeze into new laws as they left his
lips, crystallizing into aphorisms binding upon all men in all
circumstances. He spoke to the occasion, to a unique individual
with a unique problem, with the intent of redemption and restoration. All such encounters were between two living souls, not between a man and a lifeless Law.

These three general principles which illuminate the life and
teaching of Jesus cast their light upon all that he said and did,
including his sparse words on sex and marriage. One of these
words occurs in the Sermon on the Mount and is found only in
the Gospel of Matthew. 'You have heard that it was said, "You
shall not commit adultery." But I say to you that every one who
looks at a woman lustfully has already committed adultery with
her in his heart.' This verse has frequently been taken out of context to indicate that Jesus was an ascetic, condemning all sexual
desire. When the saying is seen in its proper setting, however, it is
clearly an illustration of the first principle described above, the
emphasis on intention, on motive. The passage contains a whole
series of contrasts between the Law which dealt with outward
behavior and the emphasis of Jesus which called for inward integrity, for wholeness, for unity of emotion and act. Mere restraint
of murder is not enough; the heart must be purged of homicidal
hatred. Almsgiving, however generous, means little if it does not
spring from sincere compassion. Prayers which are repeated loudly
and in public to impress the populace with one's piety are of no
avail. In each case, the point is made that conformity to the Law
means nothing if it lacks genuine motivation. If the chief aim is
to win men's approval, then one is a hypocrite, which means
literally, in the Greek, a play actor, and he has his reward, the
audience's approval. But inwardly he is divided, really wanting
to act otherwise. He dare not follow his impulses, however, from
fear of censure or punishment. Such a split between motive and
deed bars him from entrance into the Kingdom, through whose

portals only the whole, the pure in heart can pass. Jesus is saying in this word about adultery that there is no special virtue in abstinence when one is a seething mass of lustful desire, mentally ravaging every woman he meets. He is not saying anything at all about the sexual desire of persons who sincerely love one another, of married couples. That he obviously regarded as altogether normal and wholesome, as did all Jews, and he not only attended the wedding at Cana in Galilee, but even made a contribution to the wine supply. Those groups in the early Church who interpreted this particular verse to mean that *all* erotic impulses are evil simply revealed their Hellenistic bias. They obviously misunderstood Jesus entirely, misled by their underlying dualism. They knew what he meant about almsgiving, prayers, and oaths, that it was the motive which was of central concern. Had it not been for their original prejudice against sex, they would likewise have known that Jesus' concern was identical in the saying about adultery.

A second word of Jesus relating to sex and marriage is the passage dealing with divorce. It appears once in both Mark (10:2–12) and Luke (16:18) and twice in Matthew (5:27–30 and 19:1–12). Matthew presents this saying first in the Sermon on the Mount: 'It was also said "Whoever divorces his wife, let him give her a certificate of divorce." But I say to you that everyone who divorces his wife, except on the ground of unchastity, makes her an adulteress; and whoever marries a divorced woman commits adultery.' The later passage in Matthew parallels Mark's account which describes the question of the Pharisees whether divorce was lawful, and Jesus' answer. His response began with the counter-question, 'What did Moses command you?' The Pharisees replied that the Law permitted divorce by certificate. Jesus characterized such permission as a concession to human sin. God's purpose from the beginning was different. He created man as male and female, intending that the two should become one flesh in a lifelong bond. Divorce was no part of the divine plan. 'What God has joined together let no man put asunder.' Whoever, therefore, divorces his wife and marries another is guilty of adultery, and the same principle applies to the woman who remarries after divorcing her husband. Matthew puts the words, 'except for unchastity' in Jesus' mouth, but he alone does so. Both Mark and Luke leave the prohibition as an absolute.

Most New Testament scholars are agreed that Matthew's qualification represents a later addition to the text. It is wholly inconsistent with the rigor of Jesus' teaching, which was absolutist throughout. No concession is made to human weakness anywhere. The demands of God are unequivocal. Men are to take no thought for the morrow; they are to love God with every fiber of their being, to love neighbor as self. The summation is found in the verse, 'Be perfect as your father in heaven is perfect.' Jesus was not legislating for human society. He was not a social reformer in the ordinary sense. His statement of the divine command was absolutely uncompromising. So in the question of divorce, he went behind the Mosaic Law, which did recognize the relative character of human life, to God's original decree and plan, which is rigidly unyielding. Jesus' ethic is throughout, and the realm of sex and marriage is no exception, filled with what Reinhold Niebuhr has called 'impossible possibilities,' which is to say that his ethic is not capable of being translated directly into the relativities of history. The Christian perfectionist always makes the error of assuming that he is confronted with the possibility of fulfilling the command of Jesus without compromise. He paints on the canvas of life in colors of black and white, thus falsifying reality which is a series of grays. Man never deals with alternatives, one of which truly satisfies the divine will, while all others fall short. Rather, he is faced with a series of choices, all of which stand in some degree under God's judgment. The Church has recognized this fact in numerous areas, but has inclined toward an inconsistent rigor in matters of divorce. As Maude Royden has observed, 'The Church again and again has sanctioned war and capital punishment. Every bishop on the bench, every incumbent of a living, every witness in a court of law takes oaths. No country executes a man for murder because he admits he hates his brother, nor literally regards a lustful glance as adultery. Neither does the Church excommunicate Christians who refuse loans or gifts to those who ask. Yet it argues that Christians who have almost uni-

versally disregarded the *literal* meaning of every other principle
enunciated in the Sermon on the Mount must *literally* obey the
injunction against divorce on pain of disloyalty to their Lord!' [1]
The rejoinder that the ban on divorce is more plainly stated is a
frail reed which withers before the chill wind of an examination
of the prohibition against taking oaths, which could hardly be
more uncompromising than it is. This is not to say that divorce
is not an evil in God's sight. Obviously, it is, but then so is war.
Yet the Church has always known that periods in history occur
when war is the lesser of two evils, when passive submission to
tyranny would be worse than armed resistance. So it is with divorce, which at times may represent the only possible solution,
a more creative and constructive alternative than a sterile and
corrosive marriage. To seek to make any of Jesus' absolutes into
laws governing human behavior is to miss the whole point of his
message, to erect a new legalism. He always gave concrete human
need precedence over abstract ritual law. Man was not made for
the Sabbath, nor for marriage as a prison. Both were rather made
for man.

In Matthew's Gospel, there is a brief appendix added to the
word on divorce. The disciples recoiled from the rigor of Jesus'
teaching, declaring that it would seem better to be celibate than
to go through life saddled with the wrong woman. Jesus responded with the cryptic saying to the effect that there are some
who are born eunuchs, some who have been emasculated by men,
and some who have made themselves eunuchs for the sake of the
Kingdom. A few New Testament scholars regard this verse as a
later addition, the Hellenistic dualism of the early Church read
back into the Gospel record. Those who accept the passage as
genuine point out that it is not an instance of asceticism but
simply one of many places where Jesus insists that the demands of
the Kingdom are paramount, taking precedence over all ordinary
activities. A man cannot first go and transact a piece of business
or bury his father or plow a field and then repent. Jesus believed
that the response to the Gospel must be now or never. One must

1. Royden, A. Maude, 'What Is Marriage?,' in *The Atlantic Monthly,* Sep-
tember 1923.

be willing to hate his parents, to forsake his family, to sell all his possessions, or even to maim himself physically, in short, radically to remove any obstacle that bars his entrance into the Kingdom of God. Jesus was not suggesting that money or sex or the family were evil in and of themselves, to be avoided and forsworn. He regarded them as roadblocks to salvation only where they represented the source of a man's ultimate security, where they assumed the role of idols. 'Seek ye *first* the Kingdom of God, and all these things shall be added to you.' The motivation of celibacy is apocalyptic rather than dualistic. Jesus was in no way suggesting that marriage is a low or degrading estate. Such a statement would clash directly with his immediately previous declaration that matrimony is divinely ordained, a part of God's creative purpose.

All three of the Synoptic Gospels carry the story of Jesus' encounter with the Sadducees concerning marriage in the resurrection. These members of the Temple aristocracy, who did not believe in the resurrection, came to Jesus with a hypothetical question. Suppose, they said, that a woman married seven brothers, being widowed by each in turn, when the dead are raised, whose wife will she be? These Sadducees were obviously fishing with baited hooks. If Jesus denied the resurrection, he was in even greater difficulty with the Pharisees, who passionately insisted upon it. If, however, he affirmed his agreement with the Pharisees, he was presented with a patently absurd situation. His reply was consummately skillful. He at once expressed his faith that the dead shall be raised, rebuking the Sadducees for their skepticism, and then went on to say that in the resurrection, 'they neither marry nor are given in marriage, but are like angels in heaven.' This might seem, at first glance, to be Hellenistic, to imply a kind of spiritual immortality, free from the soiling flesh. But Jesus spoke specifically of resurrection, which in Jewish circles always means that the *body* is raised, an idea repugnant to any dualist. The emphasis in Jesus' answer is upon the fact that at the end of history, the exclusive relationships of this world are banished. All will love one another equally before God. He was not looking forward to release from the body and its degrading passions, regarding sex and marriage as evil. He expected the resurrection of the flesh in the tradition of Hebrew naturalism.

One further passage which merits consideration is the account of the woman taken in adultery, which appears in the Fourth Gospel but which is obviously Synoptic material. This incident represents a kind of microcosm of Jesus' ethic. His concern was not so much with her act as with her attitude. He looked upon her with a love which understood and accepted and forgave. She found in him one who did not judge her for her violation of the law but who met her with a desire to redeem and to heal. He was not shocked by her sexual sin. He did not delight in a self-righteous and legalistic denunciation. She received from him the same treatment he accorded the harlots and publicans. Sensuality was in his eyes a minor vice beside the enormous spiritual pride of the scribes and Pharisees. In this encounter, the essential naturalism of Jesus' attitude toward sex is inescapable.

Apart from these few verses noted, the Gospel records are silent with respect to Jesus' interpretation of sex. But these few verses, meager though they be, are thoroughly consistent with his teaching as a whole, and it is perfectly possible without doing violence to that teaching to draw certain implications from it. No elaborate code of sexual morality can legitimately be based upon Jesus' ethic, for such a code would perforce deal primarily with external behavior and would fail to do justice to the uniqueness of the individual. What is legitimate, however, is to say that in every concrete situation Jesus' primary concern was with the inner attitude and that he sought to lead men into a life of love. The norm, therefore, by which sexual relations are to be judged is radically different in the mind of Jesus from what it is in the eyes of society. The latter cannot deal with men's motives, except in a very crude and rough-hewn fashion, for example the distinction between premeditated murder and manslaughter, which in many a trial proves a thorny problem. Generally speaking, society must judge men on the basis of what they do. So in the realm of sex, morality is determined on the basis of one principle, the marital status of the persons involved. All sex outside marriage is taboo, while marital coitus is respectable and right. Society raises no questions about and makes no allowance for the motivation of sex. A couple may enter marriage simply to legalize what is an essentially selfish relationship, each exploiting the other's body, treating the other not as a person but as a thing, without becoming what the Bible calls 'one flesh,' except in the most literal, exterior sense. No matter, their sexual relations are respectable in the eyes of the world. They are married. On the other hand, an unmarried couple may be truly 'one flesh,' a genuine unity of two total personalities, using sex as one means of expressing that unity. It is of no consequence. They are out of wedlock and society condemns them as immoral.

This, of course, points to the close connection between the word 'moral' and the term 'mores,' which Webster defines as 'customs; specifically, fixed customs or folkways imbued with an ethical significance; customs or conventions which have the force of law.' What is moral, in other words, is determined by the mores. And sexual mores, by and large, are directed to one end: the prevention of irresponsible procreation. Man is the only animal who arrives at sexual maturity before he achieves social maturity, so that every society develops codes which are designed to prevent a man's becoming a grandfather before he can vote. There are many variations in the specific means used to attain this goal in the mores of various cultures, and the more complex the society the greater is the hiatus between the two levels of maturity. The Polynesian adolescent is ready for social responsibility long before the American or European, and Polynesian sexual morality is correspondingly less rigid. But whatever the differences, the primary concern of every society with sex is bound closely to procreation. Morality, in this sense, means that sex is used responsibly by persons who are prepared to face the consequences of their union, that is, parenthood. Certainly, no one can find fault with such a concern or with such a definition of morality as far as it goes. The Christian, however, must raise the question whether this concern and this definition go far enough. Jesus insisted that the righteousness or morality of his followers must exceed that of the scribes and Pharisees. Furthermore, it is entirely possible that a contraceptive device which is wholly effective will be developed in the near future, with far-reaching repercussions on social morality. The ability to control procreation at will would seriously undermine the sexual taboos of society. The near approach to such an ability with modern contraceptives which achieve an effectiveness of 85 to 95 per cent, has already had a profound influence.

The difficulty in western civilization, with its so-called Christian morality, is that there is considerable confusion between three factors: the legitimate concern of society with reproduction, which western culture shares with all others; the specifically Christian attitudes and norms, rooted in the Old Testament and in the teachings of Jesus; and the heritage of Hellenistic dualism, which regards sex as evil. This confusion creates great difficulties in all discussions about what is 'moral' or 'immoral' in the realm of sex. The pervasive taint of Hellenistic dualism is responsible for the uneasy guilt which attaches itself to all sexual activities. Social mores brand irresponsible coitus as dangerous to the public welfare but are relatively silent beyond that. Christian faith seeks to promote a type of inter-personal relationship which will develop integrity in sexual matters, leading to the creation of a state of 'one flesh.' All of these are involved in any thought or discussion of sexual morality, like the three notes of a triad. When any one is sounded, the vibrating overtones of the other two are heard. The negative attitude of Hellenistic asceticism is now almost universally regarded as a false note, and intellectually at least is very much out of fashion, though its emotional influence lingers on. The concern of society is legitimate and important and cannot be ignored. But morality in this sense must be distinguished from Christian morality, which is not indifferent to social problems but which represents a different orientation.

Christian faith approaches the problem of sex and marriage at a deeper level than concern for the public good. Matrimony is not simply an institution set up for the protection of women and the proper nurture of children, and sex is more than a procreative function, though certainly none of these factors can be ignored. But Biblical religion always seeks, in every ethical problem, to go beyond mere mores to the depths of the individual personality, to the realm of motivation. This was clearly the intention of Jesus, and he was simply carrying on the prophetic tradition of his fathers. He poured out bowls of wrath upon the external morality of the Pharisees and summed up the whole of God's law in the two-fold commandment of love. The unfortunate fact is that the word 'love' has become so confused, so romanticized, so torn away from its Biblical roots that any modern author uses it at his peril. It is essential to define with the greatest care what one means, lest some counterfeit image be raised in the reader's mind and all commerce become impossible. The New Testament uses three different words for love: *eros,* which means desire, not necessarily sexual, though it may be; *philia,* or friendship; and *agape,* which is the love of God for his creatures, flowing spontaneously forth from his being, uncaused by anything in the objects of his love. The greatest emphasis is, of course, placed on the last of these terms, and it is *agape* which Christians are bidden to manifest toward one another. But as Paul Tillich has pointed out in his excellent analysis of love, *agape* is the love which resides in being itself and which enters into all qualities of love on every level.[2] There is an *eros* in every relationship of love, the desire for re-union with that from which one has been separated. *Philia* simply means that there is an element of familiarity with the object loved. But the important point in all of this is that love is *not,* in Biblical terms, an emotion. It is an orientation, or attitude, of the total personality, 'heart and soul and mind and strength.' It is an outgoing concern for what is loved that seeks to serve and to give. It has an emotional content, to be sure. Without the driving force of feeling, it would be coldly and barrenly intellectual. But neither is love without its rational aspect; it involves the whole of the personal life.

The distinction drawn by modern psychology between infantile love and mature love is illuminating at this point. The former *is* almost solely emotional, and it is extremely selfish, seeking primarily its own gratification. It does not love another human

2. Tillich, Paul, *Love, Power, and Justice,* Oxford University Press, New York, 1954.

being as he really is, but as an ideal image, an image of the person as the lover needs and wants him to be. It is perfectly understandable when the small child reveals his grandiose ideas about his parents, unable to see any flaw or weaknesses in them, because he needs the protection and care of omniscience and omnipotence. But the normal course of development replaces the ideal images of parents with a more realistic view, seeing them as real persons, fallible and mortal. The child has matured in such a way that he no longer finds it necessary to endow his mother and father with superhuman powers. But many a chronological adult simply transfers his infantile love for his parents to the object of his later affections. She (or he) is regarded as the most beautiful, most intelligent, most charming creature in the world. She is not loved for what she is but for what her lover wants her to be. She is, as the mother is to the infant, simply an extension of his own ego. He must believe that she is so remarkable, because only such a creature is worthy of his love. Illusion is the standard diet of infantile love. It is, as the poets say, blind. It is so preoccupied with its needs and wants, its feelings and reactions, that it cannot see the beloved at all. The infantile lover is so busy enjoying himself in his friends' company that he cannot enjoy his friends. He defines love in terms of his inner response. 'It's a tickly feeling around the heart you can't scratch.' It is ephemeral and unpredictable. It comes and goes without warning. This is love as it is understood by many a modern, as it is counterfeited in a highly sentimentalized and even more highly eroticized currency popular on stage and screen and in romantic songs and magazine stories. Cupid appears appropriately enough in diapers.

Mature love, in contrast, is not blind. It has progressed from pablum to porterhouse. It feeds upon the raw meat of reality. The beloved is seen as he really is, with all his faults and liabilities, as well as his capabilities and assets. He is loved for himself *as he is,* in full awareness and recognition. And what the mature lover seeks is not primarily his own satisfaction, the gratification of his own desires or the titillation of his own feelings; he wants to serve the beloved, to contribute to the fullest self-realization, the most creative fulfillment of the other, and he is willing to undergo considerable sacrifice to achieve his goal. This has a close analogy in the love of parent for child, an active, outgoing concern. It springs from an inner strength, from the ability and the willingness to serve needs. One of the chief difficulties with marriages based upon infantile love is that both partners are expecting to receive all and to give nothing. They are so devoured by their own hunger that they have no awareness of the wants of others, or at least no ability to do anything about them. So life is a constant struggle, each fearful of having demands made upon him which he cannot meet, each asserting his own needs as imperiously as a squawling child. Mature love wants to serve, having learned that Jesus was profoundly right in recognizing that it is more blessed to give than to receive, to love than to be loved. The more one bears the burdens of others, the more he contributes to his own strength, and he who is the servant of all is truly the greatest of all. The mature lover, then, knows his own weaknesses and is not ashamed to accept help when he needs it, but he also knows his capacities and is glad to put them at the service of another.

A more philosophical expression of the psychologists' description of mature and infantile love has been propounded by Martin Buber, the great Jewish existentialist. Buber distinguishes two kinds of relationships, one between persons, which he calls I-Thou, and one between a person and a thing, referred to as I-It. He regards it as perfectly legitimate for a person to use or to exploit a thing, to treat it as the means to an end. That is what things are for. But it is never legitimate for a person to use another person. It is the essence of immorality to exploit another human being, to treat him as though he were a means to an end instead of an end in himself. The most elementary understanding of the law of love makes it obvious that any such a de-humanization of a person is a gross violation. The fact that a man or woman may be perfectly willing, even anxious, to be used or exploited, is entirely beside the point. The owner of a sweatshop can plead that his employees are eagerly grateful for the pittance he pays them as wages, but this does not render his abuse of them moral. He is still treating persons as things. It almost goes without saying that Buber is simply expressing in philosophical language what the psychologist uses different terms to describe. Infantile love regards people as the means of satisfying its ends and uses them indiscriminately. Mature love recognizes and values persons for themselves.

The foregoing distinctions between mature and infantile love on the one hand and I-Thou and I-It relationships on the other have, it is to be hoped, clarified to some extent at least, the meaning of love in its Biblical sense, as Jesus used it. Love, for him, meant not primarily a romantic emotion, but concern and respect, devotion and the desire to serve. God's love was not in his teachings sticky sentimentalism, seeking the 'happiness' of men without regard to cost or consequence. The divine love could be and frequently was stern and demanding, involving judgment and suffering, for sometimes it is only such a love that will best serve the needs of the other, and men are called upon to emulate their Maker. It does not at all follow that because one loves another he should fulfill the loved one's every need and grant his every request. There are times when genuine love must resist and refuse for the sake of the one loved, as every parent knows.

All of this needs to be kept in mind in the following discussion of Christian sexual morality, which is based upon Jesus' law of love. In his ethic, that which is normative in sexual relations, is *not* — as it is for society, Christian or otherwise — the external, marital status of the persons involved. Rather, the norm must be sought in inner attitudes and motives. The question must be raised concerning what sex means to the man and woman participating therein. If they are involved in an I-It relationship, each treating the other as a mere body, a thing to be used and exploited as a means to self-gratification, their marital status assumes a decidedly secondary importance from Jesus' point of view. They may enter such a relationship on the basis of an infantile love, which makes of sex, as it does of almost everything in life, the means of serving its own needs, or there may be no pretensions of love at all. There may be a frank admission that the only goal is the release of sexual tension, a mutual exploitation. In either case, again, the marriage question is far less important than the consequences of that kind of relationship to both partners, for sex so used is destructive and corrosive. The exploited one is defiled and cheapened, treated as an 'It' instead of a 'Thou,' and the exploiter is degraded from the level of an adult to that of an infant. A baby cannot escape his 'oral' attitude toward life, his mouth gaping in hunger, looking to be fed, to having his needs met. He can neither feed himself nor anyone else. But an adult with that orientation, in sex or any other realm of existence, is a real tragedy. He is capable of a far more creative experience, but he cannot enter into it because of his illusory, infantile outlook upon himself and his world. Sex which is motivated by the 'I-It' attitude, which uses other human beings as the means to the ends of one's own gratification is, in Jesus' terms, immoral even if the persons involved are thoroughly and respectably married before the law.

But what of the other side of the coin? Does this mean that Jesus would condone the sexual relations of a couple who genuinely love each other, who share an I-Thou attitude but whose coitus is conducted without benefit of clergy? There are those who answer in the affirmative, who hold the position that Jesus' sole concern was for motivation without regard to social condition or mores.[3] Before dealing with this question, however, it is necessary to raise the prior question about the meaning of marriage. Here again a conflict between society, including 'Christian' society, and the teachings of Jesus becomes apparent. Jesus spoke about marriage as 'what God has joined together.' Society, on the other hand, has little or no concern about who does the joining together. A purely secular ceremony, performed by a public official, ties a knot as legal and acceptable as that wrought by the loftiest prelate. And no ecclesiastic may celebrate connubial rites without the express permission of the state, which graciously permits him in such an instance to play the role of magistrate. Is marriage, with its consequent permission for sexual intercourse, a matter for God or the state? This has been a subject of no little controversy

3. Cf. John Macmurray's *Reason and Emotion,* D. Appleton–Century Company, New York, 1936; especially chapter VII, entitled, 'The Virtue of Chastity.'

in Christendom for a number of centuries.[4] In the Middle Ages, when the Church held undisputed sway, a marriage was regarded as consummated by sexual intercourse between betrothed parties, even if no formal ceremony had occurred. There is, in other words, something more to marriage than mere contract, more than an institution approved, if not created, by society for the protection of women and the nurture of children. That something is what the Church calls sacrament, the inward and invisible state of the persons involved which brings the whole discussion full circle back to Jesus' emphasis upon motivation. What makes a marriage is the consent of the partners, their serious intention to live together in some sense, however dimly perceived, as 'one flesh,' a union of their two separate existences into still a third existence, the marriage itself. The effective nature of consent is recognized by the state in its sanction of Quaker weddings, where no officiating magistrate, secular or religious, presides. The couple simply announce in the presence of witnesses that they take each other as husband and wife. The Church also recognizes that two persons ultimately marry each other, that no one can bind them together without their consent. No wedding ritual has the priest or clergyman say, 'I make you man and wife.' Rather he uniformly declares that inasmuch as this man and this woman have consented together in holy wedlock and have publicly witnessed the fact before God and man, 'I pronounce *that they are* husband and wife.' Furthermore, the Church will always declare null and void any marriage in which it can be shown that full consent was lacking, where any coercion was involved, or where deceit was practiced, and the state will concur in granting the annulment, even if the marriage has been sexually consummated.

If, then, a marriage is effected primarily by the partners to it with Church and state playing the role of approving spectators or parents pronouncing blessing, a similar primacy prevails in sexual relations. On one level, that of a purely individual morality, those who contend that Jesus' concern was solely for inner motivation

4. Cf. the highly instructive discussion of this in G. H. Joyce's study of *Christian Marriage, an Historical and Doctrinal Study,* Sheed and Ward, London, 1933.

are surely correct. The question of external status is entirely and altogether secondary. If sex and procreation can one day be separated in such a fashion that conception is a completely voluntary occurrence, then it will be difficult to point the accusing finger at any couple who engage in coitus outside the bonds of formal marriage, provided only that the sexual relations represent the creation of 'one flesh,' an outward and visible symbol of an inner and invisible union of two total selves. It is perfectly obvious, however, that contraception is still fallible, and that a purely individual sexual morality is not at present a realistic possibility. No man is unto himself an island, and Jesus' law of love is by no means limited to one's sexual partner. The command to love is universal, and no man and woman ever have intercourse in a vacuum. They are surrounded by a cloud of unseen and unseeing witnesses: parents, friends, school, church, society as a whole. As one student, caught in an unwanted pregnancy and a hasty cover-up marriage, remarked to the present writer: 'When we first began our sexual relations, we thought no one was involved but the two of us, but now we realize that we involved his family and friends, my family and friends, and this child who is to be born.'

The inescapably communal nature of life, to which both Testaments of the Bible bear eloquent and repeated testimony, enters with especial force into the sexual sphere in the fact of reproduction. Precisely because of the so-far inseparable tie between coitus and procreation, society seeks to prevent irresponsible coupling, however much 'in love' the individuals concerned may be. This means that any who flout the social taboos run the risk of censure, ostracism, and even punishment. In such an atmosphere, clandestine sexual relations must always occur under the shadow of anxiety, the double fear of either exposure or pregnancy, or both. Each month the days are anxiously counted until the girl's menstrual period begins. Each act of intercourse must be furtively snatched from under the nose of the watchdog of social morality. Sexual indulgence under such conditions can be and often is, far more destructive of a relationship between two persons than a frustration which is mutually endured for the sake of a later and greater good. And the frustration loses most of its sting when it is voluntarily imposed from within rather than arbitrarily imposed from without. The abstinence does not spring from any dualistic negation of sex, nor from any moralistic idea that a formal marriage sanctifies sex, but from a realistic recognition that pre-marital intercourse *under present conditions* is more of peril than of profit. The development of an infallible contraceptive device may very well, over a period of time, modify those conditions in such a way that all outer bans will be removed. The Christian will then still have to face the fact that the powers of human rationalization are very great, and he must constantly ask himself whether what he labels as love may not rather be a counterfeit excuse for sexual indulgence. But his primary concern will be with the genuineness of inner attitude. He cannot allow himself to fall into a new Pharisaism based on a Hellenistic asceticism rather than on Old Testament Hebraism and the ethic of Jesus.

Paul

The most casual reader of the New Testament is struck at once by the sharp contrast, in language, in outlook, in literary form, between the Synoptic Gospels and the Epistles of Paul. The many differences between the two collections of writings have given rise to numerous volumes and even to theological schools which have sought to distinguish between the simple teachings of Jesus and the metaphysical elaborations of Pauline Christianity. In the drama of the early Church, Paul is seen as the villain of the piece, a child of Hellenistic culture in all important respects, with only minor genes of Judaism in his intellectual heritage. Such a portrait of Paul was painted in especially vivid colors by the Biblical scholarship of the late nineteenth and early twentieth centuries. He was cast in the role of a Pied Piper, leading the children of Jesus' followers out of their simple home in the Sermon on the Mount into the dark cavern of Greek speculation. Christianity was transformed by him from an ethic into a theology, from an essentially Jewish way of life into an Oriental mystery cult, complete with cult and sacrament.

There is just enough truth in such a theory to make it highly plausible. Paul was, unlike Jesus, a cosmopolitan. Born in Tarsus, a seaport through which flowed the commerce of the Roman Empire, the seat of a large and flourishing university, Paul both spoke and wrote Greek. A Roman citizen, a world-traveler, a mind trained in speculative thought, he mingled constantly with Gentiles, with men and women of the world, while Jesus was a provincial Nazarene carpenter, who lived most of his life in the Palestinian countryside, untutored and unlettered, unacquainted with the culture of the larger world. The differences between the two men can be traced in no small degree to the contrast in their backgrounds and careers. Jesus stood within the prophetic tradition of the Old Testament. He brought together and fulfilled all that is greatest in that tradition. His terminology and his assumptions were all fundamentally Jewish. Paul's religion, on the other hand, was a Christ-centered mysticism, a quest for salvation from an evil world and an evil age, ruled by principalities and powers, by spiritual wickedness in high places. He was obviously influenced by the prevailing failure of nerve, by the longing for salvation which saturated the whole Graeco-Roman world. He absorbed more of the 'spirit of the age' than he himself knew.

But when all of this has been conceded, it is necessary, as the scholars of the last two decades have increasingly recognized, to defend Paul against his detractors, to point out that whatever strains of Hellenistic culture may be detected in his thought were minor motifs, almost completely covered by the crashing chords and mighty themes of rabbinic Judaism. He may have used certain phrases popular among the Stoics or on the lips of devotees of the mysteries, but this does not imply any intimate understanding or thorough acquaintance. Existentialism or relativity will find reference in the letters of contemporaries without indicating that the writer has any more than a superficial knowledge of either. Every culture and every age has its jargon, and Paul could not escape his environment. But in all important points, he was primarily a Jew, fundamentally at one with the man he called Master and Lord. He was not in any essential aspect of his life or thought Hellenistic. His language, his presuppositions, his method of reasoning, his imagery are all Hebrew to the core.

In the preceding section, Jesus' message was described as marked by three central characteristics: concern for inner motive rather than outer morality, the primacy of the law of love, and the recognition of the unique status of the individual as over against a legalism which ignores the individual. All three of these are to be found at the heart of the message of Paul. Outer works can never save a man; only his inner faith, his love for God is of any avail. 'Though I sell all that I have and give to the poor, and though I give my body to be burned, and have not love, it profits me nothing.' Good works which spring from bad motives are worse than nothing. Motive is everything. And the most important motivation of all is love. Paul gave to the New Testament concept of *agape* its highest expression, surpassing even the Synoptic Gospels in this respect.[5] The epistles are filled with evidences of individual problems treated as such, of respect for individual differences. Paul was strikingly inconsistent, adapting his teaching to the local situation of the person or church concerned. He was not seeking to lay down any universal code of ethics, to which all must conform. For him, as for Jesus, the only absolute was the law of love, whose specific applications are legion. God judges not the outer act but the heart. Paul discovered from his own experience how sterile and futile was the legalism in which he had been raised and he broke with it completely. Sin is not what a man does, but what he is. It springs from a wrong orientation, which cannot be dealt with by will power, by seeking to overcome one bad habit at a time, in patchwork fashion. What is required is an inner rebirth, a dying unto the old man and a rising to newness of life, a reconstruction of the total personality, which means trust in and love for God.

Paul's use of the terms 'spirit' and 'flesh,' his contrast of the two in terms of warfare give the impression of Hellenistic dualism. It appears as though he regarded the body as evil and the soul as good. But a closer examination reveals that his meaning is quite different. He was using Greek terms, pregnant with dualistic association, but he was using them not as the Greek philosophers

5. As pointed out by Anders Nygren in his *Agape and Eros,* Society for the Propagation of Christian Knowledge, London, 1932.

but as the Jewish rabbis. The words were simply translations of their Hebrew counterparts, taken from the Septuagint, the Greek version of the Old Testament. And in every case, Paul reveals his Jewish orientation. The term he used for 'flesh,' for example, is *sarx*, a rendering of the Hebrew *basar*, which does not mean the body as opposed to the mind, or soul, not even in Hellenistic literature. Liddell and Scott, in their standard Greek lexicon, can give no instance of such a use of *sarx*. Rather, the word *hule*, or matter, stuff, was the one selected by the Hellenistic writers in such a context, and if Paul were moving in that realm of thought, he would certainly have used that terminology. The Hebrew *basar* and the Pauline *sarx* both mean the totality of the person as he exists apart from God, seeking to live out of his own resources. Paul did include bodily lusts under 'works of the flesh,' but he also referred to pride, envy, malice in the same way. In fact, he even spoke of the Jewish zeal for the Law as springing from the 'flesh' which clearly means man's attempt to live on his own terms, refusing to acknowledge his absolute dependence upon God. Paul saw human nature as inescapably religious, under the necessity of finding meaning and direction in some form of worship. As Luther was later to put it, 'Man either worships God or an idol.' This gives rise to a kind of dualism in Paul, a dualism which he described in terms of 'flesh' and 'spirit,' but it is far removed from Hellenistic categories of thought. Life was not for him a warfare between the body and the mind but a constant choice between God and an idol. The substitute for God may be sexual license or alcoholic indulgence or gluttony but not necessarily so. It may also be entirely 'spiritual' in character, having nothing whatever to do with bodily appetites.

Paul visualized the entire creation as groaning under the rule of the powers of darkness, and his dualism is in this respect far closer to Persian Zoroastrianism than to Hellenistic culture. His view of sin as a force which takes hold of a man and leads him into dark and evil ways is of one piece with Jesus' concept of demon possession. Jesus spoke again and again of the evil spirits which dwell within men and which can be driven out only by the spirit of God, or *pneuma*, and Paul had a wholly similar

view. For both men, the powers of darkness are 'spiritual,' not
fleshly. For neither Paul nor Jesus is the human body evil in and
of itself. It is the use made of the body, the spirit controlling the
whole man, the character of the totality that is fundamental.
Only absolute devotion to God can save a man from bondage to
other gods. It should be clear, then, that whatever dualism there
may be in Paul is predominantly Jewish in character, however
Hellenistic it may appear from his terminology. Nonetheless,
Paul did play the villain of the piece in one respect. His own
Hebrew background made him always aware that his Greek
words were translations of their Jewish equivalents, with all of
the naturalistic and holistic overtones of the latter. But as the
Church became predominantly Gentile, moving away from its
Hebrew origins out into a world of Greek culture, dominated by
Hellenistic ideas, Paul's terms were increasingly interpreted in a
dualistic way. All unwittingly, the great Apostle to the Gentiles
marked the transition point between the healthy and positive
attitude toward the body which characterized the Old Testament
and Jesus and the negative dualism which increasingly colored
the thought of the Church of the second and third centuries.

To turn to Paul's interpretation of sex, it is obvious that he
was by no means consistent. On the one hand, he declared that in
Christ the distinctions of sex had been transcended. 'There is
neither Jew nor Greek, there is neither slave nor free, there is
neither male nor female; for you are all one in Christ Jesus'
(Galatians 3:28). At the very least, the two sexes are equal. 'In the
Lord woman is not made independent of man, nor man of
woman, for as woman is made from man, so man is now born of
woman. And all things are from God' (1 Corinthians 11:11–12).
On the other hand, Paul frequently suggested that woman is dis-
tinctly an inferior being, since woman was created from man.
The head of every woman is her husband, to whom she is subject.
Paul forbade females from speaking in church, commanding
them to keep silence, although in justice both to him and to
women it should be noted that the word he used for 'to speak'
in this context (1 Corinthians 14:33–5) was the Greek *lalein* which
means 'to babble' or 'to chatter.' In 1 Corinthians 11:5 he seemed

to assume that women would both pray and prophesy, which is a further illustration of his lack of consistency. The so-called Pastoral Epistles to Timothy and Titus are no longer regarded as Pauline in authorship, but whoever wrote them was very close in spirit to the Apostle when he counseled the ladies to dress modestly and declared that they were neither to teach nor to have any authority over men (1 Timothy 2:9-15). Various authors, usually male, have sought with considerable ingenuity, to justify Paul in all of this, pointing out the social conditions of the times, the widespread degeneration of morals, the increase of prostitution, and so on. The truth of the matter, however, is simply that he suffered from a malady with which most members of his sex are afflicted, namely male arrogance. He believed that men are superior to women, that God intended from the beginning that men should exercise authority over their wives. This is only another guise assumed by the ubiquitous pride of humanity, which hides behind a thousand faces, the white man's burden, the manifest destiny of the Aryan race, the American century. Paul was much closer to the universalism of the Gospel when he declared that in Christ all distinctions are banished, all barriers broken down.

Yet this is not all arrogance. Masculine superiority was definitely assumed by Paul, but he did not make this unqualified. Certain responsibilities and obligations were laid upon men in relation to their wives. In every case, where the woman was instructed to be obedient to her husband, the husband was enjoined to honor and protect his wife. The duties of marriage were always presented reciprocally. There is no consistent interpretation of sex to be found in Paul's epistles and one can be purchased only at the price of distortion. He wrote each of the letters to a specific church with specific problems, and he was dealing with individual problems, not setting up a legal code that would cover all situations.

Still another paradox in Paul's thought is to be found in his attitude toward marriage. On the one hand, he counseled celibacy, wishing that all men were single as he was, while on the

other, he not only permitted coitus within marriage but advised
against too long periods of continence. The central passage in the
epistles in this connection is 1 Corinthians 7. Here Paul made his
famous statement that 'it is well for a man not to touch a woman
. . . I wish that all men were as I myself am.' He urged the
unmarried and widows to remain single but admitted that he had
no such 'command of the Lord,' offering only advice, not law. He
gave two reasons for such counsel. The first looked toward 'the
impending distress,' the Messianic woes which were soon to fall
upon the earth, heralding the return of Christ in glory. In such a
time, men would do well to realize that all ordinary institutions
and relations were speeding to their doom and therefore any
time or concern spent on them was wasted. The second reason,
directly related to the first, dealt with freedom from earthly
anxieties. 'The unmarried man is anxious about the affairs of
the Lord, how to please the Lord; but the married man is anxious about worldly affairs, how to please his wife, and his interests are divided . . . I say this for your own benefit, not to lay
any restraint upon you, but to promote good order and to secure
your undivided attention to the Lord.'

Both of Paul's reasons for advising celibacy were apocalyptic
rather than dualistic. He did not suggest anything inherently evil
in sex or marriage. He merely regarded them as living on borrowed time and therefore of decidedly secondary importance.
Exactly the same attitude was reflected toward circumcision,
toward money, toward slavery, toward all the things of this world
which he believed destined quickly to pass away. The only suggestion that the already married should abstain from sexual intercourse is found in verse 29, where Paul wrote, 'Let them who
have wives live as though they had none.' But this was a part of
the general cataclysm, the turning upside down of which Jesus
also spoke in the Beatitudes. The Kingdom was to be given not
to the wise, the mighty, and the noble, but to the poor, the meek,
the disinherited. The slave was free, the freeman in bondage.
Those who mourned were soon to rejoice; those who bought
were to have no goods. Paul's whole view was based on eschato-

logical rather than dualistic presuppositions, on the conviction
that all things were passing away and therefore worthy of no
concern in the last days.

Yet there was more in Paul than mere apocalypse. He com-
forted the slave, telling him not to mind his chains, but Paul did
not advise him to refuse the opportunity to gain his freedom. On
the contrary, he was specifically permitted to emancipate himself,
and Paul did not patronize him, telling him, 'You do not sin,'
for there was no need for such a word. Nor did Paul say, 'I would
spare you the worldly anxieties of your freedom.' The man who
wished to marry, however, was grudgingly permitted his new
estate. By implication, at least, he was not 'firmly established in
his heart,' and did not have 'his desire under control.' His passions were strong, and although no censure was leveled against
him, his celibate brother was better. Here, of course, Paul parted
company with traditional Judaism, which always frowned on
celibacy, regarding marriage and parenthood as the natural way
in which every man and every woman should walk. This paradox
in Paul's thought represents the perfect example of the blending
in him of Hebrew faith and Hellenistic culture. He was a Jew,
but a Jew of the Diaspora. He took a middle position between the
extremes of his day. The prevailing dualistic thought about flesh
and spirit produced two types of reaction, in interpretations of
sex. The first was asceticism which regarded all sexual activity,
even among married persons, as evil. The second went to the
other extreme and regarded all things bodily as matters of complete indifference. These antinomians demonstrated their con-
tempt for the flesh by indulging in sexual orgies. Corinth was a
city filled with the vices common to the age, and all earnest souls,
Stoic no less than Christian, were concerned about the growing
decay of morality. Obviously, the struggling church there had
sought the Apostle's advice. Caught as they were between asceticism on the one hand and antinomianism on the other, they were
bewildered, eager to know what their new faith required of them.
Paul's reply was characteristic of him. It was primarily Jewish,
primarily apocalyptic, but there were also strong overtones of
Hellenistic influence.

He refused to command celibacy, regardless of the inner consequences as a thoroughgoing dualist might. Nor was he a complete antinomian, believing that the spirit is insulated from the flesh, indifferent to physical events. He was too good a Jew to adopt either of these positions, asserting the essential goodness of sex and marriage and recognizing the psychosomatic unity of body and soul, so that whatever occurs in one realm inevitably affects the other. Yet he was enough a child of the Hellenistic Age to rate celibacy as superior to marriage, regarding the latter as the lesser of two evils. It was Paul of Tarsus, not the Saul of rabbinic Judaism, the Apostle of Jesus of Nazareth, who wrote, 'It is well for a man not to touch a woman.' And he seemed to be dimly aware of this in some intuitive fashion, for he confessed, 'Concerning the unmarried, I have no command of the Lord, but I give my opinion.' It was truly an opinion, one which has worked great mischief in the Church, obscuring the naturalism of Christianity with a dualistic coloring for centuries.

Yet Paul's Judaism does come through. His naturalism was not entirely obscured. Very likely there were those in Corinth who were strongly ascetic, who had serious doubts about sex even within marriage. They wondered whether total abstinence might not be the ideal. Paul did not agree. He refused to condemn all sexual activities as springing from weakness of the flesh. He knew that there was no virtue in outer celibacy when inwardly one was filled with desire. Too long a period of continence would even serve as a temptation to the strongly sexed to have extra-marital relations. Therefore Paul advised 'that every man had better have a wife of his own and every woman a husband of her own. The husband must give the wife her conjugal dues, and the wife in the same way must give her husband his; a wife cannot do as she pleases with her body . . . and in the same way a husband cannot do as he pleases with his body.' No Hellenistic dualist would have spoken as positively about sex and marriage as Paul did. Jesus' concern for the inner motive found clear echo in Paul, who wrote, 'If they cannot restrain themselves, let them marry. Better marry than be aflame with passion!' Neither Jesus nor Paul found any virtue in disciplining the flesh for the sake of discipline. That is the way of the ascetic, not of the Jew. If a man is consumed by sexual desire, he ought to marry. Rigorous self-denial is of no meaning because it represents a divided self.

What is required is a single heart, a single mind, a wholeness of the personality. If a man is so intent upon other things that sexual energy is entirely sublimated, he has no problem, which seems to have been the case with Jesus himself as with Saint Francis of Assisi. But if his libidinal drives are strong, then clearly, he ought to marry and to engage in coitus. If he is 'aflame with passion,' he certainly will not be able to study how to please the Lord. Far better for him to release his sexual tensions so that he can go to his prayers at peace. This was Paul's point of view and advice. No dualist of any age would counsel so. The dualist always urges men to wrestle the more strenuously with their baser emotions, for in their victory they will become nobler and better. Paul, in contrast, insisted that 'if you marry, you do not sin,' and enjoined husbands and wives to give each other their conjugal rights, advising against over-long continence. This scarcely sounds like a man convinced that sex is evil in and of itself. Nor does the verse farther on in the same epistle give that impression: 'Do we not have the right to be accompanied by a wife, as the other apostles and the brothers of the Lord and Cephas?' (1 Corinthians 9:5). Paul did not himself exercise that right, but he gave no indication of any disapproval of his colleagues. There is considerable dispute over whether the Epistle to the Ephesians is by Paul, but certainly its author was saturated with Pauline thought and language, and the simile likening the relationship of Christ and the Church to that between husband and wife indicates a strongly positive view of marriage.

Yet when all of these entries have been made on the credit side of the ledger of Paul's interpretation of sex, there are figures on the debit side which at least betray Hellenistic coloration. One wonders, for example, why the unmarried state should be a better preparation for the coming of the Lord than marriage — unless a complete withdrawal from the world were counseled, a retreat emphatically denied by Paul in the Thessalonian correspondence. And Paul's attitude toward sexual sins was far more abra-

sive than that of his Master, who was extremely tolerant of harlots
and publicans, reserving his harsher words for sinners of the
spirit. Paul almost seemed to relish rolling the words off his pen,
as he scalded the vices and perversions of the age, a vehemence
which causes the psychologist to raise a quizzical brow. So violent
was Paul's condemnation of sexual sins that one scholar has
been led to suggest that the mysterious 'thorn in the flesh' of
which the Apostle complained but never identified was actually
an active and tempting libido.[6] Such a view, however, seems
scarcely plausible. If Paul were consumed by erotic desires, it is
more than probable that he would have married. But the frequency of the references to sexual irregularities in the Epistles
cannot be ignored. Even when allowances have been made for the
licentiousness of the Graeco-Roman world in which the struggling churches were growing up, still Paul's diatribes tell us as
much about himself as about the wickedness of the age.

Paul's attitude toward sex and marriage was marked, then,
with inconsistency. He was a Jew, steeped in the naturalism of
the Old Testament, captivated by Jesus Christ, preaching the
message of love, convinced that God penetrates the veneer of
outer act to lay his probing finger upon the inner motive. He
was in no sense a Hellenistic dualist, regarding the body and its
functions as evil, to be denied and disciplined for the sake of a
pure soul. He not only allowed coitus for those with strong sexual desire but positively advised it, warning against the temptations which follow an artificial restraint, instructing husbands
and wives to give to each other the conjugal rights. Yet his Jewish
naturalism was debased by his cosmopolitanism. He preferred
celibacy to marriage, a preference which he tried to justify apoca-
lyptically, but which betrays a dualistic bias. His statement 'It
is well for a man not to touch a woman' was almost purely Hellenistic, entirely contrary to Hebrew ethics. In Paul, as in the
Church which grew up on the foundations he laid, the two
strands of Jewish naturalism and Hellenistic dualism blend to
form a curious and complex pattern. Paul himself managed to

6. Cf. Morton Scott Enslin, *The Ethics of Paul*, Harper & Brothers, New
York, 1930, p. 228f.

keep the former as the dominant motif, with the latter a minor figure, appearing now and then in the background. But as the Church moved out among the Gentiles, the Jewish heritage and language faded into the past, and the Hellenistic influence grew. Paul's use of 'flesh' and 'spirit' were interpreted dualistically so that Marcion, the first great enemy of the Hebraic elements in Christianity could adapt the Epistles perfectly to his purposes. The Gnostics and their successors in heresy were all essentially dualistic, and although in most other respects the Church successfully defended the ramparts of naturalism, the citadel of sex fell to the enemy. Increasingly, virginity became a cardinal virtue, marriage a concession to the weak, not because the end of the world was at hand, for the Church early realized the necessity for revising the timetable of cataclysm, but because sex had become an evil necessity for the propagation of the race, to be avoided and denied by the spiritually strong. Marriage was, to be sure, an honorable estate, but unquestionably inferior to celibacy. And even those who were 'consumed with passion' were urged not to marry, to discipline themselves, to mortify the flesh, for the flesh was evil (cf. the Temptations of St. Anthony). Perhaps it is unjust to Paul to say that he was the 'fifth column' within the Church responsible for all of this. It might have happened in any case, or Christianity might have remained a small and obscure sect within the Jewish nation. But certainly Paul played no small role in the conquest of the new faith by a Hellenistic-Oriental dualism in the interpretation of sex. He played the role all unwittingly, however, for essentially he was a Jew, a brother and kinsman to Jesus of Nazareth.

II

AUGUSTINE

No SURVEY OF any aspect of Christian thought can afford to neglect Augustine. He marks the transition point between the ancient world and the Middle Ages. The father of Latin theology, the progenitor of the major ideas and terminology of medieval Catholicism, he is also a kind of spiritual grandfather to Luther and the Protestant Reformers, whom he profoundly influenced. Born in a small town in North Africa in A.D. 354, he passed through all of the major phases of ancient culture before his conversion to Christianity. He showed early promise as a student and was exposed to the best education available in his province. At the age of eighteen, while a student at the University at Carthage, he read Cicero's *Hortensius,* a book which changed his life. The work is no longer extant, but it seems to have urged upon its readers the importance of practical wisdom. Augustine was seized by a passionate desire for an all-embracing world view, an answer to the question of life's meaning. He was assured that existence has some purpose, but the particular character of that purpose was not clear to him. A persistent restlessness disturbed him and he sought release from it in a faith which would unify his life and relate him significantly to the deeper meaning which lies behind all things. It was not merely an intellectual quest upon which he embarked, but a religious one as well. Where was he to find the key to life's box of puzzles? His Christian mother pointed him toward the Scriptures, but Augustine balked. His literary teeth, cut on the master stylists of the Latin tongue — Cicero, Vergil, Seneca, Lucretius — were set on edge by the crude Hebraisms of the Old Testament. Nor could he digest the contradictions of which the Bible seemed to him to be full.

He turned, instead, to the Manichees, a mystical religious cult widespread in North Africa at the time. Typical of the syncretism of the period, the blending together of doctrines from many philosophical and religious schools, Manicheeism drew its chief ideas from the Zoroastrianism of Persia. Augustine was taught that the whole world is involved in a cosmic struggle between two primordial forces — the principle of goodness, symbolized by light, and that of evil, or darkness — and that all men must choose between them. This sweeping dualism readily lent itself to the prevailing identification of the body with evil and the soul with good. The Manichees followed a regime of rigid asceticism, severely disciplining the flesh, practicing both vegetarianism and celibacy. This was the path followed by the pure ones, or *Cathari,* who achieved a triumph over the powers of darkness and entered into the realm of light. But since all men could not attain such heights, provision was made for a lower level, those who joined the sect without the rigors of the ascetic discipline, the *auditors,* or hearers, and it was to this outer circle that Augustine attached himself. He had taken to himself a concubine and found it impossible to break out of the prison house of the flesh. So alluring was his jailer that escape was unthinkable. Yet there was a law in his mind which plagued him with strong feelings of guilt. He thought he ought to be celibate, to be able to live without the degrading necessity of sex, and this was a conviction firmly implanted in his mind long before he became a Christian. He simply shared the prevailing view of almost all savants and seekers of the age: that the wise man and the holy man must eschew the desires of the flesh for the quieter life of contemplation.

For nine years Augustine remained with the Manichees, but a growing doubt, which a visiting hierarch failed to dispel, finally led him to unbelief. In 383, he moved to Rome and in the fol-

lowing year to Milan, where he pursued his career as a teacher
of rhetoric. There he associated himself briefly with the Skeptics,
or Academics. This school of professional intellectuals abandoned the search for Truth. Absolute certainty was regarded as
an illusion, forever beyond the feeble grasp of the human mind.
The senses are notoriously untrustworthy, the eyes and ears frequently deceive; how can one know when they are really right?
The ideas and opinions of men are ephemeral, changing from
age to age. How, then, can one be sure of anything? The answer
is that one cannot. The only certainty is that there is no certainty. Some of these Skeptics went so far as to withdraw from the
world entirely, into the desert. Since they could never be assured
that their course of action was right, the wisest course was to take
no action at all. Augustine remained on the periphera of this
group, also. His skepticism was less sweeping, less radical. He
asserts in the *Confessions,* his spiritual autobiography, that during this period he never ceased to believe in providence, in the
ultimate meaningfulness of existence, but once more he did not
know what that meaning was, and he did entertain some doubts
about the immortality of the soul. His was a temperament which
could not long endure agnosticism. He was driven by an unre-
lenting quest for certainty.

But where was wisdom to be found, where the place of understanding? He still could not please his mother by embracing
Christianity; Manicheeism had been weighed in the balance and
found wanting; skepticism gave him no peace. He found the way
out of his wilderness, intellectually at least, in Neo-Platonism.
In Milan, he read Plotinus, recently translated into Latin by
Victorinus Rhetor, Rome's most eminent teacher. He had read
Plato's *Timaeus* and some of the other dialogues, but where Plato
failed to answer Augustine's questions, Plotinus succeeded. The
chief barrier to his unqualified affirmation of a meaningful world
was, for Augustine, the existence of evil. For a long time, the
dualism of the Manichees, with its assurance of the ultimate victory of the good, had satisfied him. But when that faith broke
down, his only alternative was skepticism. If the world was purposeful, why should there be suffering and evil? Why should

whatever power there may be who directs all things allow the
wicked to rage? Plotinus' answer was that evil is in itself nothing;
it is simply the absence of good. Pure goodness is pure Being;
pure evil is absolute non-being. Augustine gladly embraced this
happy solution to his problem. He adopted the Neo-Platonic
categories of thought and laid the foundations of his later theology. He saw that non-being is a logical principle, a limit for
thought. If one can speak of an existent's having being, then after
its destruction, it is by no means nonsense to speak of its not
being. But it is a contradiction to speak of non-being as evil, for
that would be to say that it had being. Everything that is, is good.
Evil is the result of the intrusion of non-being into the realm
of being. It is degradation, loss of status, sinking to a lower level
of existence. For a tiger to behave like a tiger, or a pig like a
pig, is not evil. These creatures were made to act so and are
simply fulfilling their own natures. But for a man to live like a
tiger or a pig, that is degrading. He has lost his true nature, his
true being, and that is evil. It is not altogether accurate to speak
of the *man* as evil, for he exists, and in so far as he exists, he is
good. It is rather the corruption, the loss of being, that is evil.
All things that are have been created by God *ex nihilo,* out of
nothing, and they are suspended over an abyss of non-being,
utterly dependent for their continued existence upon the creating and sustaining power of the divine. God cannot create evil,
and nothing that is, is evil. The only evil is failure, the return
to the abyss.

Augustine was able to satisfy his intellectual quest for meaning
in this way, but his emotional life was still in turmoil. He could
deal with the problem of evil in his mind; in his life it remained
unsolved. He could not subdue his lust of the flesh. He could not
conceive of life without sex, although he was still tormented by
guilt over his 'habit of satisfying an insatiable lust.' He had been
attending Christian worship in Milan and was greatly impressed
by the preaching of the bishop, Ambrose. Stirred by this impetus,
he returned to the study of the Scriptures, and in Paul's Epistle
to the Romans, he heard the voice of God speaking to him directly. His conversion resulted in the transformation of his life.

He was no longer a man divided against himself, wrestling vainly against his inner desires. His lust was gone; his tastes had been changed. His appetite was no longer for the things of the flesh but of the spirit. This was what he had sought from the beginning. He could not enter the inner circle of the Manichees because he was unable to give up sex. He felt that he could not become a Christian until he found the power to embrace celibacy. The Oriental-Hellenistic dualism of his day influenced him in such a way that his interpretation of sex was far more negative than Paul's. Yet the naturalism of the Old Testament and of Christianity also made its mark. Augustine was by no means a thoroughgoing dualist. The two strands are interwoven in his thought in an exceedingly complex pattern. But in his attitude toward sex, dualism proves the stronger of the two.

Sex before and after the Fall of Man

Augustine overcame his earlier aversion to the Hebrew Scriptures sufficiently to recognize the essential naturalism of the creation narrative in the book of Genesis. He looked upon sex and marriage as facts of creation, and to that extent he was forced to call them good. Adam and Eve, before their disobedience, walked naked and unashamed in the Garden of Eden. Their nudity was pure, as their sexual intercourse would have been, had they not sinned and been expelled from Paradise before their first coitus occurred. God obviously intended that man should be a sexual creature; otherwise he would have created a second man rather than a woman as Adam's helpmeet. But sex in Paradise would have been a phenomenon very different from its present corrupted state. There would have been no lust, no passion, no heat. The sexual urges of Adam and Eve before the Fall were entirely controlled by their minds and wholly at the service of procreation. Augustine suggested that the first parents of the race would have decided calmly and rationally to produce a child, engaged in intercourse without lust or passion, and then awaited the birth of their son. There would have been no irresistible desire, no pain or bleeding connected with the defloration of Eve, no pangs of childbirth. All parts of their bodies were controlled by the rational will, and sexual desire would have come and gone on call. Augustine's chief objection to sex in the fallen state is the fact that desire is not controlled by the reason. Of almost equal odiousness to him is the tempestuous nature of orgasm, blotting out all else in life, banishing the reason, sweeping the mind before it as a raging flood. In contrast, the sexual relations of Paradise were intended to be placid, rational, and without the imperious ferocity of passion. Augustine was never altogether clear as to whether the pristine sex of Adam and Eve would have carried with it pleasure, and if so, of what kind. Whatever joys may have been involved were clearly meant to be less intense and more moderate than those experienced now. Here the influence of the classical tradition on Augustine becomes readily apparent, in his emphasis on moderation, on the rational, contemplative life. Sex after the Fall is evil primarily because it interferes with that life, disturbing the peace of scholarship and meditation. Augustine's Neo-Platonic background, with its assurance that all things are good, together with such naturalism as he gleaned from the Bible, led him to assert that sex would have existed before the Fall of Adam and Eve, but the sex of Paradise would have been more moderate, more in keeping with the rational, contemplative existence of the sage, and it would have been entirely for the purpose of procreation.

The Bible itself, in its account of the Fall, is silent about the sexual relations of Adam and Eve in Paradise. Augustine had no Biblical evidence that the expulsion from the Garden preceded their first intercourse, and he was making a large assumption. Very probably he was motivated by his desire to emphasize the fact that the original sin was *not,* as seems to have been understood in some quarters even then, the sexual act. He spoke explicitly against such a misunderstanding of the Bible. The original sin, he said, was rather pride, which he defined as 'a perverse desire of elevation, forsaking Him to whom the soul ought solely to cleave as its beginning, and the making of one's self the one beginning.' [1] In pride and self-love, Adam and Eve chose their own wills, rather than the will of God, and they ate

1. *The City of God,* Book XIV, Chapter 13.

of the forbidden fruit. The immediate result was that 'the eyes
of them both were opened, and they knew that they were naked;
and they sewed fig leaves together and made themselves aprons'
(Genesis 3:7). Augustine remarked on the curious fact that they
covered their genitals, rather than their hands and mouths, for it
was the latter which were guilty of sin, in taking and eating. He
speculated as to the meaning of this anomaly and found the answer in the words, 'the eyes of them both were opened.' This
could not mean that before sin they were blind, for Adam had
to see in order to behold and name the animals which God
showed him. It means that they became aware of a new impulse,
independent of their minds and wills, which Augustine called
concupiscence. Fallen man was now beset by a kind of lust, a
burning desire which he did not know in Paradise, where he was
satisfied with the knowledge and the love of God. Having turned
away from God to himself, from the true source and center of his
being to a false center, he was filled with a restless longing which
affected all his thoughts and acts. All men since the Fall are
searching for that which was lost — fellowship with God, who
gives depth and meaning and purpose to life. So long as they
wander from God, they seek meaning and purpose in themselves,
or in artifacts of their own creation, in money, in power, in prestige, and so forth. They are driven in all areas of life by concupiscence, whose chief characteristic is insatiability. The more
a man gets in life, the more he wants. He is never content but
looks always for more. His thirst can be quenched at only one
spring; all else is ocean water, parching his throat still further.
'Thou hast made us for Thyself,' Augustine wrote, 'and our
hearts are restless till they find their rest in Thee.'

Concupiscence affects all areas of life but with especial force
in the sexual realm. When the eyes of Adam and Eve were
opened, they became aware of the workings of sexual concupiscence in them. No longer were they living in full harmony with
reason and nature, in control of all of their faculties. Now they
found feelings within themselves that came unbidden. Because
they were disobedient to God, they suffered the consequences of
disobedience to self, symbolized and made manifest in their

bodies. They were still able to control and direct their arms and legs and eyes, but their sexual organs acted independently. They found, as have all their descendants since, that sex lay beyond their control, the desire necessary to tumescence and coitus sometimes arriving without invitation and sometimes refusing to answer conscious summons. This, then, is the divine punishment for disobedience: man's body becomes disobedient to him. Augustine thought it peculiarly appropriate that the generative organs should be especially affected, since it is through them that the results of original sin are passed on from parent to child.

The impotence of the will to command the sexual organs gave birth to the sense of shame. Since man is no longer master in his own house, he hides the usurper from sight. He can no longer give the orders, but he can conceal his unhappy plight. Augustine was immensely impressed by the fact of shame, pointing out that even in legal and honorable wedlock, married couples exercise the utmost care to prevent their sexual relations from being observed. The children who are produced by intercourse are never permitted to witness the act. Augustine observed that it was altogether fitting for the school of philosophers who inveighed against modesty, insisting that coitus was perfectly honorable and therefore to be performed in the open, for all to see, to call themselves Cynics, since the term in Greek bears a close resemblance to the word for dog-like. A certain cultural imperialism betrayed Augustine into believing that all men were as he was. He had no way of knowing that shame and modesty are by no means universal phenomena.

Since concupiscence entered into the whole of the life of fallen man, and especially in his sexual activity, no sexual union takes place without its corrupting effect, without burning desire and compulsiveness, which is both the result of sin and the punishment of sin. All children are born out of the workings of concupiscence, and they inherit both the reality and the guilt of this lust. All men are conceived in sin and born in sin and therefore are under the devil's power. They are not evil because they are human; their humanity as such is the creation of God and therefore good. The evil lies rather in their concupiscence, which is a pollution, a degradation, a loss of being. Man's original ability to control all of his body has been lost, and it is this deprivation of being which is evil. Because this evil is transmitted through the sexual act, it was necessary for Christ to be born of a Virgin. Since no concupiscence was involved in his conception, the Saviour was free from sin. Between Mary and Joseph there was no nuptial cohabitation, for if there had been, Christ must have been contaminated by concupiscence and would have come actually in sinful flesh, rather than in the *likeness* of sinful flesh. Augustine regarded the Virgin Birth as eloquent testimony to the ubiquity of the effects of sinful lust, since only Christ was without sin, and he alone was born without benefit of sex. The development from the Apostle Paul to Augustine becomes disturbingly clear at this point. Paul also believed that sin is transmitted from one generation to the next, through the flesh. But he did not even hint what was openly stated by Augustine, that the sexual act is evil or responsible for the passing on of original sin. Nor did Paul know of any doctrine of the Virgin Birth of Christ in order to free him from the taint of sin. He believed that Christ was without sin ('He who knew no sin was made sin for us'), but in Paul's thought there was no necessity for Christ to be born asexually, as there was in Augustine's. Paul did express a preference for celibacy, but he did not condemn those who found it necessary to marry, nor did he anywhere suggest that sex within wedlock was in any way questionable.

The Good of Marriage

Augustine, of course, insisted that marriage in itself is not sinful. Marriage remains the creation of God and must therefore be good. Sin is conveyed by what occurs within marriage, not by marriage itself. To censure fleshly lust, said Augustine, is not to censure marriage. What he called 'the malady of concupiscence' is the outcome not of marriage but of sin. He used the analogy of a lame man limping to a certain place in order to attain a good object. His limping does not detract from the good of the object, but neither does the good object make the limping good. So the evil of concupiscence does not take away the good of marriage, but neither does the marriage make a good of lust. God, however, maketh the wrath of men to praise him and brings good out of evil. The divine wisdom can still extract a good out of the evil of concupiscence, in the propagation of the species. A man can direct the wild horse of lust into the bridle path of domesticity if he will exert all of his strength and allow it to run only when intent upon 'the carnal generation of children.' Augustine believed that this was actually the case with the Old Testament patriarchs. Their primary religious duty, sexually speaking, was to procreate the chosen people of God so that the prophecy of Christ's coming might be heard among them and also that 'the house and lineage of David' might be established, within which were to dwell the earthly parents of the Messiah. Under the old dispensation, the covenant of the Old Testament, the children of Israel were begotten by physical birth. Therefore, polygamy was permitted because through that agency more offspring would be produced. But, as Augustine pointed out, polyandry was not sanctioned, since that could not serve the purposes of procreation. A woman requires only one husband to impregnate her, while a man can father children on several wives. The patriarchs' practice of polygamy, however, was never for the satisfaction of fleshly lust. They acted wholly in accord with the divine will and never approached the beds of any of their wives except when intending to be fruitful and multiply. The name of Isaac means, in Hebrew, 'laughter,' and one can imagine at least a smile on the faces of the lusty patriarchs at the naïveté of the proper Bishop of Hippo. Forced to rationalize the divinely approved libidinal meanderings of the heroes of Israel, Augustine nevertheless insisted that the good of marriage is better promoted in monogamy, because God created one woman for one man.

Virginity and Celibacy

Under the old covenant, then, marriage was not only permitted but commanded for the purpose of the carnal generation of the chosen people of God. But now, since the coming of Christ, the time for marrying has come to an end, and it is better to live in virginity, for now the children of God are not produced by physical birth but by spiritual rebirth. From the standpoint of the economy of salvation, it does not matter under what circumstances children are born. The offspring of believers are conceived in sin equally as much as the progeny of pagans, the children of legal wedlock are in the same condemnation as illegitimate sons and daughters. All must be born again to be saved. The preservation of the race as well as the production of candidates for salvation may be left to the pagans. Christians can confine themselves to concern with the second birth, refraining from marriage and reproduction, for this is the more excellent way. Augustine believed all sexual desire to be tainted with evil, corrupted by concupiscence, and therefore to be avoided if possible. Not even the good of begetting children was to be compared with the blessedness of celibacy. Virginity is of such a value that not even the desire to raise up children to convert to Christ can compensate for its loss. The married are under no circumstances to imagine that theirs is an estate of dignity and sanctity equal to that of the celibate. Those who are virgins are more pleasing in the sight of God, and they will have greater rewards in heaven. Both the married and the celibate Christian will, to be sure, inherit eternal life, but the latter will be able to follow the Master into the Elysian fields of virginity, while the married must remain behind. Augustine bolstered this argument with two passages from the New Testament. He cited the parable of the workers in the vineyard, all paid the same wage at the end of the day, despite considerable disparity in the work done to show that all Christians receive eternal life, regardless of their earthly circumstances. But then he pointed to the saying in the Fourth Gospel, 'In my father's house are many mansions,' declaring that the mansions of the virginal will shine with a greater light than the less pretentious dwellings of the married. In a similar vein, Augustine urged widows not to remarry, but to remain single. His whole treatise *Of Holy Virginity* sought to persuade his readers that celibacy is better in the eyes of God than marital intercourse, however pure and loving that intercourse might be. The strong apocalyptic note in Paul has almost completely disappeared in Augustine, who interprets 1 Corinthians 7 with a dualistic bias.

Augustine did declare, however, that one's sexual status is of secondary importance to his total orientation. The virginal must be warned against the sin of pride, which is far worse than any sexual sin. 'Wherefore virginity is not only to be set forth, that it may be loved, but also to be admonished, that it be not puffed up.' [2] Precisely because celibacy is such a good, those who practice it must constantly be on their guard against the temptation to self-righteousness. After all, sinners who know themselves to be such are easily humble. There is little danger that the harlot and the publican will be unaware of their need for forgiveness. And all men, however saintly, are morally bankrupt before the throne of God, at the mercy of the divine grace. Therefore those who have kept themselves pure in carnal matters must beware that they do not soil themselves spiritually by crying, 'My God, I thank thee that I am not as other men are.' They must maintain their assurance that virginity is to be preferred to marriage, but they must not set themselves above their married brethren. They must not judge their neighbors nor compare themselves with any other humans, unless it be with the holy martyrs. They must ask themselves whether their sacrifice of sensual pleasure is to be compared with the martyr's sacrifice of his life. They must remember that many who were not virgins were nonetheless faithful unto death and therefore will follow Christ into the fields of martyrdom, while they are left behind. But no man should ever set himself beside another for purposes of comparison. Every Christian, said Augustine, must rather set himself beside his Lord and before such a measuring stick, even the most holy virgin knows himself to be a sinner in need of forgiveness. Even those who are without outer blemish are not free from the sin of inner thoughts and desires. In short, humility is a greater virtue than celibacy and pride a greater sin than lust. All Christians must know that they have nothing of their own to bring before the bar of divine judgment. They can only plead, 'God be merciful unto me, a sinner.'

Mere outer virginity is no virtue in and of itself. Augustine's Biblical orientation asserted itself in his strong emphasis upon

2. *Of Holy Virginity*, Section 22.

motivation. 'Though consecrated virginity is rightly preferred to marriage, yet what Christian in his sober mind would not prefer Catholic Christian women who have been even more than once married, to not only vestals, but also to heretical virgins?' [3] The really essential thing is to hold the true Catholic Faith, and Augustine even seemed to suggest that a prostitute with orthodox beliefs would be better than a virgin who was a heretic. But even the Christian virgin cannot indulge himself in self-congratulation, since his chastity is not his own achievement but the gift of God. True Christian virginity involves not alone mere outward abstinence from sex but purity of inner attitude as well, and this is possible only for those to whom God has given his grace. Not that God ever compels virginity. He did not make such a demand even of the Mother of Christ. She had vowed her virginity to the Lord before the conception of the Saviour, and her chastity was by choice, not by command. This is not to say that anyone is wholly delivered from concupiscent desires, not even when the voluntary vow is augmented by the divine grace. Sexual impulses come even to the true Christian virgin, but no sin is involved in such an experience so long as consent is withheld. The evil of concupiscence does no harm if the will does not agree to the promptings of the instinct.

The power of withholding consent, however, does not lie in the 'natural man,' that is, man apart from divine grace. Since the Fall, all men are born in a state of inner division, the flesh lusting against the spirit. Augustine at this point was even more inconsistent than the Apostle Paul, because his Hebraic background was weaker and his Hellenistic background stronger. On the one hand, he specifically disavowed any dualistic understanding of man, denying that there are two separable natures, body and soul. He wrote a long treatise entitled *Continence,* in which he recognized that God seeks not the subjugation of the body by the mind, a sterile and moralistic wrestling with wrong desires. The true goal of the Christian is rather a transformation of the self so that the inner warfare is ended, the character of the desires changed. Mere abstention from sex has little virtue if it springs

3. *On Marriage and Concupiscence,* Book I, Chapter 5.

from the wrong motives. In this respect, Augustine correctly understood Paul's use of the term 'flesh,' realizing that it refers to 'spiritual' sins no less than carnal ones. On the other hand, however, Augustine consistently implied that the dark powers within must be rigorously held in check and subdued by the higher powers of reason. His Manichean dualism lingered on in places, as for example where he came very close to Plato's analogy of the charioteer, striving to hold the steed of sensuality on a close rein while encouraging the noble stallion of the mind. The Bible is clear that man's nature is one, a psycho-physical unity, and there is nowhere any suggestion that the body should be controlled or ruled by the reason. Augustine's prejudice against the passions, particularly the sexual passion, is thoroughly un-Biblical, derived from Hellenistic sources. Not even Paul praised virginity in the extravagant language of Augustine. The latter simply took it for granted that God preferred his saved ones to abstain from sex altogether, graciously permitting them to marry if they could not, granting them in that case the gift of fidelity, contentment with monogamous intercourse for the purpose of procreation. Both the celibate and the married are utterly dependent on the divine grace for the right inner attitude as well as the proper conduct, and to neither is the gift bestowed once and for all. The struggle against concupiscence is never at an end, at least in this life. The grace of God is required continuously so long as a man lives. If once he thinks himself free from evil desires, so that he no longer needs assistance to fight them, he is lost, for then those desires will attack him with redoubled vigor.

Sex in Marriage

Augustine, for all his praise of virginity, insisted that the celibate must not make the mistake of regarding marriage as an evil. 'Both are errors, either to equal marriage to holy virginity, or to condemn it.' [4] Augustine built his fortress on a hill between two valleys of heresy: the Pelagians and the Manichees. The former, taking their name from a British monk, Pelagius, rejected the

4. *Of Holy Virginity,* Section 19.

whole doctrine of original sin, claiming that each child is born innocent. Marriage, for them, had not been affected at all by Adam's Fall. It remained as holy and as honorable as at creation. Against this, Augustine argued that concupiscence had corrupted marriage as it had corrupted every other human act or institution. But he did not go so far as the Manichees on the other side, who made marriage wholly evil, regarding even sex for procreation as the work of the devil, for to bring a child into the world was to imprison another soul in the flesh. Augustine replied that corrupted though marriage might be, it nonetheless remained the creation of God, with vestiges of goodness which are indelible.

Marriage is good and virginity is good. The latter is better, but the Christian is not commanded to follow the better way, which is a matter of counsel, not of command. Augustine distinguished between counsel and command, pointing out that a command applies to all men and may not be disobeyed without incurring mortal sin, while a counsel is merely a gentle suasion, a suggestion which points to the higher levels of life without compelling the believer to scale those heights. Neither marriage nor virginity is a command. The individual is left free to choose his own estate, and if he wishes to chose the better of the two, he will of course decide to remain a virgin. Marriage, however, was given to men by God and is therefore not to be despised. It is at its best when man and wife take a mutual vow of celibacy and live without sex, following the example of Mary and Joseph. This, for Augustine, was the highest good of marriage: the companionship which does not depend upon physical intercourse at all. But for those who 'cannot contain,' whose desires are such that they must allow them expression, marriage is a lawful and honorable estate. They do not sin.

There are three goods to marriage: procreation, fidelity, and sacrament. The first, reproduction, serves the purpose of harnessing youthful lust in the respectable occupation of producing children, tempering sexual desire with parental affection. To bring souls into the world is a good, for human beings are born for holy friendship with one another, and such souls are candidates for salvation. This, Augustine insisted, must be the primary motive for begetting children, the desire to produce through carnal generation that which may be spiritually regenerated, and not the egoistic wish to perpetuate one's own physical life through his seed. But such a motive must be kept within the bounds of matrimony. God's providential ordering of the world arranged that sexual desire should provide for the continuation of life. What food, therefore, is to the individual, sex is for the race. As one man requires nourishment for his preservation, the whole of mankind requires sex for its continued existence. The satisfaction of both hunger and lust are carnal delights, said Augustine, but by temperance excess can be avoided. And as it would be better to die of hunger than to eat food offered to idols, so it would be better to do without children than to seek a family in unlawful intercourse. No doubt Augustine was correct in his conclusion, but his analogy is a curious one. Even Paul found no harm in eating meat sacrificed to idols, and certainly he would not have counseled starvation in the midst of plenty, even though the food came from pagan altars. Augustine's larger measure of asceticism is plainly manifest. Marriage, for Augustine, did not require any sort of ceremony, either legal or ecclesiastical. He recognized the validity of a union between a man and a woman, provided only that two conditions were fulfilled: a mutual resolve to make the relationship permanent, lasting through the lifetime of both parties, and a willingness to accept any children born of their coitus, doing nothing to prevent the birth of any babies conceived. The first good of marriage, then, is the procreation of the race.

The second blessing of the marital state is fidelity, and under this heading Augustine dealt with sexual relations not primarily aimed at reproduction. Marriage is, of course, intended only for those who cannot contain, who find it necessary to obtain release from strong sexual tension. Augustine agreed with Paul in advising such people that it is better to marry than to be consumed with passion, that matrimony keeps the concupiscent urges within lawful bonds. This is the origin of Augustine's pharmaceutical definition of marriage as a 'medicine for immorality.' He further agreed with the Apostle that one marriage partner ought not to take a vow of celibacy without the consent of the other, lest the weaker member be led astray by his unsated desire. Augustine knew from his own experience how powerfully Eros can tug at the sleeve, and he repeated Paul's admonition to married couples to give each other their conjugal rights. But where Paul rested his case, Augustine went considerably farther. In the first place, he voiced his horror at what he called 'immoderate license,' demanding that marital coitus be moderate, limited, and altogether decorous. And secondly, he asserted that sex within marriage which is not motivated by the desire for children is a sin. Paul, in contrast, nowhere spoke of moderation in lawful sexual relations. He was realist enough to know that some persons carry a high sexual voltage, and he recognized that it was important to provide safe and legal means to deal with it. Let them marry and release their energy. He made no mention of moderation, since that would, for some at least, be as dangerous as to ask them to remain unmarried. The whole purpose of marriage, for Paul, was to quench the fires of passion, and he knew that an inferno cannot be put out with an eye dropper. Augustine, while allowing this purpose with the one hand, proceeded to take it away with the other. Nor did Paul anywhere restrict sexual relations within marriage to those entered with the intent of procreation. This Augustine could not have found in the Bible; he drew it rather from the dualism of the Graeco-Roman world, which looked upon sex as an evil necessary to the preservation of the species, an appetite which must be tempered by the golden mean of moderation.

Augustine did admit that sex for pleasure instead of pregnancy is only a venial sin, one that is pardonable as a lesser evil than extra-marital intercourse. But this was for him the lowest level to which one could sink and keep within the limits of propriety. Here, Augustine's ignorance of Greek led him astray. He was forced to read his New Testament in Latin translation, and in his perusal of Paul's 1 Corinthians 7, he encountered the passage where married couples were counseled not to abstain from coitus for lengthy intervals, 'lest Satan tempt you through lack of self control. I say this by way of concession, not of command.' The

Latin for 'concession' is *veniam,* or pardon, while the original Greek read *sungnomen,* which means rather allowance, regard for circumstance and temperament. Augustine took *veniam* quite literally and labeled sex for pleasure a venial sin, requiring pardon. Actually, this is a very questionable interpretation of Paul's teaching. The Apostle was making allowances for individual temperament, not commanding frequent intercourse but raising no objection where the persons involved seemed to require it. Paul said nothing about procreation or the motive thereto. Augustine, on the other hand, regarded all sex except that required for reproduction as venially sinful. This is one of the best examples of the way in which the somber blue of Hellenistic dualism has crowded out the bright red of Biblical naturalism in the development between Paul and Augustine. It would be unfair to lay the sole responsibility for this on Augustine. He simply accepted the tradition as it was passed on to him from earlier hands, but he did systematize and solidify it, making it definitive for the medieval Church, and it is his mind which still dominates the Roman Catholic interpretation of sex, as will become apparent in subsequent chapters. Yet many of the most important aspects of that interpretation are Hellenistic rather than Biblical in origin.

Permissible and pardonable though marital relations apart from procreation may be, Augustine nevertheless set rigidly circumscribed limits. No attempt must ever be made, 'either by wrong desire or evil appliance' to prevent procreation. Any who sink to such depths are guilty of animal conduct. Augustine could not under any circumstances allow sex which was for pleasure or the expression of love alone. There must always be at least the *possibility* of impregnation. He strictly forbade birth control, abortion, or the exposure of unwanted children. He even condemned what was later called the 'rhythm method' of birth control. This passage is worth quoting in full in the light of modern Roman Catholic teaching on the subject. 'Is it not you (referring to the Manichees) who used to counsel us to observe as much as possible the time when a woman, after her purification, is most likely to conceive, and to abstain from cohabitation at that time, lest the soul should be entangled in the flesh? This proves that you approve of having a wife, not for the procreation of children, but for the gratification of passion. In marriage, as the marriage law declares, the man and woman come together for the procreation of children. . . . Where there is a wife there must be marriage, but there is no marriage where motherhood is not in view; therefore neither is there a wife.' [5] Augustine was certain that such a practice transformed a wife into a mistress, who exchanged the use of her body for suitable gifts. This ban on any form of birth control applies equally, of course, to any other method of attaining orgasm: mutual masturbation, fellatio, cunnilingus, or pederasty, since such would be carried on for pleasure alone. All sex within marriage must be conducted in such a way that conception is always possible. If a man and his wife have intercourse without the intent of offspring, motivated by love or the desire for pleasure, the sin is venial, pardonable, provided that nothing is done to prevent the union of sperm and egg. But if birth control in any form is used, the sin becomes mortal. The only purpose for permitting sex for pleasure within marriage is to avoid the greater sin of extra-marital intercourse. This is the second good of marriage, then, fidelity, and the bodies of the married are holy if they keep faith with one another and with God.

The third and final good of marriage is the sacrament, the indissoluble link between a man and his wife. Augustine made no exceptions in the dictum that divorce is never permissible. Separation is the only resort for couples who cannot live in peace together, but no remarriage is possible while both are alive. Augustine anticipated that appeal might be made to certain Old Testament examples of divorce and remarriage on the grounds of barrenness by replying that this was under the old dispensation when reproduction was a duty to God. Since Christ, however, not even a childless marriage may be dissolved. Matrimony is a sacrament and as such indelible. Even if a husband and wife secure a civil divorce and remarry, although *de facto* they are no longer married, in the eyes of God they remain man and wife so long as they both shall live. In the case of separation by death, the

5. *On The Morals of the Manichaeans*, Chapter 65.

bereft one is permitted a second spouse if he or she cannot contain, but celibacy is decidedly preferable. Augustine followed Paul, and both were certain that they were following Jesus in regarding matrimony as an absolutely indissoluble bond. No allowance is made for individual circumstances; marriage has become a legalistic prison from which there is no escape.

Summary

When Augustine's views on sex and marriage are arranged in hierarchical form, permanent virginity, like the name of Abou ben Adam, leads all the rest. It is the highest and greatest good. When the question was raised as to how the race should be preserved, Augustine replied that the heathen would see to that. And what if all the heathen are converted to Christianity and practice exemplary purity? So much the better, for the Kingdom will then arrive all the sooner! Just below permanent virginity on the scale of valuation comes celibacy on the part of those who have had previous sexual experience: widows and widowers or married couples who vow to live together as Mary and Joseph, abstaining from all coitus. Those who cannot attain these heights must confine their sexual relations to procreative acts (presumably intercourse during pregnancy or after menopause would be taboo). Still under the law, guilty only of venial sin, are those whose primary motive in sex is pleasure or love but who do nothing to forestall conception. Anything else sexual was consigned by Augustine to outer darkness. He did not, as Thomas Aquinas was later to do, arrange these in the order of their gravity, but he made scattered references to such illicit acts as fornication, adultery, masturbation, incest, birth control, and so on. Augustine modified all such ethical judgments with one theological principle: the highest of human virtues is entirely without merit apart from faith in God. Even those Christians who are guilty of the venial sin of sex for pleasure are more pleasing to the divine than the purest pagan virgins, for the former are destined for eternal life in spite of their sins, while the latter's chastity cannot save them from damnation. Augustine was too much the disciple of Paul to regard any human works as efficacious for salvation. 'As the feasts of the Just are better than the fasts of the sacrilegious, so the marriage of the faithful is to be set before the virginity of the impious.' Augustine quickly went on, however, to caution, 'Neither in that case is feasting to be preferred to fasting, but righteousness to sacrilege; nor in this, marriage to virginity, but faith to impiety.' [6]

What about the Just, the saved ones? Are they freed from concupiscence? Augustine, despite his agreement with Catholic teaching that the sacrament of baptism removes the taint of original sin, and in spite of the strong link which he forged between original sin and concupiscence, answered in the negative. To all sin, he wrote, there are two aspects: what he called the *actus,* or the act of the sin itself, and the *reatus,* or the guilt which follows in its train. In many cases, the act of the sin is buried in the past. It is no longer a present reality, but the guilt remains, unforgiven. The *actus* is ended, but the *reatus* lingers on. With concupiscence, it is just the reverse. Baptism forgives the sin and removes the guilt. The *reatus* has been banished, but the *actus,* the force of concupiscence, remains in the form of desires. Sexual urgings and longings arise in the mind and imagination of the holiest of men, but there is no guilt attached to them so long as the will does not consent to their lecherous promptings. Concupiscence is like languor after a disease; the germ has been destroyed, but the patient feels weak and debilitated. In the regenerate, the voice of concupiscence gradually diminishes, until it disappears almost entirely with advanced years. In those who have been immoderate, however, sexual impotence in old age does not bring with it release from yearning. Lust continues to rage in the mind, even when it can no longer stir the body. In an illuminating passage in the *Confessions,* Augustine complained that free though he seemed from past evil cravings, his dreams sometimes betrayed him. His vigilant censor was able to bar the door to the remembrance of things past when he was awake, but asleep, his dreams were most alluring. 'Still there exist in my memory . . . the images of such things as my habits had fixed there; and these rush into my

6. *On the Good of Marriage,* Section 8.

thoughts, though strengthless when I am awake; but in sleep they do so not only as to give pleasure, but even to obtain consent, and what very nearly resembles reality.' [7]

The Pelagians were quick to ask Augustine why concupiscence should be passed on to the children of baptized believers if concupiscence is banished in *reatus* by baptism and diminished in *actus* by old age. Augustine was equally quick to respond that what one bequeaths to his offspring is not the condition of his spiritual regeneration, but that of his own carnal generation. He was an early advocate of the theory that acquired characteristics (of which salvation is clearly one) are not inheritable. What is seminally carried over to the offspring is that with which the parents were born, both the *actus* and the *reatus* of concupiscence. The baptized Christian, however, is freed of the guilt, and the actuality remains only in the form of involuntary impulses which he is given the strength to resist and deny.

It is obvious that Augustine looked upon sex as a highly dangerous affair. He believed the best course to be one of total abstinence. If some men's thirst would not permit such self-denial, then he urged a moderate and temperate ration within the confines of marriage and preferably the narrower confines of parenthood. It might seem that this is not so far from Paul after all, but just as there is a development between Jesus, the Palestinian Jew, and Paul, the Roman citizen, so there is considerable ground between Paul, a man lightly touched by Hellenistic dualism, and Augustine, who was strongly influenced by the spirit of the age. Paul's strongest argument for celibacy was eschatological, convinced as he was that the Kingdom was at hand. He nowhere betrayed any suspicion of bodily pleasure or praised the way of the classical sage, the quiet life of moderation in all things and contemplation of the eternal.

7. *Confessions*, Book x, Chapter 30. The parallels to modern psychoanalysis in this passage are striking, in more ways than one. Not alone is there the *super-ego*, rendering the impulses of the *id* 'strengthless when awake,' but there is the persistence in dreams of successfully sublimated energies of the past. This is a phenomenon frequently encountered by persons who have completed an analysis. Some of the old anxieties and neurotic strategies which disturbed them before analysis and which have been recognized and dissipated can come to life again in dreams.

Paul knew nothing of a Virgin Birth and said nothing of the
restriction of sex to procreation. On the contrary, his entire concern was that Christians should strive to please the Lord, and
clearly no highly sexed individual could keep his mind on Christ
when his libido was chained by a false asceticism. Augustine, however, shared the classical view of life, in this one respect at least,
that he regarded sex as both immoderate and an interference with
the contemplative life of reason. Sex did seem essential to procreation, an enterprise whose absolute necessity he was unwilling to
concede, but he was prepared to resign himself to the inevitable,
albeit not without reluctance. Augustine was not a consistent
dualist by any means. He absorbed enough of the Old Testament
to catch much of its naturalism, although he never entirely overcame his suspicion of the Jewish Scriptures and came to terms with
them chiefly by means of allegory. But he did refuse to identify the
body with evil and the soul with good. Jesus and Paul, no less than
patriarchs and prophets, made that impossible for him. His Neo-
Platonism gave him an appreciative eye for the essential goodness
of all creation, including the body. He was, like the Church, in
most important respects naturalistic, sternly resistant to dualistic
heresies. But in his interpretation of sex, he was, again like the
Church, led astray into the belief that mortifying the desires of the
flesh is good for the soul, that fasting and virginity are pathways
to God. Medieval asceticism had begun. The Oriental dualism,
which broke into the western world at the time of Alexander
the Great, though successfully resisted by the Church in the theological arena, carried the day in the struggle over the interpretation
of sex. The naturalism of both Judaism and Greek classicism found
that the thumbs of the crowd were turned down.

III

THOMAS AQUINAS AND THE COUNCIL OF TRENT

AFTER AUGUSTINE the darkness fell. The barbarian tribes of north, east, and west swept across the prostrate empire, and life became insular. Little groups of human beings huddled together, scattered all across the face of Europe, laid the foundations of feudalism, the result not so much of any social theory as of necessity. This was the best way for men to survive when communication was cut off, when every man's hand was against his neighbor. It was during this period when new threads were added to the loom of western civilization — those contributed by the social organization and mores of the Teutonic tribes. All the major strands had now made their appearance in the weaving, and it remained only for them to cross and re-cross themselves in the intricate patterns of the culture of the West.

The Church readily adjusted itself to the new conditions of life. Already, missionaries had been carrying the Gospel north across the Rhine, west across the English Channel, and east across the Danube. Already, monastic asceticism had begun to regard the conditions of this life as of secondary importance. What did it matter if the world was dark and without cheer? The only thing to do in any case was to withdraw into the peace and quiet of the monastery, there to say one's prayers, to prepare one's self for the eternity which awaited, beside which three-score years and ten were but a moment. The Dark Ages were not so dark as many still assume. There was intellectual and artistic activity of distinction and even brilliance throughout the period from the fifth century to the tenth, and the Middle Ages witnessed in the thirteenth century a kind of Renaissance, whose roots went back into the eleventh and twelfth. The period of greatest creativity, however, was between 1200 and 1300 A.D., that century which in its own way matches the fifth century B.C. for its prolific spawning of genius. This was the age of Dante, of Francis of Assisi, 'God's Troubador,' of Innocent the Third, who brought the papacy to its highest point in history, of the full flowering of Gothic architecture. This was the age that produced the master theologian of medieval Christendom, Thomas Aquinas, the 'Angelic Doctor,' who gave the scholasticism of the Middle Ages its great synthesis, its hierarchical system.

Aquinas is of especial interest to this study not only because he was the greatest of the medieval theologians, but also because his system has been officially sanctioned by papal decree as the theology of the Roman Catholic Church. His life was almost dull in its uneventfulness. After a brief dramatic episode in his youth, involving a quarrel with his parents over his career, he devoted the remainder of his comparatively few years to study, to teaching, and to writing. It was in his mind that all the activity occurred. There was acted out one of the most exciting events in intellectual history — the administration of the Christian sacraments to Aristotle, who was baptized a believer and married to Augustine. The cross-fertilization between Christendom and Islam which resulted from the Crusades had brought to light once more the long sleeping mind of Plato's greatest pupil, a mind fully explored and appreciated by Arabic philosophers such as Avicenna and Averroes. The intellectuals of Europe were rent asunder by Aristotle: the conservative Augustinians refused to have anything to do with this pagan heresy, while the radical Averroists enthusiastically embraced the new ideas. Aquinas produced a synthesis of the two schools, harmonizing the thought of the two giants of antiquity, Augustine and Aristotle. In the magnificent structure of the *Summa Theologica*, the two major strands of western culture hitherto omitted were added to the weaving: the philosophy of Aristotle and the tribal life of the barbarians. This achievement was accomplished by the man whose fellow students in the classroom of Albertus Magnus called him 'the dumb ox.'

A proper understanding of Aquinas' interpretation of sex requires some grasp of his moral theology in general. He followed Aristotle's classification of all existing things under two headings — matter and form, or potentiality and actuality. Nothing in the created world is pure actuality, with all of its potentialities fully realized. That is true of God alone. Therefore, an examination of any object at any moment will reveal both its matter and its form. An acorn, for example, has as its matter all of the unrealized future of an oak tree, while its form is that of a seed; it has only realized in actuality this much of what it is destined to become. When the acorn is planted, and it grows to a young tree, its matter continues to be the potentialities which lie before it, while its form is the actuality which it has achieved. The form of anything is always what it is up to the present; the matter is the potentiality which lies in the future, that into which it may expect to develop. Obviously, each created being has its own unique form. A dog cannot hope ever to become a man, or a tree a dog. A being can become only that which lies within its form. Aristotle called the form of a living being its soul. The soul, for him, was the sum total of the dynamic, active processes going on in the life of the creature. It was not, in Aristotle's thought, a separate substance which continued to exist beyond physical death. He did speak of a kind of survival of man's reason in the sense that each man's mind participates in the universal Mind and returns to its source at death, but this is far different from personal immortality, with individuality and recollection preserved. Aristotle looked upon individuality as secondary in importance to universality, and the soul, or reason, was simply swallowed up and absorbed in the Absolute. Thomas, on the other hand, believed that the soul does survive death in individual immortality. A disembodied soul was not for him a full 'personality.' Only the full psychosomatic unity of soul *and* body constituted a whole man, and the complete human nature would be restored at the resurrection. But the interim state of the soul between death and resurrection was for Thomas a far more blessed and happy condition than it was for the Hebrews. For them, Sheol was a miserable, ghostly existence, while Thomas placed the souls of the saved 'with Christ' in Paradise. Aquinas was naturalistic in one sense, appreciating the essential character of the body to man's full being, but he displayed a trace of dualism in his exaltation of the soul at death.

All living creatures have souls, but man alone has a rational soul. Man alone has intellect. Aquinas, with Aristotle, believed that true happiness lies in fulfilling all of one's potentialities, and since man's unique nature is rational, his highest good comes through knowledge. Aristotle was content to stop there, but Aquinas went on to add that it is not sufficient merely to say that it is good to know. The question must be asked about the proper object of knowledge, and obviously the answer is God, who fulfills not only the theoretical aspect of knowledge — the quest for Truth — but also the practical — the quest for Goodness. The chief end of man is the knowledge and the love of God. Man's true happiness and fulfillment can be found nowhere else. The theoretical question — how is truth found in Thomas' system — can be passed over, but his interpretation of sex rests upon the foundations of the ethical question — how is goodness achieved — and its answer.

In general, the good life means living in accordance with reason, for that is man's distinctive characteristic. To live primarily for the satisfaction of bodily impulses and appetites is to descend to the animal level. This is not to say that these impulses are evil. They are a part of human nature but only a part. They must be controlled and directed by the mind. This means, as Aristotle had said, that certain habit patterns must be established. Aquinas made a distinction between what he called a *facultas,* a natural capacity, and a *habitus,* an acquired or learned use of that faculty. Habits can be established in one of two ways, either by mere repetition, which is purely impulsive, or by deliberate choice and rational control. The latter way gives to acts their moral significance, for morality has meaning only in the context of rational decisions. Animals or small children or insane persons are amoral precisely because they are incapable of using the reason, and the categories of good and evil do not apply to them. The good man is he who directs and controls his natural impulses with his reason in such a way that they become habits. In the realm of sex, for example, the temperate man's *habitus* is such that his libidinal urges are fully under the power of his reason, while the continent man, although he successfully resists his passions, must struggle strenuously against the lower, animal part of his nature. Thus, temperance is a greater good than continence.

One of the natural faculties which all men possess is what Thomas called *synteresis,* the ability to recognize that good is different from evil. But this alone is not sufficient for the good life. *Synteresis* must be supplemented by conscience, which is the ability to know right from wrong in specific situations. But while *synteresis* is infallible (there is eternally a difference between good and evil), *conscientia* is fallible (one can always make errors in judging right from wrong in concrete problems). In order to guide the conscience in its decisions, the reason looks to the natural law, which is simply the eternal law of God projected into the created world, or that much of the divine law which is discernible by the reason, unaided by revelation. The natural law governs all creatures, animate and inanimate, rational and irrational. It applies to rational creatures in a unique way, since they alone are capable of awareness of its existence. They alone can consciously affirm or deny its precepts. A stone or a dog has not the capacity of awareness or of choice; each is ruled by the natural law wholly. Man cannot escape the effects of the law, but it will have a different impact upon him according as he seeks deliberately to live by it or to disobey.

The first principles of the natural law are to the practical reason what the first principles of logic are to the speculative reason: both are self-evident. For example, Aquinas regarded it as immediately apparent, requiring no demonstration, that things equal to the same thing are equal to each other. So in the practical realm, it is axiomatic that good is to be done and evil to be avoided. This is the first precept of natural law. But men can be certain that they are dealing with natural law only in the general principles. In questions of detail, of what is right or wrong in a particular situation, one cannot be certain. Therefore, God has revealed as divine law the moral and ceremonial precepts of the Old Testament as a corrective and a supplement to the natural law. For the latter, man does not require revelation; its provisions can be discovered by natural knowledge. The divine law, however, is not attainable by the mind apart from faith. That is revealed by God in a series of special acts. The divine law never contradicts or nullifies the natural law but supplements and fulfills it.

In his quest for the good life, then, the Christian uses his reason to discover what the natural law requires, looking always to the divine law as a corrective, as a guide which directs him to the proper interpretation. In principle, man ought to be able both to know the will of God and to obey it. Adam and Eve had such an ability, but since the Fall, man's capacity to know fully has been lost and his power to obey has been weakened. Hence, man requires the assistance of grace both to know God and to obey his commands. This the Church supplies through the sacraments. Man's quest for the good life finds its fulfillment in acting in accordance with his reason, developing his natural capacities, establishing good habits. He finds his knowledge of what is good partly through the natural law and partly through the divine law, following what he knows to be the good partly by his own strength and partly by the enabling power of grace. In each case, the supernatural simply completes and fulfills the natural. The natural is good and true as far as it can go on its own. There is everywhere harmony and continuity between nature and grace, between reason and revelation, between human and divine. All things are arranged in hierarchical order, moving from inanimate to animate, from non-rational to rational, from human to angelic, from creature to Creator. The whole of existence is seen as a kind of arch in which the lower is supported and held in place by the keystone. All that is below finds its fulfillment and meaning by being drawn up into the highest. It is always in this sense that Thomas spoke of man's bodily nature as lower than his rational nature. There is no condemnation implied in these terms; it is simply a matter of lesser and greater good. This is the naturalism of Aristotle which Aquinas adopted in contrast to the Platonic dualism of Augustine.

Sex before and after the Fall

In his interpretation of sex, Thomas began, like Augustine, by going back to Creation, affirming that sex was a part of the divine purpose and therefore good. Woman was made as a helper to man, according to the Biblical account, and since in ordinary enterprises another man would have been of greater assistance to Adam, it is clear that from the moment of woman's creation she was intended to serve the purpose of sex — only in that enterprise is she superior as a 'helper.' Thomas interpreted this to mean not only that God created man to be fruitful and multiply but also that woman is to be subject to man. All other creatures were made 'male and female' simultaneously, but Adam preceded Eve into existence, and she was made from him. This, said Thomas, gives the first man his proper dignity and authority. Further, man's reason is more fully developed and in greater control of his emotions than woman's, which is additional evidence of his superiority. Thomas was not alone in his male arrogance. He has ample company among the leading figures in the history of Christian thought. Most of them have regarded woman as primarily a sexual being and therefore dangerous, requiring the sovereignty of man.

Sex as a fact of creation was, for Thomas, good, but a secondary good, because in the animal kingdom, including man, the male is not found in continuous union with the female, as among plants, but only at the time of coition. By this means, the two become 'one flesh,' but man has a destiny far higher than sex — the use of his reason. Here, Thomas was following Aristotle but without any conflict with Augustine, for all three men placed great stress on the life of reason, the realm of the mind. This emphasis is derived from the classical tradition, not from the Bible. Except for the so-called Wisdom Literature, which was influenced by Hellenism, there is no suggestion in the Old Testament that man is essentially *mind,* that his highest good is to be sought in contemplation. Nor is any such view to be found in Jesus or Paul. The Fourth Gospel, which is strongly Greek, does stress the *knowledge* of God, but the characteristic Biblical emphasis is on love rather than knowledge, on obedience rather than enlightenment, on deeds rather than thoughts. The stress on communion with God through the reason found in both Aquinas and Augustine explains their suspicion of sex as an intensely physical drive which interferes with the placid, contemplative life. Both of them were naturalistic enough to recognize the good of the body and its sexual functions, but they clearly preferred a life above the weary necessities of the flesh. They could never have derived such a point of view from the Bible, nor could they have found there the notion that the reason should control the bodily impulses. The Bible seeks a harmonious unity of all man's parts, mind and body, reason and emotion, a unity which is achieved not by the dominance of one part over another but by the integration of all around the love of God.

Thomas, despite his attitude toward sex as 'the inferior appetite' which ideally should be ruled by the intellect, nonetheless saw that procreation was a part of the divine plan at creation. God was concerned, as nature clearly shows, for the preservation of the species in bodily form, an enterprise served by sex throughout the animal kingdom. He also provided this same means for the initiation of souls into life; therefore one cannot deny that sex is God-given. Aquinas agreed with Augustine that 'a certain deformity of excessive concupiscence' which infects all present sexual relations would not have been true in Paradise, where 'the lower powers were entirely subject to reason.' So firmly did Thomas hold this belief concerning the hypothetical but never-realized sex of the first parents that he was convinced that they could have determined the sex of their children by a mere act of will. And since the significance of celibacy came only after the Fall, all the children of Adam and Eve would have generated offspring; therefore, there would have been an exactly equal number of males and females. Yet there was no sexual intercourse in the Garden of Eden. Aquinas and Augustine were describing what God intended rather than what actually came to pass. Thomas quoted Augustine as his authority for the fact that it did not come to pass, repeating the assertion that the Fall occurred before the nuptials of the parents of the race had been consummated.

The close harmony between these two theologians in their view of the pristine purpose of God and the effects of the Fall comes to a brief pause, however, in Thomas' more positive view of pleasure. Augustine, it will be remembered, imagined that sex in Paradise would have been less intense than it now is. Aquinas, on the other hand, declared that intensity of pleasure is not to be excluded from the state of innocence. 'Rather, indeed, would sensible delight have been the greater in proportion to the greater purity of nature and the greater sensibility of the body.' [1] And not only was pleasure a part of God's purpose for sex in Paradise, but it remains a part of his purpose for sex in sinful man as well. Aquinas specifically dissented from the view that all pleasure is evil. There are, he said, good pleasures and bad pleasures. What distinguishes the one from the other is its source. All pleasure results from the 'repose of the appetite in some loved good and resulting from some operation.' If either the higher or the lower appetite rests in that which is in accord with reason, the pleasure is good, while it is evil only when the appetite is served by something contrary to reason and the law of God. The sexual appetite, while obviously a lower form, is morally neutral, arising from the instinctual level, and it becomes good or evil only as it is directed by the reason. And since in Paradise it would have been entirely subject to the rational mind, it would have been entirely good.

But the original sin intervened, with the ravages of concupiscence trailing in its wake. Aquinas was one with the main stream of Christian tradition in regarding this original sin as pride, not lust. In the state of innocence there was no rebellion of the flesh against the spirit, and Adam could not have sinned in body unless he had first sinned in soul. He sought to make himself the center of life's meaning which disrupted his entire existence, subjecting him to the torments of concupiscence. In fallen man the reason's sovereignty is unseated by his lust. Concupiscent desire distracts the reason through attention to bodily pleasure, by impelling man to do that which is contrary to reason, and by fettering the reason. Sexual desire which transgresses the limits of the mind is not morally neutral but positively evil. Concupiscence, though not the original sin itself, is one of its results and is transmitted from

1. *Summa Theologica*, Part I, Question 98, Article 1. All references are to the *Summa*, unless otherwise noted.

generation to generation through the sexual act, or what Aquinas called 'the seminal power.' He raised the question of whether a body miraculously created by God out of true human flesh, yet not produced by carnal generation, would be sinful flesh. The answer was in the negative, because it is the sexual act which is the carrier of original sin not the flesh itself. This again is to go beyond Paul, who never condemned the sexual act as the conveyor of sin. For him, it was rather the flesh itself, the whole of human nature, which bore the taint of sin.

Aquinas had the interesting idea that for a time after the Fall men remained relatively good. Adam had been thoroughly instructed about the divine will, and the effects of original sin apparently took some time to be felt in full force, for Aquinas believed that both faith and reason flourished in the immediate descendants of the refugees from Paradise. But about the time of Abraham, faith began to wane and idolatry to wax. Concupiscence grew in power, beclouding the natural reason, and God responded to this state of affairs by instituting the rite of circumcision. Thomas displayed considerable ingenuity in accounting both for the origin of the custom and for the hiatus between the Fall and its appearance, but his Biblical literalism together with his ignorance of the fact that circumcision was a very ancient practice, found among many primitive tribes, conspired against him. One wonders how he explained the fact that the Egyptians referred contemptuously to the Hebrews as 'the uncircumcised' several centuries after Abraham, or accounted for the Exodus narrative which makes Moses the founder of the rite in Israel. Aquinas regarded it as altogether meet and right that circumcision should be performed on 'the virile member,' and he cited numerous reasons therefore. Theologically, the rite is a sign of faith that Christ would be born of the seed of Abraham, and if this seems obscure, all is made clear by the assertion that circumcision foreshadowed the removal of corruption which was to be accomplished by the Saviour. Practically, the operation weakens the concupiscence of the penis and serves as a remedy against original sin, which is contracted through the act of generation.

In dealing with the polygamy of the patriarchs, Thomas once

more followed Augustine in regarding this as a special command from God to the holy fathers of Israel for the purpose of insuring the multiplication of the children of the Covenant. Polygamy was at that time perfectly lawful and regular. But monogamy is truly the law of God, not, to be sure, written or revealed in any divine law (as indeed it is not; the Bible nowhere condemns polygamy) but written, said Thomas, on the heart. This can be demonstrated very simply. In the animal kingdom, there are species which observe a kind of monogamy; the male has intercourse with one female and then remains with her until the offspring are born and raised. In other species the female arrives at her period of ovulation, has connection with several males, and then goes off alone to bear and rear her young. In every case, Aquinas argued, where the father's care is needed for the protection and training of the young there is what he called 'determinate union,' that is, the joining of only one male with one female. But where the mother's care is sufficient, where the father does not play the role of guardian and teacher, there is 'indeterminate union' — males and females coupling indiscriminately. Obviously, man falls into the former group. Human children require longer and more elaborate care than the young of any other animal. And Thomas pointed out that in *homo sapiens,* the nurture of offspring involves not simply physical protection but intellectual and psychological influences as well. For such an enterprise the father is especially well suited and therefore necessary. Thus it is clear that the natural law enjoins monogamy, even though the written law of the Old Testament fails to command it. One could quibble with Thomas, asking why man should not do as some of the 'determinate' animals, shift mates after the young leave the nest, but that would be captious. Aquinas adopted Augustine's three goods of marriage, the procreation of children, the promotion of family harmony, and the reception of sacramental grace. The first is common to all animals, the second is unique to humans, and the third restricted to Christians. Polygamy may serve the first of these purposes, but it does not contribute to the second, since the plurality of wives is apt to produce family friction, as it did even for Abraham. And of course Christians are bound by the sacrament to one mate for life. There was, however, nothing contrary, either to natural law or divine law, in the polygamy of the patriarchs. It was commanded by God.

The Good of Virginity

But now a new era has come. Christ has been born of a Virgin, as he had to be in order to escape the infection of original sin. His conception took place without the corrupting influence of sex. Thomas followed Augustine in this tradition, which is again Hellenistic in origin; for neither the Gospels nor the Epistles of the New Testament even suggested that Christ was born of a Virgin in order to exempt him from the taint of sexual intercourse. That is an interpretation which fairly shouts of its dualistic ancestry in Oriental-Hellenistic culture. It follows quite easily, however, if sex is a contaminating act, that virginity is superior to marriage. Thomas believed his attitude substantiated by Jesus, who gave to his followers three counsels, not commands, for those would be obligatory on all, but counsels, signposts to the more excellent way. These three are absolute poverty, absolute chastity, and absolute obedience to one's superiors in the Lord. This means that all who think marriage better than virginity are wrong. They are refuted by the example of Christ himself, who both chose a virgin for his mother and remained himself a virgin, as well as by the authority of the Apostle Paul who clearly preferred virginity as the greater good. And the reason joins in confirming the divine teaching and example, 'both because a divine good takes precedence over a human good, and because the good of the soul is preferable to the good of the body, and again because the good of the contemplative life is better than that of the active life.' [2] Such a judgment is obviously true in Aristotelian terms. Whether the Biblical view of life will support such a statement is another question. Thomas was convinced that virginity is a part of the contemplative life, a good of the soul, wherein the reason is able more fully to concentrate on the things of God, whereas marriage is a good of the body and a part of the active life, directed to the propagation of the human race. Thomas made no allowance for differences of individual temperament in this judgment, as Paul

2. Part II (Second Part) Question 152, Article 4.

obviously did in 1 Corinthians 7. He flatly asserted that it is abstractly true that virginity is superior to marriage. Here once more Aquinas revealed his aristocratic penchant for the life of the mind and his condescension for the active life, the man who works with his body, a direct heritage from the classical rather than the Biblical world. And as for the wedded folk's seeking to please one another, Thomas might have done well to study more carefully the parable of the Last Judgment in Matthew 25: 'Inasmuch as ye have done it unto one of the least of these, ye have done it unto me.'

The material element of virginity is what Thomas called 'integrity of the body,' but this is decidedly secondary to the formal element, the inner resolve to keep one's self free from sexual pleasure. In this respect, Thomas certainly followed Jesus, emphasizing inner motive rather than external condition. The word virgin, he said, comes from the Latin *viror,* meaning 'fresh,' unparched by the heat of the sun. So the virgin is determined to keep free from the heat of venereal passion. The material element, or bodily integrity, is secondary because all men are born in this condition. But the formal element, the resolve to preserve this integrity for God's sake is not a condition of birth but a solemn vow taken in faith. Further, it is possible to lose the material element of virginity through rape and yet maintain the formal element, so long as the reason does not consent to the pleasure. Even if a ravished virgin should experience pleasure in the sexual act, she remains a virgin in God's sight, provided only that the pleasure arose involuntarily from her body without the consent of her will. This same principle applies to any pleasure experienced in dreams. But if pleasure is the result of a deliberate purpose of the rational mind, then virginity is destroyed whether copulation has occurred or not. In the case of one who has lost his virginity through consent of the will, regardless of what has happened to his body, he can be restored through penance. The virgin who has lost 'bodily integrity' without assenting to the pleasure in the reason could be restored in body by a divine miracle, if God so willed. But God himself cannot change the fact that one has experienced sexual pleasure willingly.

In arguing that the formal element of virginity is more important than the material, Thomas quoted Aristotle's dictum that
man's good is threefold: external things, such as riches, clothes,
housing; bodily goods, such as health and strength; and the goods
of the soul, the highest of which is contemplation. In this hierarchy,
external things are to be used according to the dictates of reason
for the good of the body, while the body is to be used for the good
of the soul, and action is to be subordinated to contemplation.
Therefore, as a wise man will give up certain things which may
be perfectly good in their own right for his body's sake, so the
virgin gives up sex for the sake of the higher good of contemplation
of the divine. But what if the objection is raised that the natural
law is contrary to virginity, since hunger and sex are two of man's
strongest instinctual needs, and since nature is obviously concerned
with the preservation and propagation of the species? Thomas had
already admitted that none can live entirely without some pleasure
and that there is nothing wrong with the sexual appetite itself.
How, then, is virginity to be justified? Aquinas replied that the
precept of natural law which governs hunger must be followed by
all men, for the individual cannot survive without food. But the
precept governing procreation is not directed to every individual
but to the race as a whole, which needs not only to be multiplied
physically but to be enriched spiritually. It is enough if some take
unto themselves the concerns of reproduction. Others will refrain
from these in order to give themselves wholly to the contemplation
of God, which serves not only their own souls but also the whole
of mankind. Thomas used the analogy of an army, where not all
carry banners, not all fight, not all stand sentry duty. Each task is
performed by a part of the whole, yet each task is necessary to the
whole.

A married person may, however, be better than a virgin, for
his inner attitude toward his sex life may be holier. He may be
more prepared to practice virginity if necessary than the virgin,
and he may have some more excellent virtues. Virginity is by no
means the greatest of the virtues. Its purpose is to free the mind
for devotion to the divine; therefore, those virtues more directly
concerned with contemplation are higher than those that are

simply a means to contemplation. The theological or religious
virtues are superior to the moral virtues, of which virginity is one.
Martyrs and monks who renounce not only venereal pleasure but
the whole world for God's sake are more pleasing in his sight.
Thomas was not wholly a dualist in his interpretation of sex, for
he did recognize sexual pleasure as well as other physical pleasures
as good in themselves. He was strongly influenced by Aristotle's
naturalism, and yet he was not entirely free from dualism, either.
The renunciation of bodily pleasure is more pleasing in the sight
of God than the enjoyment of it. Thomas realized that not all men
could follow the counsels of poverty, chastity, and obedience. Some
there be whose disposition is 'not inclined to such things.' No
condemnation is visited upon those who do not take the vow of
virginity. Allowance is made for difference of disposition. In the
army of the Lord, there are diversities of tasks as well as of gifts.
The tasks of the married are not so noble and lofty as those of the
virgin, but they are nonetheless essential. Mary may have chosen
'the better part,' but Martha still had to prepare the food. The
non-virginal must cultivate other virtues. Thomas seemed to take
I Corinthians 12 seriously in allowing for differences of temperament and inclination. But Paul insisted that no task was more important than another, no Christian higher than another. Aquinas
again followed the aristocratic tradition of Aristotle rather than
the democratic tradition of the Bible.

Thomist Terminology

In discussing sex, Thomas used a number of terms which require some examination: temperance, chastity, purity, continence,
as virtues, and intemperance, insensibility, lust, and so forth, as
vices. *Temperance* was a virtue for Aquinas. It has to do, properly,
with 'pleasures of meat and drink and sexual pleasures.' Its task
is not to act contrary to human nature, as some suppose, but rather
in harmony with it. Temperance is opposed to the animal instincts of man but only in so far as those instincts are not subject
to the reason. Man is a rational animal, and therefore only those
pleasures in accord with reason are proper for him. He must seek
to develop the *habitus* of temperance, training his natural impulses

and appetites to follow rational paths of satisfaction. The temperate man is he whose character is so formed, whose habits are so deeply ingrained that he does not have to wrestle vigorously with his sensual desires. He has his passions firmly in hand. The opposite of temperance, its corresponding vice, is *intemperance,* which is the pursuit of bodily or sensual goods contrary to the dictates of reason. Thomas regarded it as childish and the most disgraceful of the sins of the flesh. Intemperance is childish because it will not listen to reason, because it becomes increasingly self-willed as it is catered to, and because it needs to have its demands resisted. Intemperance is disgraceful because it degrades man to the level of the lower animals and because it dims 'the light of reason . . . wherefore these pleasures are described as being most slavish.'

There is still another opposite to temperance — on its other side, so to speak — and that is *insensibility.* Intemperance is to use the things of the flesh contrary to the dictates of reason; temperance is to use them in accord with reason; insensibility is the refusal to use them under the misapprehension that all bodily pleasure is evil. Nature, said Thomas, has so arranged life that certain functions necessary to the preservation of the race and the individual carry pleasure as their reward, and anyone guilty of neglecting to perform those functions as the reason directs runs counter to the order of nature and therefore sins. Such a man is 'insensible as a country lout!' Aquinas was careful to safeguard the virtue of virginity, declaring that it is sometimes, under certain conditions, a good thing to abstain from bodily pleasures. Dieting for health, training for athletics, preparing for the ardors of a military campaign, all require a certain withdrawal from the pleasures of the flesh. Similarly, penitents and those engaged in a life of contemplation keep themselves free from carnal desire. This does not fall under the condemnation of insensibility, for it is a practice wholly in accord with right reason.

Temperance has to do in general with things pertaining to bodily pleasures, those of touch, of eating, and of sex. Under the pleasures of sex, temperance has two parts: *chastity* and *purity.* The former concerns the delights of the sexual act itself, while the latter has to do with the preludes to sexual union, 'impure looks, kisses and touches.' Chastity derives its name from the fact that reason chastises concupiscence, which is like a child requiring correction and restraint. Purity comes from the Latin *pudor*, meaning shame. Men are, as Augustine observed, ashamed even of lawful, conjugal intercourse because the sexual organs are not subject to the command of reason, and so they hide from the sight of others not only coitus itself, which is the concern of chastity, but also other sexual acts, such as kissing, which pertain to purity. Aquinas agreed with Augustine wholly in his twofold description of concupiscence: it is responsible for the insubordination of the genital organs and it is responsible for the subversion of reason.

Thomas saw that the term *continence* is used in two ways. First, he said, it sometimes designates abstinence from all sexual pleasures, in which case it is identical with virginity and is a higher virtue than temperance. But he preferred the second use, which denotes the resistance and struggle against stray sexual desires, and in this sense temperance is better, since 'the good of reason flourishes more in the temperate man than in the continent man, because in the former, even the sensitive appetite is obedient to reason, being tamed by reason, so to speak, whereas in the continent man the sensitive appetite strongly resists reason by its evil desires.' [3] The temperate person's habits and character are such that even his inner impulses give him little trouble, while the continent subdues the imperious demands of sex with considerable difficulty. But if temperance is a greater virtue than continence, intemperance is a graver sin than *incontinence*. The latter sin occurs in one of two ways: either the soul is carried away by impetuosity before the reason has a chance to operate, or the will is too weak to hold fast to the reason's judgment. But the incontinent man, having sinned, repents at once, for he has been carried away by his passion, and as soon as the ravening passion has sated its hunger, the reason can reassert itself, and he will seek to mend his ways. The intemperate man, on the other hand, inclines his will to sin by his own choice. He has developed a habit, a disposition which is pleasant to him and which is difficult to remove. In the case of both incontinence

3. Part II (Second Part) Question 155, Article 4.

and intemperance, however, Thomas insisted that the bodily desires are not sinful themselves. They are merely the occasion for sin. So long as they are resisted by the rational will, no evil is incurred. Only when the reason is carried away by lust or deliberately consents to lust can sin enter, for apart from the reason, there is no morality.

These are some of the terms Aquinas used in his interpretation of sex, and they provide important insights into his thought. He continually asserted that venereal pleasure, which he admitted is the greatest of all bodily delights, hinders the use of reason. The mind is dimmed, beclouded, and enslaved by sexual desire. Therefore the truly rational man will seek virginity first; failing that he will cultivate temperance, displaying chastity and purity. Lower on the scale, he will seek continence, rigorously resisting his evil impulses. This represents a curious blending of naturalism and dualism. Thomas recognized that sexual desires are perfectly natural and that to satisfy them in accord with reason is no sin. It is the lack of harmony with reason, the inordinateness and impetuosity which is responsible for sin. The influence of Aristotle in all of this is clearly discernible. The transgression of 'the golden mean,' the breaking through of *sophrosune,* or moderation, is what constitutes evil. This is again the classical world-view and not the Biblical one, which is utterly silent about the overthrow of the reason but eloquent on the subject of disobedience and idolatry. Aquinas elevated the reason to dizzy heights, regarding it as of the greatest importance in the quest for the good life, but this was not at all the view of Jesus or Paul, who were not rationalists in any sense of that term!

Sexual Sins

Whenever sexual desire exceeds 'the order and the mode of reason,' it becomes *lust,* which is a sin. Its effect is such that concupiscence becomes so passionately attached to the object of securing its pleasure that the reason and the will are 'most grievously disordered.' Sexual sins, which are venereal acts performed without regard for due manner and order, Thomas arranged in his typically hierarchical fashion. The worst of the sins of lust is what he called 'unnatural vice,' wherein are to be found, in the order of their gravity, bestiality, sodomy, unnatural connections between man and woman — fellatio, cunnilingus, pederasty — and masturbation. Bestiality is the lowest level to which man can sink, since it is the most unnatural of all sexual acts, failing to observe the use of the proper species. Sodomy is next, because although the species is right, the sex is wrong; nature's rule of hetero-sexuality is violated. Unnatural connections follow close behind homosexuality. Here both species and order of sex are observed, but nature's prescribed manner of copulation is transgressed. Finally, masturbation, or uncleanness, which Thomas also called effeminacy, means 'procuring pollution without any copulation for the sake of venereal pleasure.' This is the least grievous of all the unnatural vices, as it merely omits connection with another. The principle governing all of these judgments is that the gravity of a sin is determined more by the abuse of a thing than by the omission of the correct use. Incest is included among the unnatural vices, yet with a difference, for it is less contrary to nature and right reason than the foregoing acts, violating prudential considerations rather than physiological ones.

All the other sexual sins represent the transgression of right reason, but still on natural lines. These Thomas arranged, still in order of seriousness, as rape of a wife, adultery, rape of a virgin, seduction of a virgin, and simple fornication, which is the least grave among the sins of lust, since it is committed without injustice to another person. All other forms of sexual sin not only prejudice the welfare of future offspring, a characteristic shared by fornication, but injure another person besides. Aquinas regarded seduction of a virgin as less serious than adultery, remarking that it is a 'greater injustice to have intercourse with a woman who is subject to another's authority as regards the act of generation, than as regards merely her guardianship.' [4] Thomas seemed far more concerned over the injury done the husband of an adulteress and the father of a seduced virgin than over any harm done to the women. Both adultery and seduction are complicated and rendered graver if violence is used, that is, if rape is involved.

4. Part II (Second Part) Question 154, Article 12.

Adultery makes the woman guilty of three sins: infidelity to the law of God, offense to her husband, leaving him uncertain whether his children are really his, and bearing the offspring of a man not her husband. The sins of the adulterous man are only two: his union with another woman is not good for his own children and he hinders the good of another's progeny. Why he is not also unfaithful to the law of God Thomas did not make clear. Seduction constitutes a special sin not included under simple fornication, since the latter signifies intercourse with harlots or women of previous sexual experience. Seduction means sexual relations with a virgin still under her father's care. A twofold injustice is done: the virgin, though not forced, is led astray, and the father is wronged by the defloration of his innocent daughter.

Although fornication is the least grave of sexual evils, it is still a mortal sin, as are all sexual relations with other than one's own husband or wife. Every sin which endangers human life is mortal, and the inordinateness of fornication Thomas believed to be injurious to the offspring of the illicit union. He repeated, in this connection, his argument from natural law already described, to the effect that in all animal species where the care of both parents is required for the good of the children, monogamy is the rule. Promiscuity is against the best interests of human children and is thus contrary to both reason and nature. In this case, as in all others, it is not so much the natural appetite which makes the act sinful as it is the failure of the reason properly to direct the passions. There is no sin, said Thomas, in desiring that which nature requires to satisfy its needs, in either hunger or sex, 'save only where it is desired in excess as to quantity.' Of course, the crucial point here is when a drive becomes excessive. With food, this is determined with relative ease, but views differ widely as to what constitutes a 'normal' amount of sexual desire. Both Aquinas and Augustine defined the primary and 'natural' purpose of sex as procreation. Therefore, one supposes that anything in excess of what nature requires for that purpose comes dangerously close to sin.

Thomas repeatedly emphasized that it is the inner motive rather than the mere outer act which is responsible for sin. It is the con-

sent of the reason to pleasure which is either inordinate or contrary
to nature which is evil. As for kisses, caresses, touches, and so on,
Thomas declared that these do not necessarily imply mortal sin.
They can be performed without lustful pleasure, as for example,
when certain types of embraces are the custom of the country. But
when the motive behind them is lustful pleasure, to which the will
and the reason consent, then they are mortally sinful. This does
not, however, apply to nocturnal pollutions, to so-called 'wet
dreams.' What occurs in sleep, according to Aquinas, is not under
the control of the reason; therefore, no sin can be involved. These
emissions are the result of three things. They may represent the
body's ridding itself of excess semen, they may be a visitation of
the devil, or they may arise from thoughts just before retiring for
the night. Such thoughts may be purely speculative, or they may be
lustful. If the latter is true, the nocturnal pollution is the result
of a previous sin, but even then the spontaneous emission of semen
in sleep is never a sin in itself.

Sex within Marriage

Marriage, Thomas believed to be altogether in harmony with
the natural reason and the divine law, but it is not a command.
It is essential for the race as a whole, but not for the individual.
There must always be a division of labor in human affairs, and
the good of mankind requires that some should devote themselves
wholly to the contemplation of the divine, and to such contemplation marriage is 'a very great obstacle.' This is not to say, however,
that marriage is in any way unlawful or evil. The natural inclination to beget children has been implanted within men by God.
The shamefulness of concupiscence which goes hand in hand with
the sexual act in marriage is not the result of guilt; it is the punishment of original sin, the disobedience of 'the lower powers and
members' to the reason. Whatever passion and intensity there may
be to marital coitus is altogether excused by the marriage blessing,
and while the orgasm may overwhelm the husband's reason for
the moment, nonetheless his reason directed him into the marriage
in the first place, and therefore no sin is incurred. This curious
prejudice, which Aquinas shared with Augustine, against the ir-

rational state of man in orgasm is characteristically Hellenistic rather than Biblical. The Old Testament abounds in examples of a divine frenzy which seized Samuel, Saul, Isaiah, and numerous others. The reason was banished so as to give almost the appearance of insanity when the Spirit of the Lord took hold of or 'put on' a man. One wonders what Aquinas made of these incidents.

No deliberate act of the rational will could, for Thomas, be morally neutral. The marriage act, therefore, must always be either sinful or virtuous. It is virtuous under one of two conditions: a virtue of religion, when the parents desire to beget children for the worship of God, or a virtue of justice when one of the marriage partners renders what Thomas called 'the debt' to the other. This was his interpretation of marriage as a remedy for sin. If the husband has married because he is consumed with passion, then the wife must 'render the marriage debt' in order to protect him from the sin of adultery, from seeking satisfaction in the arms of another woman. Sex that is motivated by giving the debt or by the desire for children is virtuous and meritorious. But if the motive for sex is lust, then it is a sin, but the marriage blessings soften it to a venial one. By the marriage blessings, Thomas explained, he meant treating a wife as a wife, to whom honor and respect and fidelity are due. Sex without the marriage blessings involves treating the wife merely as a woman, an instrument for the gratification of lust, for which purpose almost any other woman would serve as well. The sin of marital sex which has as its motive pleasure remains venial so long as the marriage blessings are respected. But when this respect is gone, lust has passed beyond the control of reason and nature, and mortal sin has been incurred.

Thomas here showed rare respect for the female of the species, condemning a man's using his wife as a thing, as an instrument of his gratification. In another context, he was not so considerate. He did, it is true, command the husband to render the debt to his wife, even if out of shyness she does not specifically ask for it, but shows obvious signs of need. But if the wife should be menstruating, the husband is not obligated to pay the debt. The Old Testament law gave two reasons for abstinence from intercourse during the woman's menses: ceremonial cleanliness and the avoidance of harm to future offspring. The first of these reasons, Thomas held, has been nullified in the new dispensation of Christ, but the second is still valid, at least for Aquinas; modern science has rendered such an argument no longer tenable. But (and this is masculine arrogance at its worst) the wife must render the debt to her husband if he asks it, even during the menstrual period, lest he fall into sin through her refusal. This is one of the few examples of a Roman Catholic divine's displaying greater concern for a husband's sexual satisfaction than for the welfare of future offspring. The passage is worth quoting: 'If her husband ask, he does so either knowingly, or in ignorance. If knowingly, she ought to dissuade him by her prayers and admonitions; yet not so in-sistently as possibly to afford him an occasion of falling into other, and those sinful, practices, if he be deemed that way inclined. If, however, he ask in ignorance [of the fact that she is menstruating] the wife may put forward some motive or allege some sickness as a reason for not paying the debt, unless there be fear of danger to her husband. If, however, the husband ultimately persists in his request, she must yield to his demand. But it would not be safe for her to make known her disaffection, lest this make her husband entertain a revulsion towards her, unless his prudence can be taken for granted.' [5]

It seems scarcely consistent on the one hand to speak of woman as Thomas did, calling her unstable of reason, too ready to follow the passions, and then on the other, to insist that she hold her desires in check while the man is not expected to follow suit. This whole discussion of 'the marriage debt' elaborates a small bit of practical advice from the Apostle Paul into a complex array of legalism. Sexual relations become an obligation instead of a privilege, and certainly any man or woman who insists on the rendering of the debt despite the obvious lack of interest in the marriage partner is far from any understanding of the meaning of Christian love, though they may be within their legal rights, in Thomas' terms. Aquinas warned women against adorning and clothing themselves in such a way as to incite men's lust. A married woman, however, may beautify herself to please her husband so

5. Part III (Supplement) Question 64, Article 4.

that he may not lose interest in her and fall into adultery. But unmarried women cannot adorn or paint themselves without sin. If the motive is only frivolity or vanity, the sin is venial, while a deliberate attempt to arouse lustful pleasure in the male is a mortal sin.

Quite obviously, Thomas regarded marriage as a remedy for sin, a means of preventing fornication, or worse evils. Yet he insisted that this became true of matrimony only after the Fall. As God instituted it in Paradise, it was a law of nature, having nothing to do with sin. But after the expulsion of Adam and Eve, marriage took on the additional character of a medicine for immorality. Marriage consists of three parts: its cause, which is the internal consent of the two partners; its essence, which is the union of husband and wife; and its effect, which is a common family life. Carnal intercourse is not essential to a true marriage, for a full marital relationship can exist without it, as witness Mary and Joseph, or Adam and Eve in the Garden. The ability to have coitus is essential, however, because marriage gives each of the partners power over the other's body. Therefore, impotence is sufficient reason for declaring a marriage null and void. If after a three-year period sexual potency is still not achieved, the Church may dissolve the marriage. If both husband and wife wish to join in a mutual vow of abstinence from sex, nothing is to hinder them. But one must not take such a vow without the other, for in marriage each has control over the other. Consent to marriage, said Thomas, is implicitly consent to carnal intercourse, although it is not explicit, since there can be a true marriage without sexual union.

Further evidence of Thomas' view of marriage as a remedy for sin is found in his statement that the sexual act in marriage and in fornication are 'of the same species.' Therefore something must be added to marital intercourse in order to draw it to another species and render it sinless. This something he found in Paul's words in 1 Corinthians 7:6, where sex for pleasure is permitted 'by way of concession.' Here Thomas followed Augustine and his use of the Latin term *veniam,* indulgence, or pardon, declaring that only the three goods of marriage render intercourse for pleasure only venially sinful. These three goods are Augustine's — offspring, fidelity, and sacrament. These blessings, of which the sacrament is the greatest, bring the marriage act into a different species from fornication and excuse it. Sex in its fallen state must be lifted out of nature by the operation of the supernatural. Without the goods of marriage, sexual intercourse is always inexcusable, a mortal sin. Within marriage there is no sin at all to sex which is motivated either by the desire for procreation or by the wish to render the requested debt. But he who asks for payment of the debt, who seeks sex purely for pleasure, is guilty of venial sin.

One final word needs to be said concerning Thomas' view on betrothal and on divorce. What about sexual intercourse between a betrothed couple, formally pledged to one another in marriage? 'In the judgment of the church,' Thomas replied, 'carnal intercourse following a betrothal is declared to make a marriage.' [6] They are in God's sight married if the inner intention is for a true union, a lifelong bond, and they do not sin in their sex, for they are in the same state as the formally married. Concerning divorce, Thomas took the traditional position that marriage is an indelible sacrament, binding man and wife together so long as they both shall live. The ban on divorce is found both in the natural law and in Scripture. Separation is permitted in some cases, but never remarriage. There are, however, certain impediments to marriage: impotence, consanguinity, lack of full consent, and so on. If a marriage should be contracted without knowledge of these facts, the marriage can be dissolved, since the barriers prevented a true state of conjugal union in any case. But this is not divorce, not a separation of what had been joined together. It is an annulment, a recognition that nothing has been really joined.

Summary

In general, Thomas followed Augustine's interpretation of sex and marriage but with less suspicion of bodily pleasure and a greater degree of naturalism drawn from Aristotle. Yet Aristotle was a Greek, and Aquinas was influenced by him as Augustine was by Plato through Plotinus in the strong emphasis on the life

6. Part III (Supplement) Question 46, Article 2.

of reason, of contemplation. All that serves that life is good; all
that hinders it, evil. It is scarcely correct to call this Hellenistic,
since such a stream of thought flows from both Plato and Aristotle. Nor is it entirely dualistic, for Aristotle, at least, had a
healthy respect for the body and its functions. But there are
dualistic overtones in this division of man into body and mind,
or body and soul, and the aristocratic type of intellectual snob-
bery, with its preference for the life of thought to the life of action, which characterized most of classical antiquity, is highly
influential. As has been observed before, this whole outlook is
utterly foreign to the Bible. It is not to be found in the Old
Testament, nor in Jesus, nor even in Paul, for all his Hellenistic
hues.

Yet Paul was at one with both Aquinas and Augustine in believing that the wise man, the holy man, who seeks the highest
things in life will avoid sexual desire and sexual experience as
interfering with his high calling. Virginity is the best state of all.
All three of these men were unmarried. Augustine, it is true, had
had sexual experience but not in marriage, about which he was
always obsessed by feelings of guilt. All three men grudgingly
conceded that marriage was an honorable if lower estate for those
who 'cannot contain.' None of them saw the really positive aspect
of sex in marriage. They were all guilty of male arrogance, to a
degree, and were perhaps a trifle afraid of women. Certainly they
were afraid of the passion involved in sex. They were convinced
that a man is basically better off if he can get along without it.
None of them was a thoroughgoing dualist, condemning the body
or sex completely. All were enough under the influence of the
Old Testament, the full context of Christianity, and Greek naturalism so that they insisted on the goodness of creation. Yet
their inherent dualism prevented their taking the doctrine of
creation seriously and working out its full implications in their
interpretations of sex. The intermingling of these two strands of
naturalism and dualism is clear in the sex ethics of Paul, of Augustine, and of Aquinas, as indeed it is clear throughout the pattern of western civilization.

The Council of Trent

The history of Christian dogma is the story of a gradually narrowing road. At the beginning, the highway was as wide as the Roman Empire. All sorts and conditions of men set their feet in the Christian way and began to walk. The earliest credal formula of the Church seems to have been simply, 'Jesus is Lord.' Then with the Gnostic heresy in the second century, it became necessary to dig ditches on either side of the pavement, to hang danger signals, and to warn against walking too close to the edge. But except for the insistence that God was maker of heaven and earth, that Jesus Christ was truly born, suffered, and died, and that the life everlasting means the resurrection of the body (all phrases directed against the anti-materialistic dualism of the Gnostics), except for those limits laid down by the sides of the road, there was still a tremendous amount of room to walk. Then Nicaea in 325 defined the Second Person of the Trinity; Chalcedon and Constantinople limited the understanding of the Incarnation and the Trinity itself; the Fourth Lateran Council set the dogma of the sacrament of the Mass. The road became gradually narrower, with the danger of falling off into the ditches of heresy increasingly great. But the Middle Ages still found a highway with many lanes. There was room for Augustinians and Thomists and Franciscans; Nominalists and Realists could disagree sharply on numerous points of faith and morals without being ruled out of bounds. But with the Council of Trent, Catholic dogma was carefully and exhaustively defined, with narrow and rigid limits. Henceforth, the road is a slim ribbon with danger around every turn. Of course, the Reformation must bear a large measure of responsibility for such a state of affairs, since Luther and Melanchthon and Calvin were greatly concerned with precise statements of the Protestant faith. Rome had little alternative, short of embracing the ideas of the Reformers, but to reorganize her own lines, to mark her pathways more clearly, and the culmination of the Counter-Reformation, doctrinally, came with the Council of Trent. For the first time, the Catholic Church had a dogmatic definition which was comprehensive, covering almost all areas of faith and life. Prior to Trent, definitions of dogma were confined to occasions when threatening heresies made them necessary, and the dogma was restricted to the particular point at issue. Post-Tridentine Catholicism, however, was exhaustively complete and henceforth whoever would walk with Rome must walk its way. Doctrine might develop from this point on, but it could never change, according to the Vatican. For this reason, it is essential to an understanding of the Roman Catholic interpretation of sex to examine what was decreed at the Council of Trent. Two documents are important in this connection: the canons and decrees of the Council itself, and a catechism authorized by the Council but actually prepared after adjournment under papal supervision.[7] The decrees and canons are, of course, far more authoritative, but the catechism represents a popularization (for teachers, incidentally, not for students) of the doctrinal definitions of the Council of Trent, and there is no conflict.

The acts of the Council were divided into decrees, the positive statements of faith, and the canons, directed against heretical disagreement with the former. The formula for a canon, used by ecclesiastical Councils since Nicaea, was 'If any one does not confess,' or 'If any one asserts' a contrary doctrine, 'Let him be anathema.' The canon on original sin declared that concupiscence was not regarded by the Church as sin in those baptized, but 'an incentive to sin . . . left for our exercise.' It 'is of sin and inclines to sin . . . but cannot injure those who consent not, but resist manfully by the grace of Jesus Christ.' The Virgin Mary was expressly exempted from the original sin which affects all born of sexual union. This is a good illustration of the narrowing process, just described. Prior to Trent, no dogmatic definition had been made concerning original sin and its effects. There was room for difference of opinion within the Church.

7. For those interested, the canons and decrees of the Council of Trent may be found in *Creeds of Christendom*, edited by Philip Schaff, Harper & Brothers, New York, 1877. *The Catechism of the Council of Trent* has been translated into English by the Very Reverend J. Donovan, James Duffy and Company, Ltd, Dublin, 1908.

Augustine and Aquinas were individuals expressing their opinions, and one could differ with them. But henceforth the differences were limited to matters of interpretation. No one could disagree with the official acts of an ecumenical council, which were *de fide* — no one, that is, who was a Roman Catholic Christian. Needless to say, the actions of Trent were not regarded as binding on Protestants or on members of the Eastern Orthodox churches, who were not represented at the Council and therefore did not recognize it as a truly ecumenical council. It was a gathering only of the Roman branch of the Holy Catholic Church.

In Session Twenty-four, held on 11 November 1563, the Council issued its decrees and canons concerning the sacrament of matrimony. This whole question had been a source of much argument, not so much in doctrine as in problems of practical application. Both Augustine and Aquinas had believed that the inner consent of both parties to live together plus sexual union made a valid marriage even without parental blessing or ecclesiastical ceremony. Duns Scotus had argued that this was true only of the marriage as a contract; such a marriage was valid as a contract, but it was not a sacrament. All sacraments require a priest, and matrimony was no exception. A fully sacramental marriage requires a ceremony performed by a priest. Both points of view, the Augustinian-Thomist and the Scotist, were represented at the Council, and despite wide clerical agreement on the issue of parental consent, the ambassadors of the king of France, a monarch the Catholic church was anxious to please, caused a request to be read, asking the Council to declare that children in the power of their parents might not without their consent either marry or betroth themselves, or if they did, it should be in the power of the parents to make void or ratify the contract as they pleased. A compromise was reached by removing the whole issue from its doctrinal level and placing it in the section of the Council's actions designed for reforming the practice of the Church. One of the canons prepared for submission to the assembled divines, originally numbered 'Three,' proposed: 'If anyone saith that clandestine marriages made by the free consent of the couple are not true and valid marriages, or that it is in the power of the parent or the parents to make them valid or invalid, let him be anathema.' Out of deference to the French monarch and the Scotist bishops at the Council, this canon was never submitted for vote. Rather, the reformatory canons carried a declaration that clandestine marriages are *vera et rata,* true and valid, provided that the Church had not rendered them void. But the canon went on immediately to forbid such unions, prescribing that fully sanctioned marriages must take place in the presence of three witnesses, one of whom must be a priest. This satisfied all parties concerned, allowing them to interpret the ruling according to their own views. The Thomists believed that their doctrinal position had been upheld and saw the regulation as a practical means of securing adequate registration of marriages, rather than a ruling that the offices of a priest were essential to the sacrament. The Scotists and the French were pleased, also, for their interests had been protected.

The doctrinal canon on the sacrament of matrimony which the Council actually did vote defined marriage as a perpetual and indissoluble bond, established by God at Creation, sanctified and rendered a sacrament by Christ. Any who denied the sacramental nature of marriage (as the Reformers did) were anathematized. The statement that the Church had the right to add to or subtract from the laws of marriage set forth in Leviticus, was also aimed at the Protestants, as were the ninth and tenth dogmatic canons, which covered clerical celibacy. These specifically attacked Luther's position, which was that the Catholic exaltation of virginity was in effect a condemnation of marriage, and that any priests, monks, or nuns who found that they did not possess the rare gift of chastity but were in fact 'consumed with passion' were fully justified in marrying despite a foolish vow taken in youth. Luther, of course, witnessed the widespread immorality of the clergy and was convinced that the cause of Christ would be better served by clerical marriage. (For fuller discussion of this point, see chapter 4.) Trent replied to this that religious celibacy was *not* a condemnation of marriage, although Canon Ten declared that virginity and celibacy are *melius ac beatus quam jungi in matrimonio,* 'better and more blessed than to be united

in marriage,' and justified the state of the clergy by insisting that
'God refuses not that gift to those who ask for it rightly, neither
does he suffer us to be tempted above that which we are able.'
There is, of course, ample room for dispute of this question on
theoretical grounds, but the empirical evidence of the sixteenth
century was all on Luther's side, since the majority of the Roman
priesthood *was* tempted above that which they were able.

Trent ruled that a religious vow of celibacy on the part of
either husband or wife was sufficient grounds for dissolution of
the marriage, provided that sexual consummation of the union
had not taken place. Divorce and remarriage on any grounds,
even adultery, was forbidden, and whoever remarries while the
partner is still alive is guilty of adultery. Separation was allowed
'for many causes . . . in regard of bed, or in regard of cohabitation, for a determinate or indeterminate period.' The last two
doctrinal canons, Eleven and Twelve, asserted the right of the
Church to regulate the times and seasons proper for marriages,
and denied Luther's proposition that matrimonial cases are for
civil rather than ecclesiastical courts. The twelve reformatory
canons dealt with specific abuses and laid down rules for particular problems.

The Catechism of the Council of Trent, although not so authoritative, was somewhat fuller in its treatment of sex and marriage than the canons and decrees were. It defined marriage as
constituted by internal consent, external compact, and the marriage debt whereby the marriage is consummated. The nature of
matrimony is two-fold, 'either as a natural union (for marriage
was not invented by man, but instituted by nature) or as a sacrament, the efficacy of which transcends the order of nature.'
Dealing first with marriage as a part of the natural order, the
Catechism gave three reasons why God instituted marriage at
creation. First, mutual support and companionship between the
sexes; second, the desire for procreation, not so much as a means
of perpetuating one's own physical life as a wish to rear children
in the true faith; and third, as a medicine for immorality. The
Catechism made two comments about the second reason for marriage: that the patriarchs were primarily concerned in procreat-

ing children for the worship of God, and that 'married persons, who, by medicine, either prevent conception or procure abortion, are guilty of a most heinous crime; for this is to be considered an impious conspiracy of murderers.' The Catechism also elaborates on the third reason, describing concupiscence as a result of Adam's fall and marriage as a means whereby those conscious of their weakness and unwilling to bear the conflict of the flesh may avoid sins of lust. These three reasons for marriage apply to its place in the natural order.

But marriage is also a sacrament. This the Catechism 'proved' by quoting the Epistle to the Ephesians 5:28ff., in which the relationship between Christ and his Church is likened to that between husband and wife, concluding with the words, 'This is a great sacrament.' The Greek word rendered by the Latin Vulgate as *sacramentum* is *mysterion*, or mystery. Many medieval Catholics, including Cajetan and Estius, differed with this interpretation of the Ephesian passage, as did the Reformers, who rejected marriage as a sacrament and regarded this particular piece of New Testament exegesis as a very questionable foundation upon which to build a doctrine. But build the Church did, and Trent made it a matter of dogma, not of custom, that there are seven sacraments, one of which is matrimony. The Catechism used this as powerful argument for the indissolubility of marriage, calling it the most permanent of all human associations, analogous as it is to the union between Christ and Church. As a sacrament, of course, it conveys grace, which is essential if the power of concupiscence is to be overcome, enabling the married to abstain from extra-marital intercourse as well as from defiling relations within the marriage itself. By means of the sacramental grace conferred, 'sexual intercourse, which, without marriage, would be deservedly reprobated, becomes an honorable union.'

The question of clandestine marriages was also treated by the Catechism, warning that 'such marriages as are not contracted in the presence of the parish priests . . . and before a certain number of witnesses, are to be considered neither true nor valid marriages.' The door may have been left open theoretically for marriage by mutual consent, but practically such unions were forbidden, a position restated in the revision of canon law in 1917. The Catechism exhorted children to obey their parents in these matters of marriage, but the authority of parents was restricted to moral suasion. Marriage without parental knowledge or consent was not banned. The uses of sex in marriage were treated in two questions which exhorted the faithful to avoid sex that is motivated by sensuality or pleasure and urged them to abstain, at times (at least three days before receiving Holy Communion and often during Lent), from the marriage debt in order to devote themselves to prayers and meditation. The words of Jerome were quoted with approval by the Catechism: 'A wise man ought to love his wife with judgment, not with passion; he will govern the impetuosity of his desire, and will not be hurried into indulgence. There is no greater turpitude than that a husband should love his wife as an adulteress.'

Sexual pleasure was obviously regarded by the Council of Trent and the authors of its Catechism as dangerous and especially incompatible with the things of God, since the clergy were commanded to abstain altogether and the laity before receiving the Holy Communion. And Jesus' tolerance toward the sins of the flesh was apparently forgotten in the stern words 'no greater turpitude.' Paul's understanding of the strength of passion was obliterated in the insistence that once a vow of celibacy had been taken by a priest, monk, or nun, nothing could release them. The concern for the inner life was replaced by the demand for ecclesiastical conformity. A group of divines, holding themselves free from all 'venereal pleasure,' declared by fiat that theirs is an estate superior to that of the weak ones who must marry and they gave detailed instructions concerning a life of which they had had no first-hand experience.

Almost eagerly, one turns to the Protestant Reformation and its interpretation of sex. At least the bonds of celibacy and virginity were there shattered. Luther and Calvin spoke from the experience of a Christian family life. From the Council of Trent onward, the Roman way is clearly marked. Marriage is a sacrament of divine institution in which divorce is impossible. Only the sacramental grace of matrimony can remove the thorn of sin from the flesh of sex and then only when the motive is either procreation or 'rendering the debt.' But the one who demands payment, who seeks sex for pleasure, or out of love (a possibility notably absent from all the writings considered thus far), is guilty of sin, albeit a venial one. The partner who renders the debt is not in sin, for she (how obviously this is intended to mean the woman) merely submits; she does not seek pleasure. *Roma locuta. Causa finita est.* 'Rome has spoken. The matter is settled.' But it is not quite settled. Across the Alps in Germany, a young monk is studying the Bible. Martin Luther has not yet spoken.

IV

LUTHER AND CALVIN

ON THE EVE of All Saints' Day, 31 October, 1517, a monk from the Augustinian monastery in Wittenberg posted a document on the door of the Castle church, offering ninety-five theses on the theory and practice of indulgences for debate. Nothing was farther from Luther's mind than any break with Rome. He was a loyal and devoted son of the Church, convinced that the Pope was ignorant of the mercenary abuses of Albert, Bishop of Brandenburg, and his hawker Johann Tetzel, and that the Pope informed would certainly correct such abuses. Born in Eisleben thirty-four years earlier, he had been raised by his pious parents in the faith. His career as a law student at the University of Erfurt was interrupted by a traumatic experience wherein he stood in terror for the salvation of his immortal soul. Forsaking all worldly desires, Luther entered the monastery and threw himself into its ascetic discipline with abandon. Filled with self-revulsion and assuming that he was worthy only of eternal damnation, he sought to appease an angry God by intensive mortification of the flesh. The vicar-general of the Augustinian order, Staupitz, tried to release the promising young monk from his torment of soul with intellectual labor and assigned him first to study for his doctorate in theology and later to teach at the newly formed University at Wittenberg, where Luther quickly became famous as a lecturer and as a preacher in the Castle church. His duties as professor of Biblical theology led him to a careful perusal of the Psalms and the Epistles of Paul, and the deeper his shaft of insight dug into the well of the Bible, the more profoundly concerned he became about the state of the Church. He was not alone in his concern in the early sixteenth century. Voices were calling from all quarters for reforms, and Luther simply joined the chorus. But as events conspired to raise his lusty tones to solo status, he pursued his convictions with a consistency and a rigor which were unique, going beyond even earlier dissenters, such as Wycliffe and Hus. When the Pope informed proved as bad as the Pope ignorant, Luther defied the bull ordering him to recant and keep silence. The central issue for him was not, as has often been thought, the question of authority, Bible versus Church, or individual against Pope, but rather the question what does the Bible say. The medieval Church had set up an elaborate interpretation of Scripture, using the categories of scholasticism, based largely on Greek philosophy. Luther regarded this interpretation as fundamentally wrong, and he was certain that any reader could see that it was wrong if the Bible were allowed to speak for itself.

There is a school of revisionist history in vogue today which chides Luther for lacking the sweetly reasonable patience of Erasmus, as it also chides Abraham Lincoln for relieving Fort Sumter, seeing the conflicts of the past as easier of resolution than did the participants therein. Perhaps the revisionists are right. Perhaps the Roman Church would ultimately have reformed itself without the tragic rupture which Protestantism produced. Perhaps the Civil War could have been avoided with a little more patience, a little more understanding on both sides. But there are times in history when men of conviction can no longer say perhaps. They must act decisively and boldly. Such action always leaves scars and regrets. The question must always be faced, however, whether inaction at such a time might not have been worse. So Luther was convinced. He had set his hand to the plow and he could not turn back.

This is not the place for any detailed exposition of Luther's career or thought as a Reformer, but some foundation stones need to be laid for the structure which was his interpretation of sex.

His understanding of the teaching of the Roman Church is the subject of considerable controversy, but whether he was correct or
not, the fact remains that there were multitudes who shared his
view, knowing exactly what he meant. He began his career as a
monk and priest in the Church under the apprehension that he
must somehow justify himself before God. The elaborate system
of pilgrimages, prayers, and penitential acts led him to believe
that salvation could be achieved only by works of righteousness.
Escape from the devil and damnation depended on him, on his
inner feelings no less than on his outer acts. And how could he be
certain that he had done all that was required, or that he would
not perish in a state of mortal sin? His overwhelming anxiety
was typical of his age. The woodcuts and pictures of the period
are filled with threatening demons and devils who seek to rob
men of their salvation and carry them off to hell. A terrible fear,
what Tillich calls the anxiety of guilt and condemnation, held
thousands in its awful grasp. God was Judge, Christ was Judge, and
who could hope to win acquittal since nothing less than perfection
was demanded? Luther's frenzied efforts in the monastery brought
him no peace. His all-night vigils, his prolonged fasts, even his
self-flagellation only intensified his fear of God, but the love of
God he could not produce. The soothing words of Staupitz were
powerless to heal; he found deliverance finally only in the Epistles
of Paul, which is not surprising, since his agony under monastic
discipline so closely resembles Paul's torment under the Torah.
And like Paul, Luther never abandoned his conviction that man's
debt to God is so great that he can never by his own works of
righteousness pay it, not in an infinity of lifetimes. Man cannot
justify himself; he can only be justified by the grace of God.

This led Luther to sweep away the entire medieval distinction
between command and counsel, the two levels of Christian life,
with one kind of righteousness demanded for all, and the higher
righteousness of poverty, chastity, and obedience required for the
clergy. Rome taught that not only could man, assisted to be sure
by divine grace, obey God's commands, but he could also perform
works of supererogation, so that the saints by their 'super-righteous-
ness' added to the Treasury of Merit. Luther shared Paul's belief

that God demands perfect righteousness of all men and all men fall short of that demand. Man in his 'natural' or fallen state is not seeking God at all but an idol of his own making, a 'god' who conforms to the devices and desires of his own self-centered heart. God remains hidden from the natural reason, displaying only his power and his judgment. He does not, as medieval scholasticism thought, supplement and complete what the reason begins. The idea of continuity between nature and supernature is shattered by Luther. He saw God as a *deus absconditus,* speaking a thunderous 'No!' against all the natural striving of men. So long as man seeks to earn his own salvation, to barter with God, exchanging his good works for eternal life, he is attempting to control the divine, to live out of his own resources. Man's only hope, as Luther discovered, lies in complete surrender to God, in recognizing that he has no claims upon God whatever, that he is in rebellion against the Almighty. But this man cannot do until he has met the *deus revelatus,* in the face of Jesus Christ. In Christ and in him alone God reveals his love and his mercy, not openly so that the rational reason may plainly see it, but only to those with the eyes of faith. And faith, for Luther, meant not *assensus,* intellectual assent to a series of theological propositions, but *fiducia,* trust and obedience. His understanding of faith was Pauline, and it was, to use a term currently popular, existential to the core. Justification by faith meant for him not that a man believed certain things and thereby gained salvation — that would be to make of faith a human 'work,' and Luther joined Paul in total rejection of salvation by any human works. No man is ever saved because of what he is or does, but rather in spite of himself. God accepts and loves him *as he is,* a sinner. That paradoxical fact is known only to those to whom God has revealed himself, and their faith is the sign that they have been justified by God, not the means whereby they have justified themselves.

This radical denial of the Thomist emphasis upon nature and reason led Luther to the assertion of what Paul Tillich has called 'The Protestant Principle.' He believed that sin is to be found at every level of history. Not even the saint is perfect. He too stands under the divine judgment. And he is not perfect, particularly if he thinks that he is perfect. The Church, too, is condemned by God, for she is involved in sin, standing in the gravest danger of all precisely when she is sure that she is not involved in sin. The quintessence of sin is the introduction of a false absolute into history, when that which is mortal and finite tries to make itself God, pretending to be perfect and complete. The claims of the Church to final truth, to absolute authority, the assertions that the monk and the nun are more pleasing in the sight of God, the illusion that celibacy overcomes the power of concupiscence — all these were challenged and condemned by Luther. The perfection of the Kingdom of God is longed for in the Church and in the life of every individual believer, to be sure, but it is also contradicted and attacked. Luther was passionately concerned that men should not confuse their own partial, finite structures with the Heavenly City. They must know that they are men and not gods. This awareness of the pervasiveness of sin in every area of life had consequences for every doctrine Luther touched, and his interpretation of sex is no exception.

One further principle of Luther's which merits attention is his concept of 'the sanctity of all work.' He rejected the notion that one vocation or calling is higher and more pleasing to God than another. What God demands of all men is total devotion of heart and soul and mind and strength, and this can be done by the maid sweeping the floor as well as by the monk saying his prayers. Luther was strongly anti-ascetic in this respect, objecting violently to the idea that celibacy was a higher estate than marriage, or that poverty or monastic seclusion gave men a special status in the divine sight. He was far closer to Paul's counsel to early Christians to remain in whatever estate they found themselves when called (1 Corinthians 7) and to his appreciation for the diversity of gifts (1 Corinthians 12) than was the hierarchical attitude of the Roman Church. By this principle, Luther dignified secular work, seeing it as a means by which one could serve God and neighbor as well or better than the priest or monk, could. The sanctity of all work is, in a real sense, the religious foundation for modern economic life. The later Middle Ages were dominated by the Aristotelian and Thomist preference for the contemplative life, the life of reason, and by a condescension toward craftsmen and husbandmen, those who served men's bodies rather than their souls. Luther provided a new dignity and importance to the tasks of the common man. Protestantism can be regarded as the ideology of bourgeois and proletarian life, as scholasticism was of monastic and feudal life. This provides a curious twist to the weaving, for Luther's doctrine of the sanctity of all work is obviously more naturalistic than Thomism, which looked down upon the life of the flesh, the market place, and the marriage bed. Yet his justification by faith is considerably less naturalistic in its attitude toward the world and its inhabitants than that of Thomism, with its positive acceptance of the 'works of nature' and the efforts of men to live in accord with the divine will. This strange pattern resulted in Luther's rejection of celibacy and virginity in favor of marriage on the one hand, and in his continued acceptance of the traditionally dualistic interpretation of sex on the other.

It has already been suggested that unlike Jesus or Paul, Augustine or Aquinas, Luther spoke from the first-hand experience of lawful wedlock. It has been maintained by some critics, especially in Roman Catholic circles, that Luther's break with Rome was motivated by his desire to marry a nun. Of course, mere chronology refutes such a canard, since he did not even meet Katherine von Bora until seven years after the ninety-five theses. But even in less biased circles, a romantic love is sometimes attributed to Luther, which is sheer fabrication. He was forty-two years of age at his marriage, in poor health and fiercely preoccupied with his work, while Katherine was twenty-seven, a sober, industrious woman just over a strong attachment to another man. Devoted and loyal to each other they certainly were, but there was no romance, as that word is currently understood, in their relationship. Much of the coarseness and vulgarity attributed to his home life (and both Denifle and Grisar, the two leading Roman Catholic biographers have emphasized this to the full) belonged rather to the times, which were far less prudish than the modern world with its lingering heritage of Victorianism. The sixteenth century was not at all reticent about the facts of life, not even the most genteel, and as Roland Bainton has written, 'The volume of coarseness

. . . in his total output is slight. Detractors have sifted from the pitchblende of his ninety tomes a few pages of radioactive vulgarity.' [1] Whatever his interpretation of sex and marriage, Luther had in his personal relationships to his family a healthy naturalism, an earthy sense of humor. His personal experience illumined his words with a certain warmth and vitality.

Luther's understanding of sex as a fact of creation and therefore good followed closely the views of both Augustine and Aquinas. His commentary on Genesis contributed little that has not already been encountered: the conviction that marriage was a part of the original divine purpose, that the Fall preceded the first coitus of Adam and Eve, but that had intercourse occurred according to God's plan, it would have been a chaste and holy love, without the 'epileptic and apoplectic lust' of sinful sex. Nudity was no cause for shame; all would have been pure and wholly in accord with God's command. The strong naturalism inherent in the creation story in the Old Testament was inescapable for Luther no less than for his predecessors. However dualistic Christian thought became in its attitude toward sex after the Fall, it has steadfastly maintained that sex as originally created was altogether good. Luther departed from Aquinas and followed Augustine in his view of the defects arising from original sin. He insisted that man was 'totally depraved,' corrupted in mind, body, and will, rather than merely deprived of supernatural gifts, his natural self remaining as created, though tempted by concupiscence and somewhat weakened in will. But with regard to the effects of sin on sex and marriage, Luther had, in general, very little disagreement even with Aquinas. The first penalty or result of original sin was the ravages of lust. Once more, sex is regarded as evil because of the 'brute-like' quality of passion. Luther did not share the Catholic admiration for the contemplative life and he was not alarmed by the disruption of reason involved in orgasm, but he was concerned that it is not possible for fallen man, as it must have been for Adam and Eve, to enter into coitus 'in the knowledge and worship of God.' A second penalty is the pain and peril of

1. Bainton, Roland, *Here I Stand*, Abingdon-Cokesbury, New York, 1950, p. 298.

parturition and gestation, which, together with the trials and tribulations of rearing children, are visited upon women. The female bears particular responsibility and therefore particular penalty. She was created in all respects equal and similar to her husband, differing only in sex. She was not inferior in any way, mentally or physically, but now she is subject to her mate and to the especial infirmities and inconveniences connected with child-bearing and child-rearing. But even man is not altogether free from at least vicarious suffering during his wife's labor; he shares her distress and is anxious about her danger. Such inconveniences, said Luther, frighten many men away from the cares of marriage into the safer havens of temporary and illicit sexual unions.

A third punishment for original sin is the shame that attaches itself to the naked body and to all matters concerned with sex. Luther did not follow Augustine's suggestion that shame arises from the disobedience of the body to the mind and will. He attributed it to the loss of trust in God. Since all innocent confidence in God is lost, the heart is full of distrust, fear, and shame. 'If we possessed the confidence in innocency as Adam enjoyed, we should know no shame, no blush in our nakedness.' Luther did not go on to draw the obvious parallel — that in so far as trust in God is restored through grace, the shamelessness of Adam should be approximated. Any man who takes the God of the Bible seriously must accept all the facts of creation as divine gifts to be used and enjoyed. This is the very essence of Christian naturalism. Nothing is shameful or evil; all things are loved by God because 'all things were made by him and without him was not anything made that was made.' The two-fold doctrine of creation and redemption provide the possibilities for a wholly positive attitude toward the body and its sexual organs and functions, but so strong was the heritage of Hellenistic dualism passed on by antiquity to the medieval and Reformation Christians that they were unable fully to appreciate the implications of these doctrines. Luther went on to assert that the genitals are especially shameful and therefore covered with special care. Those parts of the body assigned by God to the glorious act of generation were in the state of innocence the noblest and most honorable, but in the state of sin they have be-

come the most shameful. And what in Paradise was the most
glorious act of generation, holy and pure, is now 'filled with the
leprosy of lust.' These, then, are the results of sin: shame at nakedness and all things sexual, the burning of lust, the subjection of
woman to man, the pangs of childbirth, and the heartaches of
parenthood. Luther insisted, however, that these are only the
symptoms of sin, effects of the inner condition of depravity rather
than the disease itself.

The ravages of lust and the shamefulness of sex did not drive
Luther into the general preference for celibacy and virginity. He
broke wholly with tradition and insisted not only upon the right
but the duty of all but a select few to marry. He gave two reasons
for his position: first, because marriage was instituted and commanded by God, and its glory has not been destroyed by sin;
second, because no one is free from the powerful urgings of lust,
and almost no one can resist, as witness the immoralities of the
supposedly celibate clergy — he regarded marriage as preferable
to fornication.

First, then, marriage is an honorable estate, ordained of God.
The Fall has corrupted marriage, as it has corrupted everything
human, but the glory of marriage still remains. Luther was indebted to Augustine on many accounts, and he absorbed thoroughly the belief that everything which *is,* is good, including even
sex. Not only is the woman the agent of generation, the bearer of
children, she is also the remedy of man's lust. Animals, Luther
observed, copulate only when the female is in heat, so that sex is
bound inextricably with reproduction, while man needs sexual
intercourse far more often than the few times necessary for a
family. So great was God's wisdom and goodness that he provided
a remedy for sin even before the sin occurred. And corrupt and
sinful though marriage has now become, it still carries with it
three divine blessings. First, through the seed of woman (that is,
Christ) as foretold in Genesis, the serpent is put down and eternal
life is brought to mankind. Second, the troubles and trials of
marriage break down human pride, fostering humility and patience
under the cross. And third, despite the fact that cohabitation is no
longer engaged in solely as a duty to God, even impure sexual

intercourse brings with it the blessing of children, as God intended. His original purpose cannot be deflected or effaced by human sin. Therefore, recognizing that purpose, shining through the filth of corruption, the faithful will take delight in the benefits and blessings of marriage. Despite the punishments, pains, and afflictions involved in wedded life, the divine glory remains. Pain is added to childbirth as a punishment for sin, but God does not remove the gladness of motherhood. And actually, said Luther, men should be grateful for the cares of matrimony, for they are plainly deserving of much penalty for their sin, and these woes serve as a daily reminder of God's goodness and grace.

Since marriage is divinely ordained, whoever disparages matrimony casts a reflection upon its author, God himself. But it is not a sacrament. 'There is in every sacrament a word of divine promise, to be believed by whoever receives the sign . . . Now we read nowhere that the man who marries a wife receives any grace of God.' [2] To be sure, marriage does symbolize something higher than itself, as the epistle to the Ephesians demonstrates, but symbols are not sacraments. Further, marriage has existed since creation and is still to be found among the heathen, whose marriages are sacred and good, but assuredly not sacraments. Marriage is God's institution, not man's, not even the Church's, and it is his law which rules it, not the Pope's. No special power to grant dispensations is given to the Pope. What is allowed and forbidden in these matters is clearly set forth in Scripture, and any Christian can proclaim that. Not even the Pope can forbid what Holy Writ allows, nor can he permit what the Bible bans. Luther recognized the right of the civil authorities to jurisdiction over marital affairs. The medieval Church, regarding marriage as a sacrament, had insisted on its exclusive right to deal with all questions in this sphere, a right that Luther denied. He held that marriage is, in one sense, an outward, secular matter, in the same category as food, clothing, house, and land. It is for the state to decide what does or does not constitute a legal marriage, and there are wide differences from culture to culture — 'Many lands, many customs.'

2. *The Babylonian Captivity of the Church*, in *Works of Martin Luther*, 6 vols., A. J. Holman Co., Philadelphia, 1915, vol. II, p. 215.

The priest or minister may officiate at a wedding only under two conditions: if the civil authority appoints him to serve as a magistrate in this capacity, and if the couple desire the blessing of the Church on their union. The Church has no 'rights' in marriage. It can enter only as invited, and its proper action is confined to pronouncing the blessing. Marriage does have its Christian aspects, but only for those who are Christians.

It is interesting to notice in this connection that Luther insisted upon parental consent as necessary to the validity of a marriage between two minors. He admonished the young that they must adhere to the old ways which give parents the right to control their children's lives and told them that they could not enter a valid betrothal without permission. He refused to accept the medieval doctrine that a clandestine marriage, consummated sexually before the ceremony has taken place, is lawful. For Luther, this was no marriage at all; it was simply fornication. Marriage was in his eyes primarily an external contract, entered into publicly and under the supervision of the state. Hence, children are in duty bound to obey their parents. He did, however, counsel a certain flexibility on both sides, recognizing that parents can be tyrannical and that children can be rebellious unless there is good will and understanding on the parts of both. Luther was curiously legalistic at this point, regarding marriage as an external contract, to be arranged by parents and the state, with very little regard for the internal feelings of the persons most immediately concerned. But he did not agree with the Roman position that one act of intercourse makes a marriage. There is legalism and anti-legalism on both sides of this fence.

Luther's first reason for preferring marriage to celibacy was his conviction that God has ordained that all men should live in the conjugal state. His second reason was that the power of the libidinal drives in fallen man is so great that no one can resist. This, of course, was a part of his quarrel with Erasmus over 'the bondage of the will.' Catholic theology looks upon man as substantially the same now as he was before the Fall. He has lost his supernatural or preternatural gifts; he is beset by concupiscence, and his will is somewhat weakened, but in general he is the same

man. He is able, by the divine grace bestowed in baptism, to do
what God commands, and even, with the help of the other sacraments, to do more. His will can control his life. Luther, in contrast, saw man as 'totally depraved,' a phrase which has been much
misunderstood. He did not mean that there are no vestiges of the
original righteousness. The totality had reference, rather, to his
conviction that no single part of man escaped the corrupting
effects of sin, so that his mind, his soul, his body, his reason, and
his will, all contain a mixture of righteousness and sin. And
sacramental grace does not operate magically to remove the sin.
Man is still a sinner although God has accepted him as righteous.
He is 'justified,' or made righteous, not in actuality but only in
the sight of God. The will is still in bondage to sin and no one can
avoid evil in one form or another. This is especially true with
respect to concupiscence. Man must give some release to his sexual
drives. If, Luther challenged, the will is so free, then why do not
those who possess this great gift use it to set themselves free from
concupiscence? Because, he said, their wills are captive. 'Why,' he
asked, 'do we hold concupiscence to be irresistible? Well, try and
do something without the interference of concupiscence. Naturally,
you cannot.' [3] Luther's assurance that a life of celibacy is impossible
is not surprising in the light of the conditions of the sixteenth
century, when the overwhelming majority of the clergy violated
their vows of celibacy regularly.

Luther did not make that judgment absolute. He admitted that
there are a few who can remain virginal, but those who do so for
the sake of the Kingdom are so rare that there is scarcely one in a
thousand, and they are 'a special miracle of God's own.' Luther
did not, he said, wish to disparage celibacy, or to tempt people
into the married state, for each man must decide for himself under
God the place in life whereunto he is called. He conceded that the
life of chastity is probably better, since it escapes the cares of
marriage and leaves one free to preach and to study the Word of
God. Here, of course, Luther simply echoed the Apostle Paul, and
his motive was also eschatological, seeking freedom to please God,
not negating sex as something evil. But this was Luther in one of

3. *Werke,* Weimar, H. Bohlan, 1887–1948, i, p. 374.

his quieter moods. In a more characteristic temper, he burst out with the assertion that marriage is a positive command of God, in the same order of strict necessity as the Ten Commandments. 'The conscience of the unmarried must be importuned, urged and tormented until they comply.' Again and again he declared that anyone who did not marry must misconduct himself. Speaking of his own experience with shameful temptation, he wrote to a friend concerning marriage, 'Your body demands and needs it; God wills it and insists upon it.' And he saw the Word of God as quite clear, that woman was made to be either a wife or a prostitute. It was this strong conviction which made him strike out so violently against the whole Catholic system of celibacy.

With his typical vacillation, he fluctuated between the extreme of crying out that all vows of celibacy are null and void, an insult to God who decreed that it is not good for man to be alone, and a more moderate position in which he recognized the validity of a vow of virginity yet urged that such a vow not be taken until the person had reached a reasonably mature age. In his *Letter to the Knights of the Teutonic Order,* Luther wrote that God had in his Holy Word decreed marriage for all. Yet the Church has presumed to deny this, to make virginity more blessed. To the many awaiting a church council to decide the question, Luther declared that a council was nothing beside the Word of God, avowing that he would rather 'look through his fingers' and trust to God's mercy a man who had all his life kept one, two, or even three whores than one who awaited the action of a church council to tell him what to do. The Word of God is the sole authority to be consulted in such matters, and to turn away from it to finite and fallible mortals, be they ever so lofty princes of the Church, is blasphemy, which is a far worse sin than fornication. Luther's motive was not solely the desire to attack Rome, though that was certainly in his mind, but he was concerned over the plight of the multitudes of priests who had been living in sin with their common-law wives and children, troubled in conscience and a scandal to the faith, yet forbidden to marry.

Writing to Melanchthon from his enforced seclusion in the Wartburg in August of 1521, he expressed his anxiety over the

extremes to which Carlstadt was going in Wittenberg in marrying
priests and nuns. Luther wished, also, to make celibacy a matter
of Christian liberty, but he found Carlstadt's reasons adduced from
Scripture to be frail reeds. Writing again five weeks later, he reported that he had found the answer he sought. Any who take a
vow of celibacy in search of salvation, he said, are guilty of offending God, trying to bargain with him with their 'good works.' And
since the largest number of those bound by such a vow do suffer
under the illusion that their abstinence somehow elevates their
status, 'it is clear that their vow is godless, sacrilegious, contrary
to the Gospel, and hence to be dissolved and laid under a curse.' [4]
To this argument Luther later added the fact that any vow must be
a possible one, and to him it was quite clear that for men (admitting
that angels are different), celibacy is impossible. 'As little is it in
my power that I am not a woman, so little am I free to remain
without a wife.' There may be those who by a special gift of God's
grace can remain single, but to make a general rule binding on all
religious orders seemed to Luther not only foolish but contrary to
the divine will. There could not be a law of that kind, he declared,
and insisted that any priest, monk, or nun who could not restrain
the desires of the flesh should marry and relieve their consciences
of a terrible burden. Luther was clearly at one with Paul's dictum
that 'it is better to marry than to be consumed with passion.'

It must not be assumed, however, that Luther regarded the
sexual aspect of marriage as altogether pure and holy. Marital coitus was, for him, a 'remedy,' a lesser evil than fornication. His
conviction that lust was irresistible led him to see marriage as a
necessity which was not without sin, and yet because of its necessity
'God winks at it.' Passion of the flesh is guided by God into the
paths of marriage and parenthood, and in this regard Luther agreed
with Augustine and Aquinas that the highest good of married life
is offspring to be reared in the faith. Any couple who marries with
passion as their sole aim is doomed to disappointment, for after
the appetite has been satisfied and departed, disgust comes to dwell
in its stead. Even marriage does not abate the desire of some, as
the widespread existence of adultery demonstrates. All that mar-

4. *Briefwechsel*, 3, p. 224.

riage can do is to keep libidinal drives within certain bounds, but even there 'we are so made . . . when once our passions are aroused that we forget everything.' No conjugal duty can be performed without sin, but God in his mercy overlooks it.

Despite his own marriage and his view of matrimony as a divine decree, Luther looked upon sex as somehow unclean, and though necessary, an unhappy necessity. His recognition of the strength of the sexual instinct did lend a certain realism to his moral counsels, however. This realism manifested itself in his reaction to certain penances imposed by Catholic confessors, of whom he had himself been one. It seems that the approved penance for some degrees of incest was to prohibit the guilty party from having sexual relations with the marriage partner, yet to insist that he or she continue to share the marriage bed. Luther's comment on this was explosive: 'What monstrous thing is this? What new remedy for sin? What sort of satisfaction for sin? Does it not show how these tyrants make laws for other men's infirmities and indulge their own? . . . They put dry wood on a fire and say, Don't burn; they put a man in a woman's arms and forbid him to touch her or know her. . . . No angel in heaven, still less any man on earth has the power to enjoin this penance, which is the burning occasion of continual sin.' [5] Luther wrote a friend, seeking consolation concerning chastity, that evil thoughts are the lot of all men, and one does not become unchaste because of them. If these thoughts come, as they do, unbidden by the will, no impurity is involved. A man can tell whether or not his will consents by the degree to which he experiences pleasure. But, said Luther realistically, one need not feel absolute displeasure. It is rather a state of uncertainty, at one moment willing, at the next unwilling.

His realism is also apparent in his attitude toward divorce. Marriage, he said, is obviously intended as a lifelong state, even among the heathen nations, who derive it as a conclusion from the law of nature. The Fall of man brought with it a multitude of sexual and marital evils, among them divorce. Separations and divorces Luther regarded as signs of the corruption which had come upon men through sin. He was, of course, bound by Jesus'

5. *Works,* Holman edition, vol. i, p. 100f.

prohibition of divorce. He thought it clear, both from the ordinance of creation and the teaching of Christ, that marriage is meant to last throughout life, and he confessed that he found divorce so abhorrent that he would prefer bigamy. However, he recognized certain problems obscured by the fiat of Rome. Luther found that Christ excepted adultery in his ban on divorce, and the Catholic Church allowed separation on these grounds. But the Gospel record is silent on the question whether the innocent party may remarry. The Church forbade it; Luther asked on what authority. Paul had said that it is better to marry than to be consumed with passion. But suppose the innocent one 'burns,' what then? The Church replied, 'Let him contain.' Luther was more realistic. He believed that in cases of adultery, the guilty party severed the marriage tie so that the innocent one can act as though his spouse had died and he is free to marry again.

Luther was concerned also over 'the infinite perils' of those who had been deserted by runaway husbands or wives, compelled by the Church to remain unmarried, living without sex for a prolonged period. The remedy he suggested to meet these cases was the extension of the so-called 'Pauline privilege.' Paul wrote to the Corinthians that when a Christian was married to an unbeliever, if the latter wished to depart, he should be allowed to do so, and the Christian should be free to marry again, this time within the Church. Luther said that any husband or wife who deserted the home proved themselves to be unbelievers in fact, whatever they might be in name, and therefore should be treated as such. However, he expressed his reluctance to speak decisively or authoritatively on these questions, deprecating his views as opinions only. But divorce and remarriage seemed to him permissible in the cases of adultery, of marriage to an unbeliever, and by extension of the Pauline privilege to victims of desertion.

His lusty realism asserted itself again on behalf of those whose sex life in marriage was, due to no fault of theirs, nonexistent. His remark in this connection became well-known, a scandal to many: 'If the wife refuse, let the maid come.' Luther could not bring himself to condemn a man who dealt with the frigidity of a wife's refusing to render the conjugal debt by putting away

the intransigent female and taking unto himself a more compli-
ant partner. He also heartily agreed that sexual impotence and
physical deformity rendering sex impossible were sufficient grounds
for annulment, but if a woman married to such a man finds the
ecclesiastical courts tyrannical and unwilling to release her, then
Luther suggested an alternative. She may, with her husband's
permission — though he is not really her husband but merely a
dweller under the same roof — give herself to another man, perhaps her husband's brother, in secret and ascribe any children to
her apparent spouse. If she does this in desperation because of
the injustice of human laws, she is not involved in sin, for the
divine law sets her free. She is not really married to her 'husband'
in any case. A man's impotence is an absolute barrier to a true
marriage.

Luther was confronted with the divorce problem on two occasions which had very wide implications. The first was the plight
of Henry VIII, who sought release from his marriage to Catherine
of Aragon. When Cranmer arrived in Germany in 1531, having
been sent there by Henry to seek the advice of the Universities,
Luther took the position that Henry's only course would be to
take Anne Boleyn as a second wife, since the Bible forbids divorce but not polygamy. But by 1536 Luther had found another
solution. Catherine was the widow of Henry's older brother,
Arthur, and a special papal dispensation was necessary to permit
her marriage to Henry, since the Bible prohibits a man from
marrying his dead brother's wife. Luther declared that the Pope
cannot set aside the Word of God, and that Henry's first marriage was never valid at all. This was the position already taken
by Cranmer, newly appointed Archbishop of Canterbury, when
in 1533 he declared the union void.

Luther's preference for bigamy to divorce appeared again in
the case of Philipp of Hesse. Luther insisted that whatever was
not specifically forbidden by Scripture was optional for the Christian, and not only is there no Biblical ban on polygamy, there
are positive examples of it, in the patriarchs. In January of 1521,
long before the affair of either Philipp or Henry, Luther had
written to a friend whose marital life was wholly asexual owing

to the illness of his wife and who had asked whether he might take a second wife. At that time Luther had responded that he could raise no objection if a man wished to take several wives, since Holy Scripture does not forbid it. Still, he went on to say, he would not like to see the practice become general, for Christians ought not to seize greedily upon anything to which their freedom gives them the right. This is very characteristic of Luther. He refused to legalize, he insisted on the liberty of the Christian man, but he wanted all believers to exercise their freedom with great care as to its effect upon others. He would only give advice and opinion, not command. Each man must, in the light of his own conscience, work out his course of action. Luther had been a confessor and he always displayed serious pastoral concern for those who turned to him in trouble. This was his attitude toward Philipp of Hesse, who sought Luther's help. Philipp was saddled with a homely and frigid wife. He was infatuated with a younger woman who responded to his ardor with warmth. Divorce was beyond his reach, and he wrote to ask Luther if he might take a second wife. Luther strongly urged him to try to bear his cross with patience and courage, but when it became apparent that Philipp could not do this, that it was a second wife or a mistress, the pastor gave his approval to the former course of action, telling Philipp, however, that the whole matter must be kept secret. Luther was not alone in his views on polygamy, incidentally, as they were shared by no less a person than Cardinal Cajetan of the Roman *curia,* who advised the Pope to grant a dispensation to Henry VIII to take Anne Boleyn as a second wife. Luther was convinced that some sort of sex life is essential to all men, and in special cases of necessity, he regarded bigamy as a lesser evil than fornication or adultery.

Luther's realism was such that he refused to content himself with pious exhortations to men to contain themselves. He knew human nature and he realized that for some men this is literally impossible. He thought it better in such a situation to keep sex within the bonds of wedlock, even if it be a second wife, than to let it run riot outside of marriage. His realistic appraisal of sex, however, did not lead him to regard it as good. Lust for Luther was impulsive, mad, bestial, a raging animal that must from time to time be allowed to run lest he burst his prison and destroy all. 'Do we not then, from all these considerations, feel how foul and horrible a thing sin is? For lust is the only thing that cannot be cured by any remedy! Not even by marriage, which was expressly ordained for this infirmity of our nature. For the greater part of married persons still live in adultery.' [6] Here, of course, he meant the adultery of thought and desire rather than of actuality — but this besets even the happily married. All men must marry except the happy few whom God exempts from the shameful necessity, and they are indeed few. No one must be forbidden to marry, not even those who have taken a vow of perpetual virginity. If they find that they cannot keep the vow, they are to be released and allowed to marry. Sex cannot and will not be denied. In this respect, Luther foreshadowed Freud, but where the latter looked upon the power of sex as a natural instinct, Luther saw it as the result of sin.

John Calvin

Calvin's theology was basically at one with Luther's. The differences were chiefly in emphasis. He, too, insisted upon the principle of justification by faith and uttered strong polemics against the papist doctrine of salvation by merit. Everything is dependent on the grace of God. But Calvin erected a much more systematic, more impressive theology. Where Luther was frenetic, throwing off pamphlets and letters at white heat, often contradictory, utterly lacking in system, Calvin wrote calmly, carefully, organizing and creating Protestantism's *Summa*. The central principle of his system was the sovereignty of God, the absolute dominion of the divine over all that lives and moves and has its being. Where for Luther the chief response of the believer to his Creator and Redeemer was love, for Calvin it was obedience. Calvin insisted as rigorously as the German Reformer that works are utterly without avail in salvation. That is a gift of God, totally unearned or undeserved by man. But Calvin placed greater em-

6. *Commentary on Genesis* 3:9, in the edition of Luther's works edited by J. L. Lenker, Lutherans in All Lands Co., Minneapolis, Minn., 1903.

phasis on the striving of the soul already saved toward sanctifica-
tion. Out of gratitude toward God for his redemption, the Christian seeks to know and to obey the divine will, which he finds
in the Bible. Calvin was much more rigorous in his attitude toward
Scripture than Luther. The moral law of the Old Testament had
not been set aside. It is not an agent of salvation, but it is a
directive for those who love God and seek to serve him. The
Calvinist ethic, as a result, was more positive and emphatic than
the Lutheran, as well as more specific and inclusive. The two systems reveal the Scylla and Charybdis of ethics. The peril of the
Lutheran system is quietism. Social life is a *massa perditionis*
and can never be redeemed. The individual does not try to
transform society; he merely says his prayers. The weakness of
Calvinist ethics, on the other hand, is legalism, a too precise definition of righteousness, which is always a coin with two sides —
the other being moralism, condemning any who fail to conform
to the accepted standards. This is exactly what happened in
Puritanism, which was one of the earliest offspring of Calvin,
producing a curious blend of naturalism and dualism. All of life
was affirmed as the creation of God; all aspects of existence were
to be brought under his sovereign sway. This is the strongest kind
of naturalism, but it is combined with a type of asceticism, an
emphasis on discipline of the body, which is in effect, if not in
intention, dualistic.

Calvin began, as might be expected, by affirming sex and marriage as facts of creation. He followed the traditional lines of interpretation in his Commentary on Genesis, but with some significant
differences. His predecessors had all looked upon woman as primarily a sexual being and upon marriage as principally for purposes of procreation. Calvin, in contrast, relegated these concerns
to a secondary status. To him, the decisive words in the creation
narrative were those of God's, 'It is not good that the man should
be alone.' His design in creating the woman was 'that there should
be human beings on the earth who might cultivate mutual society between themselves.' Sex was not excluded from the divine
plan but put in its proper place, subservient to the prior principle
of community. Calvin pointed out that the Hebrew word *Adam*

meant 'man,' not as distinct from woman but as human, separate from other species. The male alone does not constitute 'man'; without the woman he is incomplete. The species is only half created. The principal purpose of the female is not sexual but social. She is to be a companion to the man primarily and only secondarily the agent of generation. She is the symbol, as it were, of the gregarious nature of mankind. Calvin obviously displayed a greater appreciation of woman than any previous theologian, emancipating her from her enforced role as a mere baby factory or safety valve for male libido.

This does not mean that Calvin interpreted the male-female relationship in purely Platonic terms. Sex was definitely a part of the creative plan of God, but it is to be kept within the bonds of monogamous marriage. God has ordained that sex shall be the means of propagating the race, and he commands and blesses the use of sex. But the blessing is restricted to those who cohabit in chaste and holy wedlock. Fornicators and adulterers also produce offspring, but even though God allows children to be brought out of this 'muddy pool,' such actions tend to the destruction of the persons involved. Calvin dealt with the fact of concupiscence with considerable restraint, emphasizing always the positive blessings which still adhere to matrimony, in contrast to Luther who laid stress on what had been lost in the Fall. 'You may then take it briefly, thus,' Calvin wrote, 'conjugal intercourse is a thing that is pure, honorable and holy, because it is a pure institution of God; the immoderate degree with which persons burn is a fault arising from the corruption of nature; but in the case of believers marriage is a veil, by which the fault is covered over, so that it no longer appears in the sight of God.' [7] This passage is characteristic, for whenever Calvin spoke of the passion of sex, the strength of the libidinal drives, he immediately went on to add that marriage makes such passions at worst a thing not reckoned a fault by God and at best a means of producing offspring and of building society.

In this connection, Calvin warned of two extremes. The one is

7. Calvin's *Commentary on First Corinthians*, translated by John Pringle, William Eerdmans Co., Grand Rapids, Mich., 1948.

to abhor sex and seek celibacy, regarding all forms of sexuality as degrading. The other is to regard sex as self-justifying, to say, as he put it, 'that married persons might indulge themselves in whatever license they please.' He regarded it as essential to set forth the dignity of marriage in order to fight superstition and to combat the two-fold danger, either that the faithful may avoid the conjugal estate or that they may be guilty of lasciviousness of the flesh instead of living modestly with their wives. Any insult to marriage Calvin saw as an insult to God, its author and patron. In the attack on the whole institution of celibacy and the practice of taking vows of perpetual virginity, Calvin joined Luther with vigor. His reasons were essentially the same: that marriage is an honorable estate instituted of God, and that it is also a necessity if man is to avoid falling into sexual sins. The Roman Catholic Church justified its stand by appealing particularly to two passages in the New Testament, chapter 19 in the Gospel according to St. Matthew, where Jesus spoke of men's making themselves eunuchs for the sake of the Kingdom, and 1 Corinthians 7 where Paul said that it is good for a man not to touch a woman.

Calvin exegeted both of these verses from a different point of view. In dealing with the word of Jesus he seized upon the verse, 'All men are not capable of receiving this saying,' and declared that this shows that the choice does not lie in human hands. Continence is a special gift bestowed upon very few, and only those few who have been appointed by God can endure the sacrifices of a celibate life. For all others, and this represents the great majority of mankind, God not only permits but positively commands marriage, and any who resist matrimony are fighting against God. 'It is, therefore, a foolish imagination that celibacy is a virtue,' and no man can regard it as approved of God unless he is singled out by divine appointment for that estate, and that only on the grounds that he seeks a 'free and unrestricted meditation on the heavenly life.'

But how is a man to know whether he is one of the few exempted from marriage? Paul expressly stated that it is better to marry than to burn, and he had religious grounds for this judgment, for 'where there is *burning*, no love of God can exist.' But what does

it mean to burn? Does it mean simply to feel lust, to be aware of
sexual desire? No, answered Calvin, to burn is not to feel heat,
but to boil with lust. There are three kinds of sexual temptations
which beset us. In the first place, there is that impetuous assault
of lustful desire which is so sudden and so powerful that the will
is completely overcome and we are swept away into sexual acts.
'This is the worst kind of *burning*, when the heart is inflamed with
lust.' In the second place, men are sometimes stung with the
darts of the flesh, but they are able through prayer and the strength
of God's grace to refuse assent to the impulse; they are given the
power to resist. The third sort of temptation comes when one is
beset by sexual impulses not strong enough to overwhelm his will
but powerful enough to prevent his calling, in good conscience,
upon God for help. Any temptation which hinders one from
turning to God in purity and disturbs peace of conscience is *burning* and it cannot be extinguished except by marriage. If a man
is subject to strong sexual desires, he may know that he burns
and that God thereby commands him to marry. He is not one
who can contain, and he will best resist Satan and serve God in
wedlock. Any such who refuse the divinely proffered remedy are
tempting God. Only he who is free from burning and desires,
or who can, with God's help, put them from him with ease, is
exempted from the duty to take a wife.

In his Commentary on 1 Corinthians, Calvin dealt with the
familiar, 'It is good for a man not to touch a woman,' by observing that it is essential to know what Paul meant by *good*. The
mistake made by Jerome must be avoided, the assumption that
Paul meant to say that to touch a woman is evil. Paul had no such
intention. He was simply pointing out what is expedient 'on
account of there being so many troubles, vexations and anxieties
that are incident to married persons.' To say that it is good occasionally to refrain from eating or drinking does not mean
that those things are evil, nor that there is any virtue in mere
abstinence. A temporary withdrawal from such activities for the
sake of prayer is beneficial, but this in no way implies that they
are questionable. Every hour spent on food or drink or sex is
that much less time occupied with the duties of Christian life,

and since there are many impediments and entanglements in married life, Paul regarded it as good for a man to remain single. But his motivation was apocalyptic, not dualistic, and he was speaking only to those who had been given the power to forego sex, a small number of men indeed. For the great majority, Paul directed that they should have recourse to the remedy. And, said Calvin, if the question is asked, is this the only reason for entering into marriage, the cure for lust, the answer is that it is not a matter of the reasons for matrimony but rather of the persons for whom it is necessary. God's original institution of marriage had nothing of a remedy about it, since there was at that time no disease. Its sole purpose then was procreation, but after the Fall this second purpose was added.

Calvin admitted that there are advantages to the celibate life, even as Luther did. He knew that there are many trials to marriage and 'the man who can exempt himself from them ought not to refuse such a benefit.' Even those who marry must be warned of the cares of the conjugal state so that they enter it without illusions. Both Luther and Calvin, despite the fact that they were married (or perhaps because of it), dwelt at great length on the sorrows of wedded life and spoke as though, were it not for the power of concupiscence, they would gladly be delivered from it. Calvin regarded virginity as an excellent gift, but a gift received by very few. Therefore, men should be careful not to rush headlong into a vow which is not in their power, lest God punish them by sending 'secret flames of lust' and 'horrible acts of filthiness.' Calvin was evidently thinking of the gross immoralities of the clergy and not simply of their fornication and adultery, but of homosexuality as well. Like Luther, he simply appealed pragmatically to experience, calling upon anyone who thinks celibacy is really feasible to look at those who have taken the vow. Are they really celibate? Calvin thought it scarcely possible to find one convent in ten that was not a brothel rather than a house of chastity.

He summarized the teaching of Paul concerning sex, so strongly appealed to by Rome, in three articles. First, he conceded that celibacy is better than marriage, because the unmarried have greater freedom to serve God. Second, however, there must be no necessity imposed; men must be free to marry if they feel the need. And third, marriage is a divinely appointed remedy and ought to be used by all who have not been blessed with the gift of continence. The central thing in life was for Calvin, as it was for Paul, the glory of God, and if a man could devote all of his energies to that task, he would be truly blessed. But if he burns with sexual desires, he is far better off to marry and quench the flames of his passion than to suffer the distracting pangs of frustration. It is not enough for a man merely to keep himself free from sinful acts in sex. That is not continence, in the New Testament sense of the word, Calvin insisted. A man must also keep a chaste mind — 'Not only the eyes but even the concealed flames of the heart render man guilty of adultery.' Anyone who has sexual thoughts, then, is not exempted from the necessity for marriage, unless those thoughts be weak and easily dispelled.

Celibacy is for the very few. But what of marriage for the multitude? What is its purpose, and what is the character of sex within wedlock? The original purpose of marriage, as has already been pointed out, was companionship and the production of offspring. To these was added, because of sin, a third purpose, 'a remedy for avoiding fornication,' and almost all men must have recourse to the remedy. But does this mean that all sex within wedlock is lawful? No, Calvin insisted upon due moderation and modesty. He pointed out that Paul spoke of cohabitation 'by way of concession' in 1 Corinthians 7 lest the Apostle's readers should 'loosen unduly the restraints of lust.' Married couples must not gratify their desires by every means, without measure or modesty. Paul was merely considering the infirmity of human beings and making allowances for them, not urging them into 'alluring delights.' Calvin evidently shared the general fear of intense pleasure. It is as if he and all the Church fathers were saying, Sex is necessary, and it is better to use it in marriage, rather than to become involved in all sorts of sins (although really you would be much better off if you could get along entirely without it), but even in marriage, take care that you do not enjoy yourself too much for that is a very great evil! This can obviously be traced to the source of Hellenistic dualism, with its deep suspicion of all bodily pleasure, and it stands in the sharpest contrast to the naturalistic attitude, which springs from Hellenic-Hebraic origins. There is an interesting passage in this connection in Calvin's Commentary on Deuteronomy, where the law expressly directs that a newlywed male shall be exempt from military service and other types of tribal duties for a period of one year so that he may remain at home and 'cheer the wife whom he has taken.' Calvin's comment on this is fascinating, for it reveals his ambivalence of feeling. It seemed very generous of God, yet the Reformer was not altogether sure that he approved. 'That God should permit a bride to enjoy herself with her husband affords no trifling proof of his indulgence. Assuredly, it cannot be but that the lust of the flesh must affect the connection of the husband and wife with some amount of sin; yet God not only pardons it, but covers it with the veil of holy matrimony . . . nay he spontaneously permits them to enjoy themselves.' [8]

Yet for all his counsel of moderation and modesty, Calvin displayed a certain realism in his advice on sexual problems. He regarded the husband and wife as equal with respect to the conjugal bed, though they differ in duty and authority in other areas. He rejected any false prudery, for such shame beguiled devout minds. It is Satan who tempts the faithful into believing that they are polluted by intercourse in marriage, leading them to abandon coitus. The truth is that the marriage act does not pollute or corrupt. On the contrary, only a false sense of shame leads to the kind of enforced abstinence which in turn produces thoughts and acts that really do pollute. That is why Paul required mutual consent for a period of mutual abstinence. And he rightly, said Calvin, set up three provisos. First, the agreement must be mutual, since it involves the abstinence of both and not one only. Second, any such arrangement must be for a temporary period lest the partners attempt to exceed their powers and fall into Satan's trap. Third, married persons are not to abstain from sexual intercourse under the illusion that their abstinence itself

8. Calvin's Commentary on *A Harmony of the Pentateuch*, Eerdmans edition, Deuteronomy 24:5.

is a good thing and pleasing to God, but only in order to have leisure for divine things. Since all abstinence must be by mutual agreement, the wife does not have the right to refuse her husband the use of her body. This is putting the matter somewhat crudely, but Calvin strongly counseled a reciprocal understanding. Husbands and wives must consider each other's sexual needs. There is a strong tendency in everyone, said Calvin, toward self-love and selfish concern only for his own gratification. Many a husband, having satisfied his own lust, treats his wife 'not merely with neglect but with disdain; and there are few who do not sometimes feel the disdain of their wives creeping upon them.' But this is to be resisted. Men must be aware of the mutual obligations of married life. The husband is not an entity unto himself, nor is the wife. Each is but a half of the totality which is their union. Each is to show consideration for the other and neither is to act as if his body were at his own or her own disposal. The sexual aspect of marriage is mutual; it is a good in itself, not to be shunned as impure or corrupt, but it must be regulated, kept within bounds, and not allowed to run riot.

It is clear that the only justification for sex lies in marriage, as a means of producing offspring, as ordained by God from the beginning, and as a way of avoiding fornication, as permitted by God since the Fall. All else is forbidden as sinful. Calvin had some difficulty with fornication. Despite the fact that he was more literal with Scripture than Luther, he did extend the sense of the Bible when it suited his purpose. He pointed out that the Law nowhere forbids simple fornication, but went on at once to say that it is unthinkable that God would condone what mankind condemns, and that even though every age in history has been filled with lewdness, human society has continued to regard fornication as a scandal and a sin. This is rather dubious reasoning, since God has frequently condemned what mankind condones, and there is little reason to believe that he simply ratifies the prejudices of men. Calvin, however, could not believe that God would under any circumstances fail to vent his anger against fornication, and he extended the sense of the seventh commandment to cover that as well as all other forms of sexual vice. Its essence was regarded by Calvin as an exhortation to sexual purity in general, for he regarded it as patently absurd to permit fornication, forbidding adultery only. Any sexual act outside of marriage is accursed.

Adultery is worse than fornication, however, because by it the sanctity of marriage is violated and 'a spurious and illegitimate offspring is derived.' Calvin hated adultery almost more than any other sin. He never forsook an opportunity to condemn it in the severest language possible. It is the breach of a covenant consecrated by God, and where such lasciviousness prevails men descend to the level of beasts. He thought the Old Testament quite right to provide the death penalty for adultery, though he was never successful in winning the civil authorities in Geneva to his position. The actual penalty there was nine days' imprisonment on bread and water and the payment of a fine, unless the parties were unmarried, when the penalty was reduced to six days on bread and water and a fine of sixty sous. Quite obviously, this did not represent Calvin's own wishes in the matter. To those who pointed to Christ's forgiveness of the woman taken in adultery, Calvin replied that the Lord was content with the limits of his vocation. He was not a magistrate, charged with the maintenance of public morality, and any judge who follows Jesus' example does so out of gross ignorance of his own responsibilities.

Sodomy Calvin regarded as a particularly heinous crime, since not even the beasts, he said, are guilty of such a perversion of nature. Calvin had clearly no experience with the sexual behavior of animals. Bestiality, sexual relations with a member of another species, is another sin repugnant to the modesty of nature itself, and the Law very properly prescribes the death penalty. The enormity of such a perversion is seen in the fact that even the innocent animal in the case is commanded by God to be executed. Calvin listed two other sexual sins and spoke with approval of the severe punishment meted out by Hebrew Law: sexual intercourse during menstruation, called by the Old Testament 'uncovering the woman's fountain of blood' (Exodus 20:18), and immodesty. The former sin was punished by exile, and Calvin felt the punishment fit the crime, for he regarded any guilty of this as downright degenerate, since even the beasts respect such a barrier to intercourse. 'Men are warned against all indelicacy which is abhorrent to the natural sense, and . . . married persons are exhorted to restrain themselves from all immodest lasciviousness, and that the husband should enjoy his wife's embraces with delicacy and propriety.' [9] Here, Luther proved somewhat more realistic, recognizing that the character of sexual enjoyment is little ruled by 'delicacy and propriety.' The other sexual sin, of immodesty, brought comment from Calvin in connection with Deuteronomy 25:11–12, where it is prescribed that if a wife inadvertently touches the genitals of another man as she seeks to help her husband in a fight, her offending hand is to be cut off. Calvin admitted that this seemed harsh, but its very severity demonstrated to him how pleasing to God is modesty. He regarded it as 'inexcusable effrontery' to touch that part of the man's body 'from the sight and touch of which all chaste women naturally recoil.' The reader cannot help wondering if chaste women are supposed to recoil from their husband's penis as well.

All sexual relations, then, are to be confined to marriage and even therein they are restricted. Only holy matrimony can draw the veil over the sin of sex. Yet Calvin joined Luther in rejecting the sacramental character of matrimony. It is a good and holy ordinance of God, like agriculture, shoemaking, architecture, and many other exercises, but none of these is a sacrament. The distinguishing mark of a sacrament is that it is both a work of God and an external ceremony ordained by him for the confirmation of a promise. It is true that matrimony is a sign of the spiritual union between Christ and his Church, but there are many signs which are not sacraments, as, for example, the mustard seed, the vine, the shepherd.[10] All of these are analogies used by Jesus, but they are not sacred and holy ceremonies. As for the well known passage in Ephesians, Calvin made short work of showing that the Vulgate mistranslated *mysterion* for *sacramentum* and completely misunderstood Paul's meaning. In a paragraph which

9. *Op. cit.* Leviticus 20:18.
10. *Institutes of the Christian Religion,* Presbyterian Board of Christian Education, Philadelphia, 1936, IV, XIX, 34.

scalded and scolded, Calvin turned a biting satire on Rome for
her inconsistency in declaring with one voice that marriage is a
sacrament while with another she denies that same sacrament to
those who serve her best, the priests, monks, and nuns. He laid
his finger on a further absurdity in the fact that Rome claims
that the grace of the Holy Spirit is conferred in every sacrament,
while denying that the Holy Spirit is ever present in the marriage
act. Calvin agreed with Luther that the regulation of marital
affairs is a matter for the state, but he was stronger in his insistence that the state be guided by the Church. The minister is
a magistrate appointed by the civil authority and as such he
performs weddings. All citizens of the state are also members of
the Church. Calvin was no free churchman; his was the established order. He also joined Luther in forbidding the recognition
of marriages contracted without parental consent. The Geneva
laws carried a statute forbidding the betrothed to cohabit before
the marriage was celebrated in the Church on penalty of being
treated as adulterers. Marriage is not made by consent plus sexual
consummation. Parents and the state must approve.

Marriage is not a sacrament, but it is a lifelong union. The
sacred bond cannot be dissolved at will, for it is reinforced by
the hand of God. Although the Old Testament law granted divorce
to the Jews by way of indulgence, Christ went behind the Law to
creation, pointing out that divorce was never in accord with
God's will, which made the tie between husband and wife stronger
than that between parent and child. Calvin saw the divorce legislation of the Torah as a protection to women, who were by its
terms given a bill of divorcement, attesting their chastity. Man
and wife are, according to the Bible, one flesh, and whoever divorces husband or wife tears his own body in half. The Law may
permit divorces and provide no punishment for them, but any
who remarry are adulterers. Man cannot put asunder what God
has joined together.

Calvin did not, however, make this as absolute as it would
appear. He accepted as genuine the verse, 'except on account of
adultery,' declaring that an unfaithful wife cuts herself off as a
rotten member and sets her husband free. Calvin's conception of

marriage as a living organism is an interesting and highly significant one. So long as all parts of the organism remain sound, to sunder it is to tear one's self to pieces, but if one of the parts becomes diseased, then it must be amputated in order to save the whole. This is true of both parties, for Calvin thought of the right of divorce for adultery as belonging equally to husband and wife. Rome, of course, permits separation for adultery, but not remarriage. Calvin, in contrast, asserted that adultery renders the marriage void, and the offended is free to act as though the guilty spouse were dead. In several places Calvin suggested that adultery is the only grounds for divorce, but his own regulations in Geneva reveal three other sufficient reasons for separation or divorce. The first agreed with both Luther and established Catholic practice: sexual impotence renders a marriage void and an annulment is granted and the potent partner is free to marry another. An extension of this principle permitted a man who could not endure sex with his wife because of some bodily defect which she refused to have remedied, to have the marriage nullified after examination had shown his complaint to be valid and not a mere excuse for freedom. Secondly, desertion was regarded as grounds for divorce. If a partner had been missing and unheard from for ten years, the deserted partner might apply for and receive a divorce, with freedom to remarry. Calvin joined Luther in extending the so-called 'Pauline privilege' to those deserted by partners who were motivated by ill-temper or bad affection and refused to return though entreated to do so. The innocent party, after having made every effort to persuade the wandering one to come home and resume the marriage, might apply to the Consistory and receive his or her freedom. Finally, Calvin allowed the Pauline privilege itself to a Protestant married to a Roman Catholic, although he seems to have granted a larger measure of freedom in this respect to men than to women. In general, however, Calvin was quite just to the female sex. Husbands were forbidden to beat their wives in Geneva, and in all marital relations the wife had equal rights with the husband.

Unlike Luther, Calvin was strongly opposed to polygamy even in the face of its Scriptural warrant. He denounced the practice

and forbade it as contrary to God's will. Creation reveals that
God intended that two shall become one flesh, not three or four.
Calvin even went so far as to reprove the patriarch Abraham for
his failure to trust God to remedy Sarah's barrenness. God punished him by making him drive his own son into the wilderness.
Jacob was also reprimanded for his lust; God visited him with the
retribution of a life of contention and strife. Monogamy was for
Calvin an ordinance of creation, a matter of natural law, and on
this basis he ventured to censure the holy patriarchs, another curious example of Calvin's rare freedom with respect to Scripture,
an area where Luther forsook his usual liberty with the Bible.

In summary, it is evident that Calvin was less pessimistic about
sex than Luther. He believed that it could be harnessed and set
to constructive uses, whereas Luther simply sought to confine its
raging within marriage. But Calvin's attempts at controlling the
sexual drives led him into moralism and legalism, the parents of
prudery. Sex is not really to be enjoyed even in marriage but
kept within the rigid bounds of 'delicacy and propriety.' In fair-
ness to Calvin, it must be said that he was more just to women than
any of his predecessors, and he did possess a realistic understanding
of the importance of sex in life, although it was not so important
in his own life as in Luther's. This difference of temperament
between the two men undoubtedly played an important role in
their varying interpretations of sex. Although both were married
and rejected the Catholic teaching on celibacy and virginity, they
did so not on naturalistic grounds, out of a conviction that sex is
good. Rather, they believed that sex is inevitable. Both men
clearly felt that celibacy is ideally better and that if a man were
free from sexual passion, from 'burning' in the Pauline sense,
he could serve God better by remaining single. Luther made
some place for the disciplining role played by the cares of wedded
life, but neither he nor Calvin had very much appreciation for
sex as a means of expressing conjugal love, of symbolizing physically a union of two personalities. Procreation remained for them,
as for Augustine and Aquinas, the only really positive purpose
of sex. Any pleasure was still sullied, and it matters little whether
one says that it is only a 'venial sin' or that God 'winks at it' or

'draws the veil of holy matrimony over it.' Sex was still far from being accepted as the natural gift of God. Dualism remained the dominant motif in Wittenberg and in Geneva, even as in Rome.

The day of naturalism had not yet come, and when it finally does begin to appear in the weaving of the centuries in large stripes and bold patterns rather than here and there as tiny threads, it is placed upon the loom by secular weavers. To be sure, the modern naturalists either assume that they have introduced the thread for the first time or that they have discovered it in the ancient weaving of Greece, obscured and overlain by the work of Christianity. They do not realize that the thread derives equally from Israel and from Nazareth, and that the 'fall' of western man occurred at the advent of the Hellenistic Age, not of the Christian era. But the debt of Christians to them is nonetheless very great in that they have forced attention to what was there all the time, the fact that 'God looked upon *all* that he had made, and behold, it was very good.' This leads directly to the next two chapters, in which the interpretations of sex in contemporary Christianity are to be examined.

V

CONTEMPORARY CATHOLICISM

From very early times the authority of the Bishop of Rome has been very great. His supremacy over the whole Church, however, was not recognized from the beginning. In the first centuries of the Christian era, the Bishops of Jerusalem, Antioch, Ephesus, Alexandria, and Constantinople claimed equal authority. All were heads of ancient and important churches, and each insisted that his office carried as much prestige and authority as that of any other. The authority of any patriarch was limited to his own diocese, although an individual like Athanasius of Alexandria or Ignatius of Antioch might influence many in the Church at large. But he wielded such influence by virtue of his personal power, not out of any authority vested in his office. Every bishop was sovereign in his own diocese but his rule stopped at its boundaries. This was the view generally accepted in almost all quarters, except in Rome. There the Bishop proclaimed that he was the successor of Peter as head of the Roman congregation, and since Christ himself had bestowed upon Peter the primacy among the Apostles (Matthew 16:13–20), so all Peter's successors were chief among all the successors of the other Apostles. This claim was not really made good until well into the fourth century, when the barbarian tribes brought chaos into the western half of the Roman Empire and the civil authority virtually collapsed. The only stable institution left in the West was the Church, and at its head was the Bishop of Rome, who took the title of Pope, or 'Papa,' the Holy Father. The Eastern churches, with a strong secular authority at Byzantium, never recognized the authority of the Pope, giving him at best only the title of *primus inter pares,* first among equals, or chairman of the board. But the chair could only preside at meetings and count the votes; he could not act alone. In the West, however, where there were no other apostolic churches, the Popes made good their claims and grew in power and influence until Innocent III (1198–1216) was master of Europe. The Pope's infallibility in matters of faith and morals, though claimed by almost all occupants of the papal throne, was not, however, made a matter of dogma until 1870. The decree was made retroactive, applying to all Popes past as well as future, but the Vatican Council marks a kind of watershed. From that point on, any Pope who speaks *ex cathedra,* for the whole church, on a matter of faith and morals, *knows* that his words are absolutely binding upon all the faithful; they are *de fide.* The only such papal pronouncement since 1870 was Pius XII's proclamation of the Assumption of the Virgin as a matter of Catholic dogma.

There is some dispute over the force of a papal encyclical. There are some Catholics who hold that though it deals with faith and morals, the Pope is not speaking *ex cathedra,* and therefore Catholics are not absolutely bound to agree. They must give serious attention and thought, but they are free to differ, for the Pope is a mortal and can make mistakes when he speaks under circumstances other than those rigidly circumscribed by the dogma of infallibility. Pius XII however, in his encyclical *Humani Generis,* issued 12 August 1950, had this to say: 'If the Supreme Pontiffs in their official documents purposely pass judgment on a matter up to that time under dispute, it is obvious that the matter, according to the mind and will of the same pontiffs cannot be any longer considered a question open to discussion among theologians.' Whatever interpretation is placed upon the papal encyclicals, they are documents of immense importance, and any discussion of contemporary Catholic views of sex and marriage must begin with the two letters to the whole Church which deal extensively with the subject, the *Arcanum* of Leo XIII, issued on 10 February 1880, and the *Casti Connubii,* issued by Pius XI on 31 December 1930.[1]

The 'Arcanum' of Leo XIII

Leo began by reaffirming the position of Aquinas and the Council of Trent, that marriage is a divine institution created by God as a means of union between one man and one woman, a union which is to last for life. The pristine character of marriage was lost, however, at the Fall and although the Jews had the divine Law to guide them and therefore did not go so far astray as the pagan Gentiles, even they forsook the divinely ordained monogamy-for-life and introduced polygamy and divorce with remarriage into their customs. This decline in marriage resulted in a decay in all areas of sexual relations, creating moral anarchy, although a legally organized anarchy. Women were degraded to the position of chattel, and the wife sunk 'so low as to be reckoned only a means for the gratification of passion, not for the production of offspring.' Christ restored marriage to its original purity, by condemning the Jewish practice of divorce, declaring that man cannot rend asunder what God has joined together. He raised matrimony to the level of a sacrament, so that husband and wife might attain to holiness in the union which was patterned after Christ's own mystical marriage to his Church. He perfected the love which derives from the natural order and added to it the grace of the divine love, so that man and wife are brought even more securely together. More than this, through him marriage became a means of generating sons and daughters of the Church. The regulation of marriage Christ entrusted to the Church, and this trust she has faithfully carried out through the centuries. The efforts of the Gnostics, the Manichees, the Montanists, and many others to abolish marriage or to pervert its true ends have all been successfully resisted by Holy Church, a task which she continues to perform in the present time. The

1. The *Arcanum* of Leo XIII is available in *The Great Encyclical Letters of Leo XIII,* New York, Benziger Bros., 1903. The *Casti Connubii* of Pius XI can be secured in pamphlet form through the same publishers.

history of the Church is the strongest possible argument that she is the institution best suited to act as guardian of all that pertains to human marriage.

Leo then turned his attention to what he regarded as the modern attack on marriage, which lay primarily in the claims of those who asserted that the state should have supreme authority over matrimonial matters. Since this whole question lies beyond the limits of the present study, the argument may be passed over, noting only two points made by Leo in this connection. First, he declared that all marriages, whether of believers or unbelievers, are sacred and religious. 'Marriage is holy of its own power, in its own nature, and of itself, and ought not to be regulated and administered by the will of civil rulers.' The second point was Leo's denial that any separation can be made between contract and sacrament, the state supervising one and the Church the other. The contract, he maintained, is inseparable from the sacrament in Christian marriage.

In the third and final section of the encyclical, Leo discussed the unhappy results of the false theories of modern secularism. Chaos and disorder in the sexual realm were inevitable once the Christian religion was rejected and repudiated, for without that saving fear of God, 'marriage of necessity sinks into the slavery of man's vicious nature and vile passions.' Man's natural goodness is of little protection against the assault of concupiscence without the bolstering power of sacramental grace. Leo's primary concern seems to have been the increasing incidence of divorce, resulting from the relaxation of the rigid legislation which had previously made it virtually impossible. He called upon the state to seek the guidance of the Church and to check this alarming trend lest marriage become a mockery, the home undermined, and the state weakened. He thought divorce illegal under any circumstances, even for non-Catholics (as it still is in Italy and in Spain) and demanded that the civil authorities should enact laws to that effect. Leo was especially worried about what would happen to women if divorce became increasingly easier to obtain. He was convinced that wives 'run the risk of being deserted after having ministered to the pleasures of men,' and he was certain that multitudes would seek release from their marriage vows. Accordingly, the Pope warned the world in general and instructed Catholics in particular of the dangers threatening them, adding a special admonition to the faithful that in the eyes of the Church, a civil marriage 'cannot be more than a rite or custom introduced by the civil law.'

There is little in Leo's *Arcanum* that bears directly on the Catholic interpretation of sex; the encyclical is significant for what it implies rather than for what it says. It is clear that in the mind of Pope Leo, Catholic teaching on these questions comes directly from God and is infallible and binding upon all men, Catholic and non-Catholic alike. Marriage is sacred and indissoluble and should be so regarded by every society. Divorce is one of our greatest social evils and should be absolutely forbidden. Although the dignity of woman is loudly proclaimed, a condescending attitude still prevails; she is an inferior being who requires special protection. And over all arches the conviction that the Church is holding its finger in the dyke restraining the flood waters of a hellish torrent of sexual evils. Once remove that finger and all will be lost. Secular man, or natural man, will very quickly revert to the state of the beasts, a prospect, incidentally, that would have delighted Rousseau. There is little confidence in methods which seek to teach rather than to constrain, to train people for marriage so that they will freely and spontaneously work through their problems. The matter must be handled by fiat, by absolute prohibition of divorce, no matter what hardship it may work on the multitudes. Legalism reigns supreme.

The 'Casti Connubii' of Pius XI

This encyclical, like Leo's *Arcanum* (and like all Gaul) is divided into three parts. In the first, Pius set forth the dignity and the beauty of Christian marriage. In the second, he dealt with such evils as birth control, companionate marriage, the emancipation of women, and divorce. He concluded by suggesting the appropriate remedies for the current difficulties. The encyclical is one of the longest Pius issued and merits careful attention. He began by recalling the *Arcanum* of Leo and uttered a hearty

'Amen!' to its sentiments, reaffirming the indissoluble character of marriage, an estate created and instituted by God himself. But the human will also plays its part, for without the individual consent of each person, no marriage can take place. This must not mislead men, however, into believing that the sacrament is a subjective affair, dependent on the human will. God and man together constitute a marriage; man enters the marriage by his consent, but he cannot leave it at will, because God has made him subject to its divine and eternal laws.

The blessings of marriage are, as Augustine said, threefold: offspring, faith, and sacrament. The child, of course, holds first place, and Pius repeated the Augustinian position that the generation of children is not merely for the preservation of the race but for the increase of the Church, the raising up of fellow citizens of the saints and members of God's household. The blessing of offspring consists both in having children and in educating them. Pius quoted the code of canon law which declares that 'the primary end of marriage is the procreation and education of children' and then went on to observe that 'the faculty given by God for the procreation of children is the right and privilege of the married state alone.' Any sex outside of marriage is a mortal sin. The second marital blessing is faith, or conjugal fidelity. This means that each partner has a responsibility to fulfill the marriage contract, to 'render the debt,' which may not be denied to the spouse or offered to anyone else. Pius also reminded his readers that nothing contrary to the laws of nature or of reason is permissible in the sexual relations of marriage. Fidelity demands absolute monogamy, and the control of one's thoughts as well as acts, and this end is best served in an atmosphere of mutual love, which Pius defined as not 'the passing lust of the moment . . . but the deep attachment of the heart . . . expressed in action, since love is proved by deeds.' This true love will make the rendering of the debt not a matter of justice only but also of charity, and it will help wife and children to give proper obedience to the husband as the head of the family. Woman is not to live in subjection but in devotion to the good of the home. The third blessing, the sacrament, signifies the indissolubility of the relationship and confers grace upon those who receive the sacrament. All marriages are indissoluble, even those between pagans, but the sacramental character is confined to those rites celebrated between baptized persons, those who have received a previous sacrament and are therefore at least partially in a state of grace. The addition of the sacramental grace of matrimony opens up a treasure to husbands and wives from which they can draw to enrich and adorn their marriage.

Pius turned, in the second part of the encyclical, to the current attacks of the secular world on the true Catholic doctrine of marriage. First, regarding birth control, the Pontiff rehearsed all of the familiar arguments for it, the difficulties of the mother or of family circumstances, the weariness of children, and the desire to gratify sexual desire without its consequent burden. All of these he refuted with one major thesis: 'the conjugal act is destined primarily by nature for the begetting of children.' Therefore, any who frustrate the intention of nature are guilty of a sin which is shameful and intrinsically vicious. He went on to observe that Holy Mother Church is fully aware of the health of mothers of children, but this is no excuse for breaking the laws of God. The so-called 'rhythm method' of birth control he declared to be legitimate in certain circumstances. They are not acting against nature 'who in the married state use their right in the proper manner although on account of natural reasons, either of time or of certain defects, new life cannot be brought forth.' Marital sex has secondary ends, such as mutual love and the quieting of concupiscence, and these may be pursued with impunity so long as they are subordinated to the primary end of marriage. Abortion is always to be condemned, even if performed to save the life of the mother. Man has no right to take the life of an innocent soul, and doctors must work to save both child and mother, but under no circumstances are they deliberately to abort the fetus, merely to protect the mother's life. This is 'a pretence at practicing medicine.' Pius also spoke out against the eugenicists, those who would sterilize the unfit for the benefit of the race, ignoring the fact that the family is more essential than the state. Public magistrates have no direct power over the bodies of their subjects, and where no crime has been committed no punishment or damage can be rightly inflicted. The Pope turned his attention next to such errors as those which counsel a greater laxity in standards of marital fidelity and those which proclaim the emancipation of the female sex, undermining the subjection of woman to man. The latter seeks a threefold freedom for the female: physiological, so that the woman is released from the burden of childbearing, save at her own pleasure; social, whereby released from the cares of children she can devote her time to business and public affairs; and economic, enabling the woman to conduct and administer her own finances without the consent or knowledge of her husband. Pius declared emphatically that such was no true emancipation of women but rather a debasing of the character of femininity, causing the whole family to suffer. Further this 'false liberty and unnatural equality with the husband' injures woman herself, for it removes her from her exalted position in the home and places her in jeopardy of returning to her role under the pagans: 'the mere plaything of man.' The suggestion that the Church seeks to keep woman in feudal subjugation was flatly rejected by the Pope. Her equality as a soul is fully recognized by Catholic teaching, which calls upon the civil power to protect the economic status of the wife and mother. The second section of the encyclical concluded with a restatement of Leo's polemics against those who assert the legality of divorce.

In part three, Pius set forth his suggestions for dealing with the current problems of sex and marriage. First of all, he wrote, men must study the divine plan so that they may conform to it. This means that man must subject himself to God, for only so can he hope to subject his own concupiscent lust to himself. The carnal desires cannot be curbed by the devices of the natural sciences but only by the faithful performance of one's religious duties including the frequent reception of the sacraments. Only the Church can properly teach men the divine plan, the laws regulating sex and marriage. The light of reason is not sufficient: that leads down too many individual byways of interpretation. All the faithful sons of the Church will be guided and directed in all these matters by her teaching, and not only in areas where dogma has been infallibly defined but also in questions which are apparently open. For these are not really open. The Church knows whereof she speaks, is thoroughly conversant with current circumstances, and hers is the voice of true authority which she sends to the world through the medium of 'the Supreme Pastor the Roman Pontiff, who is himself guided by Jesus Christ our Lord.' The first step in remedying the current evils in sex, then, is for men to turn to God. And how are they to know what God requires of them? The Pope will tell them, for God has told him. Therefore the Church must undertake a widespread campaign of education, teaching the world the true nature of marriage. Central in such an educational program must be the recognition that Christian instruction on sexual matters will be quite different from the exaggerated physiological emphasis of modern secular sex education, 'in which is learned rather the act of sinning in a subtle way than the virtue of living chastely.' Pius listed the characteristics of marriage which were to be extolled and urged upon the faithful: mutual love, chastity, and so forth, warning husband and wife to use their sexual rights carefully, especially in the early years of wedlock so that they may be prepared for the necessity for continence in later life if circumstances should require it. Pius apparently shared the almost pathological anxiety of his Catholic predecessors that young married couples are going to *enjoy* sexual intercourse. He concluded the encyclical with a section on the importance of the economic aspects of marital life and called upon the state to insure proper conditions of employment and housing, as well as to provide laws for the protection of chastity and conjugal fidelity. Such laws would help, but not even their strict enforcement could suffice. There is still required the religious authority of the Catholic Church, and the civil authorities are exhorted to consult, to co-operate with, and to make use of that authority for their own best interests.

This completes the collection of the basic materials which comprise the Roman Catholic interpretation of sex: the Bible, Augustine, Thomas Aquinas, the Council of Trent, and two papal encyclicals. These are the essential documents, the definitions of the dogma, and they reveal a harmony of outlook. The doctrine indeed develops but does not change. The authority of the Church is supreme. What Rome teaches about sex and marriage is binding on all men everywhere, and what she teaches is that the only justification for sex *of any kind,* even of thought, is marriage, which is monogamous and lifelong. The primary purpose of sex is procreation. A secondary end is recognized in pleasure, which may be sought at the cost only of venial sin so long as it is pursued in such a way that the primary aim is not thwarted. Because the pleasure, or rather the desire for it is likely to become so intense and preoccupying, those whose lives are given to religion and contemplation are compelled to eschew all sexual experience altogether. Virginity and celibacy are definitely preferable, more pleasing in the sight of God than marital union. It is not surprising that there is a widespread feeling in the modern world, among Catholics as well as non-Catholics, that the Church really regards sex as an evil — necessary to the continuance of the race and the Church but evil all the same. It is to correct this impression that the British priest, E. C. Messenger, has written his three-volume work entitled *Two in One Flesh,* a summary of the Roman teaching on sex and marriage. This book represents one of the fullest treatments of the subject from a Roman Catholic point of view in recent times. Published in 1948, it is contemporary and merits careful consideration.

Messenger's 'Two in One Flesh'

The work is divided into three parts, each making up one small volume. Part One is entitled 'Introduction to Sex and Marriage,' Part Two 'The Mystery of Sex and Marriage,' and Part Three 'The Practice of Sex and Marriage.' The first volume begins with a discussion of the general prejudice against sex and the supposed indecency which cloaks the sexual organs and an attempt to dispel such misapprehensions by demonstrating that the teaching of Scripture, of natural science, and of philosophy is altogether inimical to any derogatory attitude toward sex. Volume Two presents an historical survey of Christian teaching about sex, through the Fall of man, the Old Testament Law, the Immaculate Conception, and the Virgin Birth into a survey of the New Testament and the Greek and Latin Fathers of the Church. The volume concludes with an exposition of the developed Catholic interpretation of sex and marriage, relying heavily on Thomas Aquinas. Volume Three deals with the practical, ethical problems of sex in modern life, including sections on courtship and engagement, sex in marriage, birth control, and so on.

The first part begins with a discussion of the common prejudice against sex and an effort to understand it, offering several suggestions about its origin. One possible source is Platonic dualism, with its elevation of the soul and devaluation of the body. Another is best summarized in the old Latin proverb, 'Inter faeces et urinas nascimur omnes' ('Between feces and urine we all come into the world'). The uncleanness of the evacuative organs attaches itself to the sexual life. But regardless of its parentage, says Father Messenger, the Church must regard any negative attitude toward sex as an illegitimate child. The Bible reveals God as the Maker of all things, including the human body, and, as Augustine has shown, it is utterly impossible for God to create anything at all evil. Even the devil and his fallen angels, are, in so far as they are beings, good. Their wickedness does not lie in their creation but in their fall; it is not their powers but the misuse of them which is evil. All bodily organs and functions are therefore clean and healthy in and of themselves, and Father Messenger cautions that instructions to children about modesty should studiously avoid any suggestion that organs or acts are dirty or unclean. This general argument is bolstered by numerous citations from Old and New Testaments, showing that God created Adam and Eve with sexual organs intended for use, and that the Bible is altogether frank, sometimes to the point of bluntness, about the 'facts of life.'

This Cook's Tour of Holy Scripture is followed by a trip through the museum of modern science, including exhibits of asexual reproduction in unicellular life and in certain types of mosses, concluding with an educational lecture on the birds, the bees, and the flowers, strongly reminiscent of that anguished moment when the conscientious parent seeks to initiate the embarrassed adolescent into the mysteries of life and love. In this connection, Father Messenger casts the authoritative aura of science about several statements which stand shiveringly nude before the brazen gaze of the actual scientist who refuses to be impressed by the finery. For example, 'The woman ovulates every month, and it seems to be established that sexual desire is then at its height. Correspondingly, it seems to be lowest at the time of menstruation . . . Thus, a woman desires sexual intercourse most at the time when in fact conception is most likely.' [2] Any sexologist could tell Dr. Messenger that this is simply not true. Not only is there little or no correlation between ovulation and sexual desire, but also there are many women who experience their most intense libidinal urges during menstruation. Another 'fact' which at least is made uncomfortable by unabashed scrutiny is Messenger's assertion that man possesses certain inherent characteristics which border closely on the instinctual, performing in his sex life the same function as the instincts in the animal kingdom. Three such human instincts are described: the existence of the hymen in virgins, which is supposed to make sexual intercourse difficult before maturity; the presence of shyness and shame, which act as 'brakes upon the impetuous sexual instinct'; and the moral virtue of chastity which resides in the human will. This last is regarded as a 'natural' virtue, the ability of man to control and direct his sex life in accord with reason, quite apart from any supernatural gift of grace.

Examining these in reverse order, there does seem some justification for the third category, since scientific investigation has revealed that the higher centers of the cerebral cortex seem to take over, in humans, functions performed in the lower animals by instinct. Castration, for example, will render a male rat completely impotent for the rest of his life; without the gonads or their secretions, he is sexless. In man, however, castration has no such dire results. He may continue to be potent, though sterile, for a number of years, unless the psychic damage of the privation produces a psychogenic impotence, which is in the same category as any hysterical paralysis, without organic basis. Unfortunately

2. E. C. Messenger, *Two in One Flesh*, 3 vols., The Newman Press, Westminster, Md., 1948, vol. I, p. 48.

for Father Messenger, however, this is a characteristic not limited to men; it is shared by most of the higher anthropoids, who remain, in Catholic theology, without reason and therefore without morals. As for the argument from shyness and shame, it would be difficult to secure the testimony of science to their innate or instinctive character. The anthropological evidence is far from clear and undue dogmatism on either side is unwarranted by the facts, but surely one cannot claim that science supports the statement that shame is so universal as to be well-nigh instinctive. The reference to the hymen as a barrier to sexual intercourse is again curious, for if it survives into maturity, its very age and texture constitute a far greater handicap to coitus then than in childhood when it is still tender and easily ruptured. This stripping away of the protective coloration of science is not undertaken in a spirit of captiousness but merely as an illustration of the tendency of many Roman Catholic thinkers, especially when they are dealing with natural law, to confuse cultural factors for things which are 'divinely ordained' or 'orders of creation,' and to use only such evidence as supports their theories, conveniently ignoring data to the contrary. When it is convenient, they emphasize man's kinship with the animals (as in Aquinas' argument for monogamy), and when that fails to suit their purposes (as in the definition of what constitutes a 'natural' sexual act), they stress man's uniqueness.

Messenger concludes the first volume of his study with a chapter on sex according to philosophy, which, he says, is concerned with the *why* of things rather than the scientific *how*. Here he makes some excellent observations about the religious aspects of sexual love, describing the sexual union as 'the highest union possible between creatures' and sexual love as 'the reflection, on the created plane, of the love of God for his creatures.' He is somewhat unfair to the animals in his comparisons of animal and human love, failing to recognize that the 'lower' forms of life are also capable of deeds of self-sacrifice for the sake of their loved ones and obscuring the fact that much of human love is also instinctual in character. On the whole, however, Messenger succeeds admirably in his purpose of demonstrating that on the basis of Scripture, science, and philosophy, sex must be regarded as a fact of nature which is good, and that negative attitudes toward it are unsound and harmful. Unfortunately, he does not stop there. He adds a one-page postscript entitled 'Conclusion to Part One' in which he distinguishes between sex as a fact of creation and sex since the Fall of man. 'The Catholic Church,' he writes, 'adopts a realistic attitude in these matters. She has had a long experience of human nature, and she is painfully aware of the great and ineluctable fact of sin, and of its consequences upon the human race. She knows that sin has led to a perversion of what in itself is a noble power, and it is precisely in order to combat this perversion that she preaches in season and out of season the necessity of mortification, temperance and self-control. She is not opposed to the rightful use of sex in marriage — far from it. But she knows that this rightful use can be secured only by rigorous measures of self-discipline. A drastic evil calls for an equally drastic remedy.' [3] Having begun by explicitly disavowing Plato's metaphor of the soul or reason as rider and the body as an unruly horse, Messenger ends by introducing the same dichotomy under different names. Whenever the terms 'mortification' and 'self-discipline' make their appearance, they betray their parentage of moralism and asceticism, the twin offspring of an essentially dualistic outlook.

The main portion of the second volume is devoted to an examination of the two chief sources of the Catholic interpretation of sex, Scripture and Tradition. Messenger follows Augustine and Aquinas closely in discussing sex in Paradise, the Fall, sex under the old dispensation, and so on. There is little point in restating those theories, for they are described in Chapters II and III of this present work. The historical section may be passed over for the final part of Part Two, entitled 'The Developed Theory of Sex.' Messenger begins by repeating the familiar position that marriage is a sacrament instituted by Christ, citing Augustine's three blessings of matrimony. Now there are many in the modern world, he says, who think that offspring represent a *secondary* effect of marriage, the result of companionship and love, which

3. *Ibid.* p. 57.

is the *primary* purpose of marital sex. If one takes this view, then of course no objection can be raised to birth control, since there is nothing wrong in seeking the primary good of sex without the secondary. The teaching of the Catholic Church, however, is precisely the reverse. The Church does not deny the secondary ends of marriage — the satisfaction of the sex urge, the companionship of husband and wife — but the primary purpose of marriage is first, last, and always the procreation of children, and the other ends of marriage must be subordinate to that overriding consideration. There are two terms used in this connection by Roman theologians: the *finis operis*, the end or purpose of an act viewed in itself, and the *finis operantis*, the aim consciously intended by the person performing the act. A similar distinction exists in the doctrine of transubstantiation, where the sacrament is said to be valid both *ex opere operato*, out of the rite itself, regardless of the attitude of the celebrant or recipients, and *ex opere operantis*, in which a further, secondary good is obtained by those who participate in a proper state of faith. The primary end of a work, however, may be different from what is consciously intended by him who acts in it. Sinful man may have for his *finis operantis*, his conscious intention in the sexual act, the satisfaction of libidinal urges or the expression of mutual love without thought for the procreation of children. But the true and primary *finis operis*, the natural end or purpose of sexual intercourse, is always the production of offspring. This is not to say that the quieting of concupiscence and the expression of love are not *finis operis*, intended by God as an integral part of the sexual act. But they must never become *finis operantis*, conscious and deliberate aims in such a way that they exclude or subordinate the primary purpose of marriage. The Roman Rota in 1944 dealt specifically with the notion that the secondary ends of marriage are 'not essentially subordinate to the primary end, but are in fact equally primary and independent.' Such a view was labeled as altogether false.

The basis for the Catholic teaching that procreation is the primary purpose of sex is to be found in the so-called natural law. This is true of all animals: they cohabit in order to reproduce, and this much, says Catholic theology, man has in common with the animals. Biologically, man is an animal; what distinguishes him is his reason, his intellect, his capacity for choosing what he shall do with his biological inheritance. And his reason directs that he shall follow nature's obvious intention, using his sexual activities for reproductive purposes. This whole question of nature's 'obvious intent' in sex is a peculiar one, because it involves a discussion which scientists in general and biologists in particular are loath to enter. Whether the primary purpose of sex is pleasure (as Freud asserted) or procreation (as Rome maintains) is a problem which involves certain teleological presuppositions unwarranted by the evidence. Obviously sex involves both, but no one can state definitely which is primary and which secondary on the basis of a *scientific* analysis of the data. Of course, anyone is entitled to an opinion on the question, but there is no more empirical evidence for one side than for the other. If Rome wishes to assert that her position is a matter of revealed truth, delivered to her by God himself, that is her privilege. But her insistence that that position is not based on revelation but on natural law is exceedingly questionable. No one but God himself knows what is nature's primary aim in sex. Some contemporary biologists are inclined to think that sexual reproduction evolved out of asexual life as a more efficient means of producing fit survivors in the struggle for existence, that greater variability was nature's 'purpose.' But they advance this theory as an hypothesis, not as established fact. They confess that as yet they do not know. Therefore, one is inclined to offer a humble suggestion to Rome: that she make her doctrine on the *finis operis* of sex a matter of revealed truth rather than of natural law. Non-Catholics will still disagree, as they disagree with other aspects of Roman dogma, but the Church would find itself on far firmer ground.

To return to Messenger, he goes on to discuss the secondary ends of marriage, the place of sex pleasure and passion. He insists that these were created by God, both as an incentive to the sexual act and as a reward for its performance. Therefore any act of coitus which is performed for pleasure has also a *finis operis,* an end which God intended. And so long as the primary end is not positively excluded, there is no sin. This brings Messenger into difficulties with Augustine and Aquinas, both of whom declared sex for pleasure to be a venial sin, but he pieces together certain quotations from Aquinas on insensibility, which enable him to say: 'Both passion and pleasure are natural concomitants of the sex act, and so far from diminishing its moral goodness, if the sex act is willed beforehand according to right reason, the effect of pleasure and passion is simply to heighten and increase the moral goodness of the act, not in any way to diminish it.' Messenger admits that Aquinas does not anywhere make such an explicit assertion, but he thinks that it follows from Thomist principles and he has no hesitation in drawing the inference. Concupiscence and turpitude are to be found in the strength of the instinctive sex desire and of the antecedent impulse which introduces the sexual act itself. In a typically tortuous example of scholastic reasoning, Messenger demonstrates that the passion of the sex act is not in itself evil, but rather the passionate desire that leads up to the act. This concupiscence, or passionate desire, is a penalty resulting from Adam's fall, but it is not a fault in Adam's descendants.

Attention is next turned to the sense of shame and the existence of modesty. Some form of shame, Messenger claims, is natural to man and would have been found in Adam and Eve even without sin, if they had not had the preternatural gift of immunity from concupiscence. In this natural sense, shame is the human counterpart of shyness in a female animal prior to coitus and serves as a kind of brake on the impetuosity of the sexual drive. But shame is more than a mere creation of nature; it is the result of sin. Adam and Eve in the Fall lost their immunity to concupiscence and with it their control over their bodies. Their sexual desires and organs established independence from their wills, and this rebellion produced shame. However, says Messenger, in so far as a man can bring his sexual impulses under the control of his reason he need not be ashamed, since it is only the lack of such control which breeds shame. Of course, no one can hope fully to achieve the rational control enjoyed originally by Adam and Eve in Paradise, but such a state can be approached. No good Catholic husband and wife, loving each other both in a religious and a human fashion, who are desirous of bringing children into the world for the glory of God, need regard their sexual union as indecent in any way.

So far as nudity is concerned, Messenger admits that there must of necessity be widespread differences from age to age and from place to place in what is regarded as modest and immodest. He confesses that the almost universal practice of nakedness by primitive tribes constitutes a genuine difficulty for Catholic theology. This cannot be explained as a temporary obliteration of the secondary precepts of natural law or as moral degradation, since the primitives prove on the whole to be without guilt or shame. The question therefore rises about the relevance of Augustine's dictum that man is ashamed because of concupiscence. Assuredly, the savages are also descendants of Adam and Eve; therefore they should be suffering from shame and clothe themselves. But they do not. Messenger offers the possible solution that it is 'the custom of the country,' and that although they do not have a 'local' sense of shame, pertaining to their bodies, they do display a 'functional' shame, pertaining to the sexual act, which is performed in privacy. But this is not true of all primitives, so the argument breaks down. This is the difficulty of natural-law theology. What is thought to be universal turns out to be local, and the most ingenious and devious reasoning must be used to prove that it is, after all, universal. How much simpler to admit that Augustine was wrong. Part Two concludes with a chapter on sex in the world of spirits, where, as might be expected, sex is transcended. In the resurrection, sex differences will be preserved in the risen bodies, because this is a part of the perfection of humanity, but there will be no need for the sexual act, nor any desire for it.

Part Three, 'The Practice of Sex and Marriage,' comprises the practical, ethical section of Messenger's work. He returns to the 'scientific' aspect of sex, declaring that it is clear that nature's primary purpose in sex is reproduction, refuting all who disagree. In the name of science, purely on the basis of a rational examination of the natural world, without reference to revelation, he thinks it possible to demonstrate that monogamous and lifelong marriage, the restriction of sex to that estate, and the further restriction of marital sex to the primary purpose of reproduction (or at least so that the primary purpose is never excluded or prevented) are all 'natural,' following irresistibly from the facts. The psychological as well as the physiological differences between the sexes are discussed, again with a tendency to overlook anthropological data. 'This essential differentiation, both physical and mental, between male and female cannot be destroyed by human efforts. . . . Who can admire a weak and womanly man? And who can admire a woman who apes masculine ways?' [4] Messenger here falls into the error of generalizing from the standards of western civilization. There are widespread cultural variations in this area, and even within western culture. Stereotypes can be dangerous. As Margaret Mead has pointed out in her *Male and Female*, it is important to compare type with type in terms of general personality rather than real persons with some cultural ideal. A shy, fluttery and nervous man seems, of course, effeminate when seen beside a muscular athlete, but beside his female counterpart he is clearly masculine. The efficient, business-like type of woman seems masculine in the company of soft, seductive sirens, but in an office full of hard-driving male executives, she will emerge as very much a woman. There are many different types of personality within both sexes, and these must be respected. Generalizations about basic differences between the sexes are apt to be misleading and positively harmful to the fullest development of personality.

In a chapter on the social aspects of sex, Messenger asserts that while the normal relationship in life is marriage and parenthood, not all human beings are called upon to live in this estate. Since the primary purpose of sex and marriage is the procreation of the species, sex is not so much concerned with the individual as with the race as a whole. Sex has social implications, but not everyone need serve society in this way. Not all humans are driven by an irresistible libido, and this provides the natural basis for the supernatural virtue of virginity, undertaken for the

4. *Loc. cit.* vol. III, p. 9.

sake of prayer and contemplation. Celibacy which is the result
of a mere disinclination to sex is not a virtue, but religious virginity undertaken for religious motives is also social in its implications, for it also benefits the whole of mankind spiritually. The
religious orders pray constantly for the world, and their prayers
are heard and answered. Each individual must decide for himself
whether he is called to a life of celibacy and contemplation or to
a life of marriage and parenthood. If the latter, then the utmost
care must be exercised in choosing one's mate, as Pius XI suggested. When the engagement has been arranged and announced,
then certain problems arise. Naturally the young couple are in
love and their love will seek expression. But they must take care
to avoid any expression of affection which arouses sexual feelings
or desires lest they be tempted beyond their powers to resist, because pre-marital intercourse is morally wrong.

The marriage takes place, and Messenger devotes a chapter to
a description of the ceremony, the Nuptial Mass, and its significance. This is followed by a discussion of the sex act as an expression of love, which is one of the legitimate and secondary ends
of marriage. The union of heart and mind and soul and will
is now expressed in this physical union, a perfect blending of two
bodies and souls in a mutual giving, each to the other, not in
sensual lust which seeks only its own gratification, but in yielding,
unselfish love. 'Viewed in this light, the sex act becomes at once
a sublime and noble expression of mutual love, and essentially
suitable for the divine choice as a symbol of the love between
Christ and the Church.' [5] An exhortation is given to married
couples to display patience, tenderness, and understanding in their
sexual relations. This is the familiar discourse to husbands found
in most modern marriage manuals, urging slow courtship, caresses,
expressions of love before the actual union of the genital organs
occurs. In this context, Messenger cites the three principles of
moral theology governing those acts preparatory to coitus. First,
anything which contributes to the generation of a child is perfectly lawful. Second, whatever is not directly related to generation but is not against it is at worst a venial sin and can be without

5. *Ibid.* p. 28.

sin if it is performed for a good end, such as the expression of love. Third, whatever is against the generation of a child is a mortal sin, so that the use of contraceptives, *coitus interruptus,* and the achievement of orgasm by 'unnatural' connections are excluded.

The sex act is not only a means of expressing mutual love; it has a religious character as well. It is a function in which humans are allowed to share with God in the creation of new life, a means of adding to the number of those who worship the true God, a contribution to the growth of the Church, and a sign of the union between Christ and the Church. The performance of the sexual act is in a real sense a religious function, and the old medieval rules which banned a couple from receiving communion for three days after intercourse have, in recent years, been relaxed, and married persons are encouraged to come to the altar without sense of uncleanness or shame. This leads to the question of the frequency of intercourse, and Messenger counsels due moderation, warning that an immoderate sex life results in enslavement to the appetite with the consequent destruction of all joy in intercourse. Newlyweds especially are cautioned to be patient, but every marriage partner is in duty bound to 'render the debt' when it is demanded. Intercourse during menstruation is permitted but not advised, as is coitus during pregnancy, when special care must be exercised lest the fetus be harmed.

In the closing chapters of his book, Father Messenger deals with the size of the family, with birth control, and with the sex education of children. Those who are married have the duty to be fruitful and multiply, and abstinence from sex is in them no virtue. Since not everyone marries, and not all who marry produce children, and not all children live into maturity, it is incumbent upon all who marry to do more than reproduce themselves. They should have more than two children and not less than four. They are allowed to space the arrival of their progeny, and in certain instances to limit the size of the family, but only by means of self-restraint. The use of contraceptives is morally wrong because it is 'unnatural,' involving a full use of a natural function and the satisfaction of a natural instinct, but frustrating the natural purpose of the function. Therefore, the practice of birth control represents a sin against nature, a misuse of nature. The whole argument rests on the assumption that the primary aim of sex is procreation and breaks down as soon as this assumption is questioned or rejected. Messenger points out that the divine law as well as the natural law forbids coitus which deliberately frustrates conception, referring to the sin of Onan in Genesis 38. There is, however, some difference of opinion about the meaning of Onan's punishment. Roman Catholic interpretation uniformly insists that his sin was *coitus interruptus* and extends the prohibition against 'spilling the seed on the ground' to masturbation also. Protestant commentators, on the other hand, see Onan's transgression as his refusal to raise up a child for his dead brother in accordance with the custom of the levirate marriage, which makes the 'divine law' a question of interpretation. Messenger does admit two 'natural' and legitimate means of limiting the family: complete abstinence and the limitation of sexual intercourse to times when conception is practically impossible, due to the rhythm of the woman's ovulation. But, as Messenger declares and as Pius XII made manifest in a recent proclamation, a good and sufficient reason is required for resort to the rhythm method of birth control. The mere inconvenience of children does not provide such a good and sufficient reason. It is the duty of Christian parents not only to produce children but also to instruct them about the facts of life in private and with all due modesty and discretion, lest the passions be aroused and inflamed. Such education is emphatically not the responsibility of the school. Only the parents can perform this task, taking care to train the will along with the mind.

This marks the conclusion of Father Messenger's three volumes. His aim is certainly worthy: to remove the prejudice surrounding sex, and much of what he has to say seems altogether sound and good. But he is under the necessity of conforming to Catholic dogma, and that dogma can never be reconciled with a completely positive view of sex. So long as virginity and celibacy are regarded as superior to marriage; so long as the primary end of sex is said to be the procreation of children, with sex for pleasure or for love subordinated to a secondary status; so long as woman is kept in subjection to man; so long, in short, as celibate and ascetic males continue to control the moral theology of the Church, Rome can never wholeheartedly give its full benediction to human sexuality. Father Messenger's book is extremely illuminating in this regard, for he has tried desperately to justify the Church's teaching and still adopt a thoroughly positive attitude toward sex and marriage. His failure is testimony, not to his lack of ability or desire, but to the basic intransigence of the Roman tradition. Dualism proves stronger than naturalism.

Fulton J. Sheen

Writing in a somewhat more popular fashion than Father Messenger, Bishop Sheen has dealt with the interpretation of sex in two of his many books, *Peace of Soul* and *Three To Get Married.* His point of departure is the familiar scholastic division of man into body and soul, or instinct and reason. In proper Thomist fashion, he asserts the primacy of the intellect over the passions. But he is at great pains to affirm the dignity of the body and to refute the charge that the Church is anti-sex. He thinks that identifying asceticism of the body with a negative attitude toward the body is like equating housebreaking a dog with being anti-dog, which makes it necessary to recall some Christian truths about the dignity of the body. Seven of those truths follow. First, the body is honorable because it is the channel through which all knowledge flows into the mind. Here, of course, Bishop Sheen follows the Thomist-Aristotelian line that there is nothing in the mind which did not come from the senses. Second, the body is the means by which men communicate with each other, verbally, artistically, sexually, and religiously. Third, the body by its inner conflicts teaches humans to recognize their need of a teacher who is more than human and who can resolve the conflicts and bestow peace. Fourth, the doctrine of the Incarnation, the fact that Christ became man, taking upon himself a human body, serves as a reminder that the material flesh has been blessed and consecrated by God. Fifth, sacramental grace is made available through the body, in the water of baptism, the bread of the Eucharist, etc., all of which are 'earthen vessels,' carrying the divine love and power. Sixth, the belief in the resurrection stands as a further testimony to the Church's positive attitude toward the body. Although the soul departs from the body at death and continues in an ethereal state until the Last Judgment, it is not the full personality, which is composed of the unity of soul and body. This fullness will be restored in the final resurrection of the dead when both the spirit and the flesh will be immortal. Seventh, the body is regarded with reverence because there are two bodies in heaven: that of Christ and that of the Blessed Virgin. All of this is cited as evidence that Christian Faith is not, as is so often maintained, negative in its attitude toward human flesh. 'There is no such thing as a choice between the flesh and the soul, because there is never flesh without the spirit, and never spirit without the flesh. Christianity is not against anything (except evil, and that is not a thing, but a privation), whether it be body, or soul, flesh or sex or mind.' [6]

Bishop Sheen insists that man is more than mere body, more than an animal with a highly developed cerebral cortex. Man has many things in common with the animal world, to be sure, but he is distinguished from other forms of life in his possession of a soul, which gives him a will. Man is not merely a soul; he is a body as well, but his soul is the activating agent of the body, the unifying, purposeful force which directs it. Within the unity of flesh and spirit, the sexual drive is an extremely important component part, but by no means the most important one. It is simply one aspect of an inner energy which is called *Vita,* and which may be regarded in three ways, as man has a relationship to himself, to other men, and to the universe. Under the first heading, *Vita* appears as the instinct for self-preservation, the inner sense of self-worth and dignity. In relation to others, *Vita* takes its form as the sexual drive, which results in the propagation of the species and is therefore the basis of community. *Vita* manifests itself in man's relation to the universe as the need for possessions, the desire for private property and the security which that provides.

6. Sheen, Fulton J. *Three To Get Married,* New York, Appleton-Century-Crofts, Inc., 1951, p. 132.

All three of these facets of the basic instinctual equipment of man are in themselves good because they are the gifts of God.

But with the Fall of Adam, the relationship between soul and body became disturbed. A force called libido, or concupiscence, appeared within the human *Vita,* a burning desire which transgresses the limits of reason. All three instinctual drives were disrupted. Self-preservation was transformed into self-love in the form of egotism and selfishness; sex became purely physical, a thing in itself, divorced from its intimate connection with spirituality and procreation; and the right to private possessions was warped into monopolistic capitalism and communism. This derangement is not inevitable, for man can still use his freedom to control and direct his instinctual drives in accord with reason, but concupiscence gives added strength to the lower passions which are more difficult to restrain. The libido, or desire itself, is not a sin but merely the temptation to sin. If the will resists the impulse no evil is incurred. Sheen's understanding of the libido is that it comprises the totality of human desires: for food and water, for self-preservation and property, no less than for sex. But all of these desires are to be guided and directed by man's rational faculty. It is obvious that the rational purpose of eating is the nurture of the body; so it represents a derangement when eating becomes an end in itself, an act carried on solely for pleasure, as in the ancient Roman practice of using the *vomitorium.* In like manner, Sheen regards it as obvious that the rational purpose of sex is procreation, and when the sexual act is divorced from that primary purpose, it is a sin. The libido has overcome the reason; the instincts have run away with the mind. 'Planned unparenthood is the deliberate and willful decision on the part of husband and wife to exclude from God the opportunity to create another to His image and likeness. It is the human will freely frustrating Divine Will.' [7]

This is what leads the Bishop to his statement that it takes *Three To Get Married,* or, as he puts it in another way, that all love is triune. Fleshly love involves father, mother, and child; spiritual love unites lover, the beloved, and love itself; while the

7. *Ibid.* p. 211.

divine love embraces Father, Son, and Holy Spirit. Sex is mere duality, two persons bound together for pleasure, while love is always a trinity. It is not simply that true love, which includes sexual love, always moves in the direction of producing new life, the union of two creating a third. In all genuine love, whether there is actual procreation or not (e.g. in marriages which are child-less — from natural causes, of course, not from the use of contra-ceptives), the third party is present, namely God. There is a thirst for the infinite in all men which persists through all their actions, though many are unaware or fearful of their thirst. They seek the satisfaction of their desires in counterfeit experiences, in sex, in egoism, in possessions. But, as Augustine observed, the restless human heart can be set at rest only in God, who alone is 'the consummation of all desires.' This fact the Christian under-stands, and Bishop Sheen believes that in a true sacramental mar-riage the erotic love diminishes with the years, while the religious love grows from more to more. In the first months of matrimony all is swallowed up in the joy of possession, which is a natural effect. But as time goes on, the pleasure of taking gives way to the happiness of giving, first of one's self to the other and then of the two together to God for his divine purposes. They offer their unity to someone outside themselves: to their children and through them to God.

It is this search for the infinite, this hunger and thirst after God, which gives meaning to virginity and celibacy, when they are assumed by Christians. Instead of seeking to find the divine love through human love, through their marital relationships, religious celibates pursue it directly. In Sheen's terms, the motive is not dualistic. There is no negation of sex or the body; holy celibacy is simply a response to a call from God to love him wholly, with everything in the Christian consecrated to his service. This is why the Virgin Mary is the inspiration of both the celibate and the married, because although she gave herself solely to God, as do the virginal, she also conceived and bore a son, as do the married. One could raise the question with Bishop Sheen whether this does not tread perilously close to a mystical rejection of the world and the flesh for the sake of God, forgetting that love of neighbor is not in any sense in conflict with love of God. On the contrary, the New Testament is quite explicit that the latter requires the former. But certainly Sheen comes very close to the naturalism of Saint Francis. There is little if any dualism in his presentation of the desirability of celibacy; the motive is largely eschatological.

Yet he does insist that the element of shame connected with sex is inevitable, at least in fallen man. This is not, however, because sex is evil or unlovely but because it is a mystery. Educators who think to abolish the shame and guilt attached to sex are doomed to frustration, because while they are right to regard sex as natural, they are blind to its mystery quality which can find fulfillment only in obeying the divine will. It is because sex is inextricably bound to the mystery of creating new life that it is surrounded with awe and reverence and therefore should be kept sacred and private, not openly practiced or discussed in the same way that one deals with other natural functions. Of course, it may be said, in rejoinder to Bishop Sheen, that the whole process of nutrition in the body is equally mysterious, in one sense. The growth of cells, the constant replacement of old tissue by new, the strange breaking down of ingested food to create new life in the body — certainly as much is known scientifically about reproduction as about growth and nutrition. Both are parts of the mystery of the life process, which generates awe in the observer. But both should be understood as thoroughly as possible and accepted as 'natural and nice,' an enterprise to which the Bishop seems reluctant to lend support. As with Father Messenger, Bishop Sheen seeks to interpret sex as a positive force, natural and acceptable, but the undertones of dualism in Roman Catholic thought and practice render this an exceedingly difficult task to carry through consistently.

It is these same undertones which make Sheen so violent when he attacks Freud and what he regards as the modern 'cult' of sexuality. He does at one point concede that what he calls Freudianism has gone beyond what Freud himself stated. But one gets the distinct impression nonetheless that Freud is the real *bête noir,* and one cannot escape the impression that the Bishop's reading of psychoanalytic literature has been at best superficial. He has far more in common with the analysts than he realizes, as, for example, when he says that 'sex is a function of the whole personality, and not of the body alone, much less of the sex organs alone. . . . It is not the sex organs which have sexual desires; it is the self, or human personality. Hence, their use or abuse is fundamentally a moral problem, because it is the act of a free being.' [8] Yet Sheen insists that it is Freud, or Freudianism which is responsible for the entire modern attempt to separate sex from the rest of the personality and make of it a thing apart. Actually, the whole enterprise of psychoanalysis represents an effort to integrate the sexual functions within the total personality. The difference lies in the methods advocated, not in the goals sought. Psychoanalysis seeks to relieve conflicts within the personality by a process of inner awareness, of insight. Sheen, and Roman Catholic practice in general, on the other hand, speaks of mortification and discipline. For all his explicit disavowal of Platonic dualism and the analogy of horse and rider or, as Sheen adapts it, a man rowing a boat, he opens the rear door to what he has loudly ejected from the front. He says that disciplining the errant impulses of the body no more means disrespect for the body than putting a bit in a horse's mouth means disrespect for the horse. Both are merely devices for bringing out the best in beast and man for the sake of the Master. It may not imply disrespect, but it clearly indicates what the Bishop thinks of the relationship between soul and body. He is much closer to Plato than he knows.

This is the fundamental difficulty with all Roman Catholic interpretations of sex. Although Thomas and his successors inherit a certain naturalism from Aristotle, so that they are insistent that the body is essential to full human nature, yet the body must always be subject to the soul, or the intellect. In other words, there is a basic mind-body dualism inherent in Thomism which cannot be overcome. It is always the task of the mind to control and discipline the flesh, which is regarded as an inferior part of man. This kind of dualism is rejected by modern psychology on the basis

8. *Ibid.* p. 130. Sheen's *Peace of Soul* is published by McGraw-Hill Publishing Co., New York, 1949.

of scientific analysis. The psychosomatic approach becomes increasingly dominant in all fields, from biology to medicine. Adolph Meyer's contributions to the understanding of the psycho-biological organism, Cannon's work in homeostasis, and Freud's integration of social and biological factors have all undermined the old dualism. Thomism does maintain that only the unity of body and soul constitutes the full human personality, but it allows independent existence to both in the interval between death and the resurrection. The immortality of the soul is an important Catholic doctrine. The Hebrew outlook of the Old Testament has almost nothing to say about immortality. That is essentially a Greek idea. The Bible speaks rather in terms of the resurrection of the body. No more than modern psychology can the Biblical writers conceive of the existence of a disembodied spirit, because man *is* a body. The Roman Catholic dichotomy leads ultimately to a less naturalistic view of sex than is possible in a theology more solidly grounded in the Bible. Since Protestantism is, theoretically at least, built upon that foundation, an examination of the contemporary situation there is next on the agenda.

VI

CONTEMPORARY PROTESTANTISM

IN THE YEARS following the Reformation, Protestant ethics developed along two major lines: pietism and Puritanism. The sectarians experimented spasmodically with a radical perfectionism which usually manifested itself in one of two extremes, sexually speaking. Either a kind of sexual communism was practiced, with the breakdown of monogamous marriage, or an absolute celibacy was adopted, looking toward the imminent arrival of the Kingdom. But such experiments were rare and unrepresentative of the main stream of Protantism. There pietism dominated Lutheran ethics, while Puritanism became the characteristic mode of Calvinism. The latter was far more concerned about public morality than the former, which restricted itself to the inner life of the individual Christian, leaving the larger issues of the behavior of the population as a whole to secular control. But both were highly moralistic in their attitude toward sex. Clerical celibacy and religious virginity have never been Protestant ideals, but with the exception of these and of the absolute ban on divorce, the Catholic interpretation of sex remained for the most part unimpaired in the Reformation churches. The only justification for sex was still marriage and procreation; all else was taboo. Sex continued to live under a shadow, and the less attention called to it the happier the Protestant divines. The romanticism of the nineteenth century had its echoes in the theology of the period, and Schleiermacher

162

adopted a radically unconventional interpretation of sex, but the revolt within the Church was small and insignificant. Victorianism reigned supreme in Anglo-Saxony, and moralistic pietism in the lands of Lutheranism. Sex was squashed, smothered, and sat upon.

Outside the churches a revolt was brewing. Rousseau called for the destruction of the chains of civilization and the emancipation of the happy savage from the slavery of culture. Romanticism produced a series of rebels, culminating in the late nineteenth century in the work of Sigmund Freud and Havelock Ellis, both of whom dared to call a spade a shovel, thereby bringing upon themselves the vilification not only of the churches but also of decent, right-minded citizens. Freud was vigorously attacked by the medical profession, which in Germany and Austria, at least, was free from ecclesiastical influence or control. The doctors were scientists who were free from theological bias, but they shared the prevailing prudery.

The nineteenth century gave way to the twentieth and Victoria was dead. The influence of Freud and Ellis spread, and the view that sex was 'natural' grew, especially among intellectuals, so that the 'flaming youth' of the era after the First World War was emboldened to throw off all restraints, and wild oats were strewn broadside. Protestantism viewed with alarm and waggled a protesting finger, even as Rome, but the long reign of dualism was reaching its end. The more thoughtful individuals who took the trouble to read Freud and who were not horrified by his attacks upon religion began to realize that there was much truth in what he said. The Biblical criticism of the modern era produced a revival of interest in the Bible itself, and its essential naturalism was registered. The study of intellectual and cultural history revealed the strong dualism of the Hellenistic Age and its influence in the early Church. All of this began to come to focus in the late 1920's and early 1930's, and many Protestant parsons adopted an increasingly naturalistic interpretation of sex. They were then, as one fears they still are, a minority, and much of their speaking and writing on the subject was naïve and still dominated by moralism, for all their enlightenment. But progress is being made, and the advance of naturalism will be readily apparent in the attitudes of the men considered in this chapter. The millennium is not yet here. There is still a sizable deposit of dualism with its negative interpretation of sex in contemporary Protestantism. This book itself will shock many. The pale blue of dualism is, however, gradually being replaced in the latest weaving on the loom of western civilization with the bright red of naturalism, and the Biblical orientation of modern Protestantism has its own contribution to make.

It is always far more difficult to discuss any aspect of Protestant thought than of Roman Catholic thought, because Protestantism covers a multitude of phenomena. There is no official position set forth in any area of faith or morals. Protestantism has no Pope, and there are no encyclicals on sex and marriage. Any documents issued by the National Council of Churches (or its predecessor the Federal Council) or by the World Council of Churches represent in a sense only the opinions of those who wrote them. These opinions have no authority and are binding on member churches only as they voluntarily assent to the sentiments expressed. It is impossible to speak of *the* Protestant position on any issue. There are rather Protestant positions, and even these do not divide conveniently along denominational lines. On many questions, there is far more common ground among conservatives in all denominations than between the conservatives and liberals within a single church body. Any attempt at a survey of the interpretation of sex in contemporary Protestantism must, of necessity, be highly selective. A few reasonably representative figures must be chosen, with the realization that each man speaks only for himself, that no one will agree with everything that any one of them says. But among them are stated various interpretations which are widely held in Protestant circles today. Leslie Weatherhead has been selected as a representative of the so-called 'liberal' school of Protestantism; Otto Piper for his attempt to derive a Biblical view of sex; Emil Brunner as the spokesman for 'neo-orthodoxy' or dialectical theology; and Reinhold Niebuhr, one of the outstanding American theologians, to represent a kind of synthesis between American liberal Protestantism and continental orthodoxy, between the 'social gospel' and the traditions of the Reformation. There is no intended implication that other men are less important or less representative. There are great gaps left — men who cling to a traditionally negative interpretation, men who have enthusiastically embraced the newer insights of science. But some must be included and others left out, and the choice has been made. Any other would suffer equally.

Leslie Weatherhead

A British pastor-psychologist, Leslie Weatherhead has long had a keen interest in psychology. He has taken special training in the field and done extensive work as counselor and psychotherapist throughout his ministry. His books reveal his concerns: *Psychology in the Service of the Soul, Psychology and Life, The Mastery of Sex through Psychology and Religion.* He seeks to combine science and religion in such a way that men and women in trouble may be helped. He displays the typical willingness, not to say eagerness, of the modern liberal Protestant to accept and to use all of the insights and techniques of modern science. He is convinced that the truth is one and that good psychology is good religion and vice versa. He occasionally apologizes for using too much psychological and too little religious terminology, but he sees no real conflict.

He begins with a plea for sexual enlightenment and education, urging an end to the old atmosphere of repression and ignorance. He recognizes that the emotional milieu in which sex education is carried on is as important as, if not more important than, the facts which are transmitted, that how one *feels* about sex is far more fundamental than what he *knows*. Warning is issued to parents against creating the impression that enlightenment about sex is a kind of primitive tribal initiation wherein the adolescent is led into a mystery. However complete the knowledge conferred, such an atmosphere will convey the attitude that sex is mysterious, dangerous, and something set apart from all the other areas of life which are healthy and natural.

Weatherhead presents a rather interesting thesis about the social evolution of sexual behavior. He looks upon primitive culture as a time when children were an economic asset and hence of great importance to the family and the tribe. This meant that the economy required large quantities of sexual energy to bring forth offspring, each one of whom was to become a soldier, a worker, an additional unit of energy in the uneven struggle against nature. Polygamy was simply a means of adding to the population, and sex was no problem to either men or women because copulation was not only a pleasure but a duty. In modern times, however, children are an economic liability. The world is overpopulated and each new babe is another mouth to feed rather than another pair of hands to work. But man is still possessed of a large amount of libido as in earlier times, and he does not know quite what to do with it. This is another way of expressing Reinhold Niebuhr's epigram: 'Freud says that the sexual impulse is excessive because it is repressed, while as a matter of fact the sex impulse must be repressed because it is excessive!' The same idea, clothed in different language, is encountered in C. S. Lewis's little book *Christian Behaviour,* where he compares the instincts of sex and hunger, observing that both can go astray. But while one can eat only enough for two or possibly three at most, a healthy young man can, says Lewis, indulge in sex enough for fifteen or twenty. This idea of sex as an excessive appetite seems to be a popular one in modern Protestantism, but it requires a careful analysis. Just exactly what constitutes too much sex? Weatherhead cites cases known to him where married couples practice coitus twice daily. Is this excessive? Evidently not, for the persons involved show no ill effects. There is as wide a variation in appetites and capacities in the realm of sex as in that of nutrition, and it is questionable whether one can go to excesses in one area any more than the other. The physiological limitations are rigid in both. As the intestines can hold only so much food, even those of a compulsive eater, the body can produce only so many orgasms, even that of a sexual athlete. There is a kind of 'wisdom of the body' which simply paralyzes sexual desire when the limit has been reached. The notion that man has more libido than he can handle seems to be a vestigial remnant of the prejudice against sex for pleasure. It is rather strange of Weatherhead on the one hand to assert that sex is a God-given instinct which is thoroughly good, with nothing naughty or evil about it, and on the other hand to complain that we have more of it than we know what to do with. One is reminded of the Hindu who prayed for rain and got a flood. How cruel of God to give his children too much of a good thing.

Weatherhead summarizes what every growing child should know about sex and then turns to what the British call 'flirting,' which is known in American parlance as 'petting.' He points out that such intimate caressing is meant to serve as a prelude to intercourse and orgasm and that it is a foolish and dangerous practice outside of marriage. He allows himself to be carried away a little into flights of rhetoric which fairly drip sentimentality, as in the following advice to young ladies: 'Don't arouse the fires of passion which a young man cannot control, which you cannot control, and which the tears of that man's mother will not be able to quench. Whatever the standard of the set in which you find yourself, men who flirt with girls end by despising the very girls who have given them a few hours' "pleasure." ' [1] An otherwise sensible and thoroughly sound consideration of the problem is impoverished by such melodramatics. Weatherhead does, however, rise above the usual moralistic treatment of pre-marital intercourse between engaged couples. He sees it as more involved than simply a problem of youthful lust and recognizes that dismissing such intimacy as 'wrong' or 'immoral' is not enough, because there is a level where the couple knows that their sex is *not* wrong. There are several factors which must be kept in mind, however. First, Weatherhead calls attention to the fact that the satisfaction of the sexual instinct is quite a different thing from satisfying the instinct for food. The latter can be done with little change in the total personality, but sexual intercourse has deep and abiding effect on the personalities of those who experience it. It is the most complete kind of self-giving of which human beings are capable, and unless a man and woman are bound by vows of lifelong fidelity, such a mutual surrender is cheapened and corrupted. And if the young couple plead that they have exchanged such vows but cannot, for economic reasons, establish a home together, Weatherhead replies that the kind of union which sex represents and symbolizes de-

1. Weatherhead, Leslie, *The Mastery of Sex through Psychology and Religion,* The Macmillan Company, New York, 1932, p. xxii.

mands that all aspects of their life be shared together. The economic tie which constitutes the home is as important as the sexual one. Further, unless the vow has been made publicly for all to witness, the little irritations and frictions which are bound to characterize any intimate human relationship are likely to be divisive, and the couple may drift apart and on into another such liaison. Add to this the fact that no contraceptive is absolutely effective, which means constant fear of pregnancy as well as the apprehension about possible exposure. Weatherhead strongly urges, for all these reasons, the practice of pre-marital continence.

But what about repression? There is a rumor to the effect that sexual abstinence produces the direst psychological results. Here Weatherhead distinguishes between *re*pression which is unconscious, compulsive, and rigid, and *su*ppression which is conscious and voluntary. The former *is* harmful, but its antidote is not expression but recognition. Suppressing certain desires for the sake of later and greater goods is not only psychologically harmless but also a positive sign of maturity. Weatherhead tries to correct the all too common misunderstanding of Freud at this point, declaring that it is completely false to assume that sexual expression under any circumstances is beneficial to the personality. If the sexual experience is not in harmony with the total character and nature of the individual, it will produce only a temporary physical relief to be followed by guilt, shame, and self-hatred, which are far more damaging than frustration. And if there is no sensitive conscience, which is hardly a happy state, then there will be little genuine satisfaction from sex, for it will be corroded by a selfishness which makes self-giving impossible. Sexual intercourse, Weatherhead concludes, should be confined to persons who have given themselves to each other wholly, economically and publicly as well as physically and privately.

In dealing with unhappy marriages, Weatherhead discusses several causes and cures, two of which are of particular interest. First, he says, difficulties are created by the 'survival of that ancient superstition which some might call "the lordship of the male." ' He does his best to deliver an effective *coup de grâce* to male arrogance and female subservience. The respect, sympathy, and assistance of the husband are demanded for the wife in her thankless, never-ending task of housework and child-rearing. The second cause of unhappy marriages is what Weatherhead calls 'physical refusal,' or the positive distaste for sex, more frequently on the part of the wife. He observes that women often divert much of their sexual energy into the care of their children and become less interested in intercourse, while fatherhood does not have such an effect on the male. He is essentially polygamous, and an unresponsive wife runs the risk of sending her husband in search of greener pastures. Wives are therefore counseled to be pliable and obliging, while patience and understanding are urged upon husbands. Caution is advised with respect to *coitus interruptus,* the practice of withdrawing the male organ just before orgasm, since it frustrates complete orgasm and may produce neurotic symptoms.

Weatherhead, however, does express himself in favor of birth control. He lists both the assets and liabilities of the use of artificial contraceptive devices. Among the former are the protection of maternal health from the ravages of continual childbirth, the enabling of persons with disease or undesirable heredity traits to have intercourse without passing on their affliction to another generation, and the advancement of a happy family life, in which couples can express their love as often as they desire without fear of producing children who cannot be properly cared for. This represents one of the chief differences in the interpretations of sex held by contemporary Protestants and Catholics. Although Catholicism, largely under Jesuit influence, now minimizes the venial sin involved in sex for pleasure and permits the so-called 'rhythm method' of birth control, thanks to Pius XI, the Church remains unalterably opposed to the use of any contraceptives. Protestantism, freed from the dictum that procreation is the primary purpose of sex, with sex for love or pleasure in a secondary and subsidiary role, is forced into no such position. Modern Protestants recognize the two functions of sex as at least equal. Both have been ordained by God and no venial sin is involved in married persons' expressing their love sexually even if they do so in such a way as to provide for the proper spacing of children with economic considerations in mind. Therefore, contraceptives are accepted and widely used in Protestant circles without guilt or sin, which marks an advance of naturalism over the old dualistic attitudes.

Weatherhead also lists the arguments against contraception. He cannot agree with the charge that it is an 'unnatural' practice, nor is he impressed with the dangers of immorality which are supposed to threaten. This, he says, is the same principle as arguing that gas stoves should be prohibited because some people use them to commit suicide. Any device which is beneficial may carry with it the possibilities of harmful use, and treating the whole matter as a secret would be to build a morality on ignorance of sin, a very unstable foundation. The one objection to birth control which has some validity is that the use of an artificial device detracts from the spontaneity of the sex act. But, Weatherhead thinks it far better to forfeit a certain spontaneity than to bring unwanted children into the world, and there are aesthetic advantages to a careful and unhurried preparation for coitus which banishes fear and greedy haste, making room for leisure and beauty. He issues a word of caution against the selfish use of contraceptives purely for one's own gratification and the consequent shirking of responsibility for the propagation of the race. But if that responsibility is remembered and fulfilled, Weatherhead finds no reason, physical, psychological, or spiritual, why full use of scientific methods should not be made.

To the unmarried, that is those who have realistically given up hope, who have reached the stage in life where most probably they will remain single, the word is sublimation, the redirection of sexual energies into other channels. Weatherhead warns against acting as though libidinal drives could be put away in a box and the lid closed. That is like boiling water in a teakettle with the spout and top soldered up; an explosion is inevitable. Sexual energy is like steam; it must have some outlet. If the circumstances of life are such that a normal married life is impossible, then one cannot act as though he were sexless. He must learn to direct libidinal impulses into other channels of activity. This process of sublimation must begin by a conscious facing of one's instinctual hunger, and at first will require deliberate effort, but after a time it becomes unconscious and spontaneous. Sublimation does not, Weatherhead insists, mean the rise of instincts from a lower to a higher level. There is nothing unclean or evil about the sexual drive. Like hunger for food, it is natural, God-given, and good, but it can be sublimated. Great numbers of men and women, including Jesus himself, have lived without direct sexual expression without developing serious emotional disturbance. On the contrary, many of them have been extremely creative.

Writing on the 'Mishandled Sex Life,' Weatherhead treats such aberrations as masturbation, homosexuality, sadism, and masochism, etc. His attitude toward masturbation is in sharp contrast to the Roman Catholic view, which regards it as an 'unnatural' act and hence worse than fornication, adultery, or rape. Weatherhead states flatly that in the act itself he can find no wrong. 'It is the non-biological use of a part of the body for the purpose of obtaining enjoyment. So is smoking. And viewed as *detached acts* the one is no more "wicked" than the other.' [2] The difficulty with masturbation, he says, is that one usually conjures up all sorts of lewd mental pictures as accompaniments to the act, and this is 'sinful,' making self-control and sex adjustment harder to achieve. He admits that we are not altogether responsible for our thoughts. Men are not wicked because certain thoughts rise unbidden from the depths of the unconscious. Humans cannot help who knocks at the door, but there is no necessity to invite every visitor in and give him the liberty of the house. When lascivious thoughts are deliberately entertained in company with masturbation, then that is a sin. Weatherhead offers various therapeutic measures for dealing with sexual aberrations, and he reveals his psychological training in regarding these conditions, including masturbation, as disturbances calling for treatment and help rather than as sins evoking condemnation and punishment. This is somewhat closer to the spirit of the man called the Great Physician than certain other attitudes thus far encountered among his followers.

So far as divorce is concerned, Weatherhead holds the position that the teaching of Jesus is absolutist in principle, unsuited to

2. *Ibid.* p. 125.

serve as a rigid code or as legislation in any society. An attempt to translate his ethic directly into public morality would land most church members in jail. What is required rather is the effort to catch the spirit of that ethic and to apply it to the problems of life as far as is possible. Weatherhead thus rejects the legalism of the absolute prohibition of divorce encountered in Catholic circles. He does, however, give the place of highest honor to those persons who endure all kinds of anguish, standing by their legally wedded spouse, seeking to redeem the situation through love rather than escaping through divorce. This is not the self-righteous 'forgiveness' sometimes manifested by a militantly innocent wife which Weatherhead characterizes as 'indecent,' but a genuine attempt in all humility to restore a marriage. Such an effort, however, must be a matter of freedom, not of law. No one has the right to demand or compel another's course of action. There must always be the right, the freedom to separate, and divorced persons should be able to remarry. Weatherhead has some excellent suggestions for remedying the present unhappy situation of marital difficulties which unfortunately cannot be considered here.

In conclusion, Weatherhead's definition of the 'mastery of sex' proves considerably more positive than the phrase would suggest. Those who have had all their questions about sex frankly and honestly answered as they were raised, who are without unhealthy curiosity, libertinism, or prudery, who regard sex as a natural and holy thing, have achieved the mastery of sex. Anyone obsessed by feelings of guilt about his drives and desires needs to be taught that these are just as normal and without sin as his hunger at mealtimes. He should be brought to realize that sex is God-given and good. But mere psychological knowledge is not enough. There must be 'the power to become,' which comes through the grace and love of Jesus Christ. Weatherhead is quite typical of much of modern liberal Protestantism in his interpretation of sex. Thorough education of the young in sexual matters is advocated; the old feelings of shame and guilt are to be banished utterly; and sex is to be regarded as clean and holy. There is here as much of modern secular rationalism as of traditional Christian theology and ethics. The Reformers, no less than Aquinas and

Augustine, have a somewhat questionable attitude toward sex. For them it was primarily lust, and it has been only in recent decades that the more positive appreciation of sex as an expression of love has come to the fore. This appreciation has its origins, for the most part, outside the Church, in secular romanticism and naturalism. Liberal Protestantism has enthusiastically adopted the positive attitude, claiming that it is true to the essence of the Christian message. There is, however, another strand of contemporary Protestant thought which is suspicious of 'psychological religion' and 'naturalistic religion,' even in the interpretation of sex, and this also demands consideration.

Otto Piper

One of the most ambitious attempts within modern Protestantism to construct a Christian interpretation of sex has been made by Professor Otto Piper of Princeton Theological Seminary. He openly rejects what he calls 'naturalistic' theories of sex found in contemporary psychology as inadequate and criticizes many Protestants for going too far in their acceptance of such theories. Instead, Piper seeks to build his interpretation on the Bible because it contains 'the only satisfactory ontology of sex, i.e. an interpretation of its nature, which in all respects is in harmony with the facts of experience.' With this as his starting point, Piper derives five principles which he regards as fundamental to the Biblical interpretation of sex. First, in sexual intercourse there is forged an indissoluble unity out of two separate persons. Such a unity, which the Bible calls 'one flesh,' springs from no other source except sex. Race, social status, religion, have no influence, either positively or negatively, in the fusion of two persons. Neither does human will affect the relationship, not even love. It is immaterial whether sexual partners love each other; they are by the act itself, even if it occurs only once, under the most casual circumstances, bound together physically as one flesh, and their unity lasts all the rest of their lives. The doors are opened to wider possibilities of unity — of mind and heart — but these are not necessarily involved in sexual intercourse. Piper's second Biblical principle is that sex does not require justification by procreation;

it has a significance of its own in the personal relationship which it establishes. The fundamental purpose of sex is the creation of one flesh between a man and a woman, and children come as an extra blessing, a kind of bonus. Piper specifically rejects the Roman Catholic view of the primary and secondary ends of marriage.

The third fundamental notion found in the Biblical interpretation of sex is that 'in sex life one attains knowledge of the inner secret of one's own physical being.' This is the core of Piper's system around which he develops his entire discussion. He points out that the Old Testament frequently uses the word 'to know' as a means of describing sexual intercourse. This is not a delicate euphemism, for the Bible is in general detailed and explicit, displaying little reticence in its treatment of sex. The phrase is deliberately chosen, says Piper, for in sex human beings achieve a self-knowledge not attainable in any other way. This knowledge is existential rather than theoretical, and this is exactly the kind of knowledge about which young adolescents are curious. It is not sufficient merely to tell them about sex; they want the experience itself. Words cannot convey the revelation. The secret of sexuality, of masculinity and femininity, can be discovered only in actual coitus. The man discovers what it means to be a man in relationship to a woman, and the woman finds her own self in relationship to a man. The disclosure is mutual. Each discovers that he is created not as an isolated individual but as part of a couple. Alone he is incomplete; he finds fulfillment only in sex. This is why Piper places such strong emphasis upon the first act of intercourse, for it is in the initial experience that the mystery is opened, the secret made known. It is on the basis of this mutual revelation also that he condemns homosexuality and masturbation, the one because it violates bi-sexuality, the other because it tries to solve the riddle alone.

Piper describes certain characteristics of masculinity and femininity. The woman plays the role of lover, companion, and child-bearer. The man pays honor to the one he loves and serves as a guide to his companion as well as a guardian to her who bears his children. Man is the leader, as the Apostle Paul has directed. 'History and sociology know innumerable shades of authoritative relationship in marriage. But they all agree that in instances where the two differ in respect to their union, he (the husband) has to take the lead if their marriage is to be satisfactory.' [3] Piper evidently regards matriarchal societies as 'unsatisfactory,' confusing the mores of bourgeois culture with what is divinely ordained. He displays a similar confusion with respect to parenthood. The mother, he says, gives the children love and understanding, while the father is primarily the source of authority. She treats the offspring as her own flesh, whereas he regards them as extensions of his wife, deriving his authority over them from the ontological and practical sovereignty he exercises over her. Here Piper might learn something from the 'naturalistic' psychologists, who could tell him that the so-called maternal instinct rests upon a very simple principle: what men tend they love. In western civilization, the care of children has fallen largely upon the wife and mother so that she has been more tender in her feelings than the father, to whom parenthood is an avocation. But where fathers share, as they do increasingly in modern life, in the feeding, bathing, dressing, they love their children in the same way. Under such conditions, paternal love is much more similar to maternal devotion than Piper suggests.

The fourth Biblical principle is that sex finds its completion and perfection in love sustained by faith. Piper denies that love is the *sine qua non* of either sex or marriage, both of which have from primeval times been satisfactorily built on other foundations, but both are structures attaining perfection only when crowned by love — especially Christian love or *agape*. Mere physical attraction forms the base upon which successive stones can be and often are laid, raising the edifice to the heights of personal love and the apex of Christian devotion, where the individual is cherished not for himself alone but because Christ died for him. Because he has become one flesh with Christ, the lover finds in him 'not merely a fellow-man but also Christ himself.' The chief differences among these various levels of love are to be found in their power over the soul. The highest creates a strength of will and a bond of unity

3. Piper, Otto A., *The Christian Interpretation of Sex,* Charles Scribner's Sons, New York, 1941, p. 65.

unknown by the lower echelons. Piper's principal example of this power is man's ability to help the woman in overcoming the daemonic nature of sex. Despite his previous remonstrances that sex is God-given, clean and holy, he reverts to the ancient prejudice that woman is the temptress. 'There is, as it were, a "daemon" of sexuality in a woman's life. This is seen by the fact that, by contrast with the man, the entire physical being of a woman is conditioned by the sexual function, and she can therefore make sex into a self-sufficient sphere of life, or rather, it gains such power over her that her conduct is unavoidably determined by it. She may become a prostitute, i.e. a sexual being as such. . . . There is nothing corresponding on a man's side.' [4] Such a woman can be redeemed only by Christian love, and only when that is mediated through a man, who appeals to her true womanhood, to her honor, and thereby enables her to resist the temptation which is inherent in her as 'the sexually attractive sex.' Piper's estimate of Christian love is no doubt pure and without blemish, but his examples of its power in action are unfortunate. He reveals not only a rich deposit of masculine bias with a conglomerate of suspicion and fear of women, but a sizable vein of uneasiness about sex itself. The higher proportion of female prostitution can more easily be attributed to a large male sexual appetite than to woman's status as a sexual being as such. Piper concludes his exegesis of his fourth Biblical principle with the assertion that sexual love points beyond itself to its fulfillment in Christian love, where individuals so related to one another discover that they are one flesh in all aspects of their lives, that sex is only one of many possible relationships between them. Sex is never an end in itself, but simply a means to the fusion of two personalities, a key which unlocks the door into the mystery of life. The symbolic character of sex as well as the permanent unity which it establishes are to be seen in the Biblical metaphors of the marriage between God and Israel, between Christ and his Church.

The fifth and final principle derived from the Bible is that although sex is both natural and good, it is not indispensable to a full human life. Sex is not self-justifying, as in the animal kingdom,

4. *Ibid.* p. 74.

where instinctive impulse flows spontaneously into activity. Human society creates conditions where sexual impulses must be disciplined to a higher end, the service of God and neighbor. This is not to say that the Bible counsels ascetic self-denial for its own sake or regards virginity as a virtue, but there are individuals who are called to live out of wedlock and without sexual liaison. The religious orders which practice celibacy suffer very little from the suppression of sexual desires, whereas in secular society such suppression seems to be a major cause of nervous disorders, which leads Piper to the conclusion that successful sublimation is possible only in the perspective of Christian faith. Jesus spoke of eunuchs who were born so, those emasculated by men, and those voluntarily accepting asexuality for the sake of the Kingdom. But, says Piper, no man can easily decide for himself whether he has been divinely called to such a vocation. Anyone who has powerful erotic drives would obviously be mistaken to condemn himself to constant struggle and self-denial. Only those whose libidinal urges have been overpowered by a vastly stronger spiritual impulse can truly regard themselves as destined for celibacy, and they must not deceive themselves that they are more pleasing to God than the married. Piper is a thoroughgoing Protestant, with vigorous emphasis on the sanctity of all callings.

The application of these five Biblical principles of sex to some concrete problems involves the discussion of such questions as love, fidelity, chastity, marriage, decency, and self-discipline. Two points are of particular interest: one dealing with the determinative character of the first sexual act, the other with the question of premarital intercourse. In his treatment of fidelity, Piper maintains that the unity of flesh established by coitus is permanent because the unlocking of the inner secret of one's sexuality is so unique that it cannot be conveyed by any other person or event. He cites Paul's words to the effect that he who lies with a prostitute makes himself one flesh with her as support for this contention. Piper recognizes that many a marriage in modern times does not represent a first union. Both partners frequently come to the marriage bed with previous sexual experience, and it is almost expected that the bride will find her husband schooled in the art of love, learning gleaned not from books but from life. But Piper does not admit that this vitiates the principle involved. Marriage for such persons is not meaningless. The public marriage vows have a penitential significance, and although fidelity is really owed to the first sexual partner, since to him or her is owed the secret of life, the spouse is now regarded as the one to whom faithfulness alone is due. Piper quite rightly seeks consistently to derive the principle of marriage from sex, rather than the reverse, as is so often done by Christian writers. It is not that sex is justified only by the conditions of marriage and procreation; it stands in its own right. But Piper carries this process too far. What he is in effect saying is that the first coitus constitutes a marriage and the partners owe one another lifelong fidelity, and in that assertion he is trying to make sex carry more than it actually does. The sex act in itself, divorced from all other considerations, does not join a man and a woman into one flesh, except in the most crudely literal sense. That is a state of union which comprises more than mere bodies; it involves the blending of two personalities in all respects in such a way that the physical coupling symbolizes and to some extent deepens, the unity. Not that Christian love or even romantic love is essential to such a fusion. Obviously in cultures and ages where considerations of social status, parental approval, and so on, are preponderant, love plays little or no role in the making of marriages, and yet stable and satisfactory relationships are established. The term 'one flesh' is far more applicable to such situations than to the casual union formed by sexual intercourse between a man and a prostitute, even if the man is thereby initiated into the secrets of masculinity. It seems absurd, even in Biblical terms, or rather particularly in Biblical terms, to describe the latter liaison as that which God has joined together. Piper seeks to rescue the house of fidelity from the shifting and unreliable sands of transitory emotion, but the enduring rock is not first coitus but a genuine intermingling of two total personalities.

In his chapter on marriage, Piper understands that there is a difference between an outward ceremony and a union divinely established. What constitutes a marriage is the mutual consent of the individuals to belong together for life, and not even a church wedding renders their relationship more acceptable to God than it was before. Therefore there is no divine condemnation on those who have premarital intercourse provided they have taken the vow before God that they intend to keep each to the other so long as they both shall live. They are married in the sight of God, regardless of their status before Church or society, but Piper warns of the dangers of such intercourse and urges a revision of social mores to permit earlier marriages for the young. This coincides with the interpretation of Jesus' teaching set forth in chapter I of the present work, and is the only one consistent with the ethics of the New Testament. But Piper too uncritically accepts the conventional attitude toward the absolute indissolubility of marriage. He correctly observes that the deeper insights of Christian faith carry unrealized potentialities for salvaging marriages and that those insights are commonly ignored in the general rush to divorce. Self-examination in humility and penitence will frequently reveal that there are other, more creative possibilities, but sometimes, despite all that faith and love can do, a unity of flesh is in fact torn asunder. In such a circumstance, it is legalistic cruelty to deny the opportunity for a full and harmonious union with another partner to the unfortunate parties, sentencing them to a lifetime of bondage.

Of course Piper acknowledges the fact of human sin, recognizing that all men fall short of the counsels of perfection to which they are called by the will of God. Yet this does not spring from man's physical nature, from his animality. His sin is not born in his body. No instinct, sexual or otherwise, is evil. The naturalists, Piper concedes, are to this extent correct. But what they neglect is the ineluctable tendency of man to go his own way in defiance of the divine will which has clearly marked the road intended for human feet. This rebelliousness affects all areas of men's lives, including the sexual, and results in self-defeat and unhappiness. All stand condemned before the bar of God's justice, if not in deed then at least in thought. The mere acceptance of the inevitability of guilt and sin, however, the admission that human power is inadequate, is insufficient, leading to resignation or Stoic fortitude. What is required is a faith in forgiving grace, which does not mean that one is delivered from all his difficulties, but rather that an inner transformation takes place; one is born again. Faith means not that one's sins are blotted out, not that he will suddenly be made good and pure, but rather that his life is determined by the power of God; he is no longer left to the expedient of his own nature. He who takes the love of God revealed in Christ seriously experiences not simply a superficial change of outer behavior but a radical transformation of inner orientation. Instead of a self directed solely toward its own ends, its own desires, he finds a self striving toward love and obedience to God. This does not mean that all sins are at an end, a life without temptation or failure, but it does mean that these are no longer man's essence. They are displaced by his earnest desire to live in love, a desire to which God's grace may grant fulfillment in growth of strength and purity of heart. Then every sphere of life, including sex, may be made new by the divine mercy and love.

Emil Brunner

Emil Brunner's ethics is built upon what he calls the 'orders of creation,' which are analogous to the Roman Catholic natural law. This order is given along with that which is created in such a way that it is dimly perceived by the natural man, although sin distorts his vision so that he cannot fully apprehend it. He requires the clarification of faith in order to appreciate its full meaning, to see it as the will of God the Creator, the divine order of creation. Now, what is the divine order with respect to sex? It is simply this: that one man should be united in holy wedlock with one woman. There are two facts which need to be seen in this connection, facts which cannot be said to be 'proof' of the divine will, since only faith can provide that, but of which even unbelief has some awareness. The first of these is the trinitarian relationship of man-woman-child. All humans, says Brunner, are products of the unity of one man and one woman, and this is not meant simply in a biological sense. Every father knows that he has a special and unique relationship to his wife and child, and every mother and every child are similarly aware of the character of this unity. If the child were mere object, then the union between father and mother could be broken as soon as the child was born. But since the child is a subject, just as the father and mother are subjects, the parents know that their act is irrevocable, their union is irrevocable, and thus three human beings stand united to each other in a relation without parallel. Of course, the mother or father can drift away and separate, as can the child, but none of the three can ever escape the knowledge of this fundamental bond, although he may deny it and attempt to evade it throughout his life. This is an existential fact, a fact of subjective experience. It is not the same as to say that physically and psychologically the child needs his parents in order to survive and to grow into a human being, although that secondary fact emphasizes and underlines the primary truth.

The second fact underlying the order of creation for sex is human sexual love, which is in essence monistic. Brunner admits that there is a polygamous instinct, especially in males, but he maintains that when two people love each other, they want full and sole possession without the intrusion of a third party. 'Two's company: three's a crowd.' And when love is strong and genuine, it is recognized as a permanent bond. There is, to be sure, an impulse toward variety, but that is a result of love's weakness, not its strength. In so far as love is intense, the lover wants no one else. He feels that fate has brought him to this meeting, that this is a unique relationship, which is the theme of all romantic literature. And this experience foreshadows the uniqueness of the other bond which is involved in procreation.

But true marriage can never be based solely on love. This is to build on sand, for love is ephemeral. Where there is only love, there is selfishness and desire for possession or self-gratification. The real bond of marriage is fidelity, the sense not merely of being together but of belonging together in the unique structure of human existence. This 'lifts the sense of having been thrown together by Fate into the sphere of that which is personally free and unconditional.' Both in the realm of fidelity — the trinity of human relationships — and in the realm of love, marriage is a uniquely *personal* matter, in which two subjects are related to one another not as 'I-It' but as 'I-Thou.' Such personal relations are different from all others, for it is always legitimate to use an 'it,' an object, as the means to an end. But it is always degrading to both individuals involved, to use or to treat a 'Thou,' a person, as merely a means, a thing. And that can be understood only from the standpoint of faith in creation. As the Creator is 'personal,' so his children, made in his image, are personal, unique, set apart from all other creatures. This fact only faith can appropriate. Unbelief sees only the similarities of man to nature (naturalism) or it finds man's uniqueness in the wrong place (idealism). All life can be properly understood solely from the vantage point of faith, so sex and marriage are likewise correctly interpreted only in faith. Sexuality has an objective meaning, procreation, and it has a subjective significance, in erotic attraction. The subjective and objective are properly united and related in the personal dimension — in marriage, where persons live for each other. This is the mystery of sex and marriage, that it is the threshold of human community. Through its experience men learn that they are created to live with and for each other.

But this is merely the *idea* of marriage. This is sex as it was intended at Creation. Since the Fall, an entirely different situation prevails. No more than human beings correspond to the original Divine Image in which they were made, do actual sex relations represent the order for which they were meant. There are only sinful men, and there are only sinful marriages. This actual, existential situation of sin Brunner discusses in terms of the rent, the shame, and the longing. The rent is the tearing asunder of sexuality and personality. The two were created in union and harmony, the one serving the other, but now sexuality is a thing in itself; man confuses his sex nature with that of the animals. The awesome mystery of sex is reduced to 'a mere trifle.' Man enters into sexual relations which are impersonal, solely for the purpose of sensual gratification. Even in the most personal of fallen man's sexual relations, even between married partners bound to each other by love and fidelity, there is an impersonal element, a degree of lust. This rent gives rise to shame and to longing. Brunner maintains that shame is not artificial, a product of cultural conditioning, but a genuine feeling with deep roots in human nature.

The absence of shame is a sign not of emancipation but of perversion, for some sense of guilt characterizes even marital sexual intercourse, where the personal-love element is at its height. The more self-determination a man develops, that is to say the more personal he becomes, the deeper is his awareness of shame. 'We cannot think of our Lord as married, although we are not in the least jarred by the fact that he ate and drank like the rest of mankind. Even the doctrine of the Virgin Birth points in this direction — whatever we may think of it from other points of view. It would appear that in sexuality there is something which is fundamentally and irreparably out of order, that is, out of the divine order.' [5]

The rent between personality and sexuality is witnessed to not only by the fact of shame, but also by the tremendous erotic longing in man which cannot be satisfied. There is in sex an intense yearning for full union with the beloved, a desire to be literally one flesh. This is the effort of all lovers, and the sexual act itself represents the passionate striving to achieve that ideal. But the longing is always frustrated; whatever union is realized is partial and transitory. In this connection, Brunner raises the question whether this very longing does not indicate that there is a mental and spiritual division which not even the most intimate physical union can overcome. In other words, is the Gnostic myth of the Androgynes correct? Was humanity originally created as a man-woman, and was one of the results of the Fall the splitting of this androgenous nature into male and female? The answer is emphatically in the negative. Against such a notion Brunner sets the word of the Bible 'male and female created he them.' It is not sufficient to point to nature as such, for God could have made things otherwise if he chose. Things are as they are because he willed them so. But is this not to say that the longing for one another is a fact of creation rather than a result of sin? No, replies Brunner, the fact of creation is the natural instinct of bi-sexuality, which can be satisfied. What is sinful is the greed, the desire, the unquenchable longing. And it is not alone

5. Brunner, Emil, *Man in Revolt*, Charles Scribner's Sons, New York, 1939, p. 348f.

the desire for full union with the beloved which is involved, but the longing for true community. All of the problems of sex spring from the rent, the split between sexuality and personality, which gives rise to shame that cannot be overcome and to longing that cannot be fulfilled.

This means that all men are sinners in the realm of sex as in every other sphere of life. All men are adulterers, violators of the Seventh Commandment, when viewed from the perspective of Jesus' words concerning the lustful look, the lecherous heart, and the recognition of this fact has the utmost importance in the treatment of specific problems in sexual morality. Here the ways of Evangelical ethics and Catholic legalism divide irrevocably. Protestantism recognizes that all men stand condemned and bases its standards upon an attempt to deal with the moral relativities of life, while Catholicism takes its stand upon natural and revealed law. The Protestant recognition of the universality of sin results in 'a new definition of the purpose of marriage . . . as a *remedium concupiscentiae.*' The sexual impulse, which, like all things created, was originally pure and good, has been perverse and must be restricted. But asceticism is not the best way to control it, for that would be to go to the opposite extreme. The sexual drive is too strong and powerful in men to be long denied except under unusual circumstances. Here, a middle way must be sought between uncontrolled self-expression which allows the sex impulse to run riot and thus destroys man as man, and celibacy which disturbs physical and psychic balance and also annihilates man. This *via media* is the divine order of creation — monogamous marriage. The chief blessing of marriage is that which the erotic regard as its chief blemish, its tempering and domesticating of the libido.

This is the first consequence of the recognition that all men are sinners in sex — the definition of marriage as a remedy for concupiscence. The second consequence is the relationship of the different orders of sex. This does not mean that there is *no* difference between a man who preserves a monogamous marriage in love and fidelity to his wife and one who is a promiscuous fornicator or adulterer. But who can see with the eyes of God? It may be that the 'righteous' husband and father is inwardly a seething mass of sensual desire, while the 'sinner' is penitent and genuinely torn asunder. The outer, objective, static law, even if it be the divine law, must not be confused with the personal, dynamic will of God. This is always the mistake of legalism, whatever guise it may assume, Pharisaic, Roman Catholic, or Puritan. It fails to recognize that God may actually command a man to act *against* the law, as for example, where the dissolution of a marriage might be a positive duty. The legalist sees only the law against divorce and regards the question as closed, while the evangelical sees the overarching fact of the divine love and grace which can, in concrete situations, break through a general law. 'Above all "orders," even above the order of Creation, stands the will of God, which here and now requires nothing of me save that I should meet my neighbor in the spirit of responsible love. But no universal law can anticipate what this means in a world confused and corrupted by sin.' [6] Each man must work out his own course of action in a dynamic, personal relation to God, and no man can instruct another concerning his duty and responsibility to the divine.

The difference between Roman Catholic and Protestant ethics is strikingly illuminated by this whole discussion. The former is characterized by a more generally optimistic anthropology which issues in legalism. The results of the Fall are regarded as comparatively slight: man has lost none of his natural powers. His reason remains intact and his will firm, though somewhat weakened, especially in the sexual realm where concupiscence operates independently of rational control. But his reason is able to discern the divine will in the natural law, and for the most part he can obey. Whatever gaps there may be in his knowledge or weakness in his will are filled and overcome by the grace supplied by the Church. Protestantism, on the other hand, at least in its traditional aspects,[7] has a much more pessimistic anthropology, regard-

6. Brunner, Emil, *The Divine Imperative*, The Lutterworth Press, London, 1937, p. 355.

7. Of course, twentieth-century liberal Protestantism, especially in America, became even more optimistic about man than Rome, accepting on the whole a Renaissance anthropology, breaking almost completely with the Reformation. The most recent trend seems to favor a return to the more traditional view.

ing man as totally depraved, his reason corrupted so that he rationalizes and his will weakened so that in Augustine's terms he is not able not to sin (*non posse non peccare*). All men are condemned and judged by the Law, which cannot save. The only hope is to be found in the divine mercy, in freedom from the bondage of the Law, in the direct, personal encounter with God. It is love not law, forgiveness not obedience, dynamic will not static command. Protestantism sets the relative character of all legislation, even the so-called orders of creation over against Rome's absolute and immutable natural law. For Protestantism, the individual stands before God in a unique situation, where the divine love can dispense with all rules. For Rome, all mankind stands before the divine law, and the regulations cannot be set aside for individual exceptions. If the line is broken at one point, it cannot hold. For then it must break at all points. The ethic of Protestantism is 'Christian liberty,' where the ethic of Rome is natural law.

Brunner denies that marriage is a sacrament. Like Luther and Calvin he regards it as a holy ordinance of God but not as a means of grace. Like the Reformers also, he admits the legitimate concern of the state with marriage. He recognizes that the modern emphasis on the individualistic nature of matrimony is a justified reaction to the traditional emphasis on the collectivistic, social aspect of wedlock. The tendency to view the family almost wholly from the standpoint of society, regulated by law and custom, did real violence and worked genuine injustice to individual personalities. But to go to the opposite extreme, as much of the modern discussion of marriage is inclined to do, is no solution. For the purely individual approach, the romantic attachment of two lovers is not a sufficient basis for a sound marriage. There must also be fidelity, which includes love but goes beyond it to social obligation. Any marriage, as any sex act, has implications wider than the lone persons involved. The community as a whole has a concern for the institution of the family and has the right to regulate family life. It is a mistake to regard the outer ceremony of marriage as simply a conformity to social custom, a mere formality, and to characterize the civil magistrate as a ridiculous interference on the part of the state. The civil authority cannot, of course, create a marriage; it frequently gives the blessing to that which is not a marriage at all. Nor can the state annul a true union between husband and wife, and any laws which made such an attempt would be without real force. But no Christian marriage is complete without the consent of the state, for the Christian is also a citizen and respects the social character of sex. The blessing of the Church upon a marriage is desirable, but in principle such a blessing is not indispensable.

Virginity and celibacy are rejected by Brunner as false goals, arising from the corruption of Christianity by Hellenistic dualism, and he gratefully acknowledges the contributions of modern secularists to the growth of positive attitudes toward sex. He regards certain of the contentions of romanticism and psychology as exaggerations in the direction of self-expression and the sole importance of love, but he understands them as thoroughly comprehensible reactions against the unhealthy repression of the centuries. In discussing divorce, he agrees with the Roman Catholic position that *in essence* marriage is an indissoluble estate, an unbreakable relationship of fidelity. Here the natural law and the order of creation agree, but Brunner insists that the Gospel transcends law, that it includes the realization that men are sinners, in need of the divine love and grace. Obviously, divorce is a sign of weakness, an indication of a sinful and adulterous generation, but to generalize from that to a universal law binding in every individual case is legalism. There may arise situations when not to divorce would be the greater sin, involving in some cases direct disobedience of the divine will. A free paraphrase of Brunner's position might run something like the following: A father makes certain rules for his children, governing their behavior. In general, he expects conformity to these rules and will punish disobedience. But his love far surpasses his concern for conformity, and if he sees that real violence will be done to one of his children by a slavish adherence to the law, he will remit the regulation in that particular case. In dealing with the infinite variety of humanity, Brunner insists that no universal law is adequate to cover all possible exigencies. Only the dynamic, personal will of God which may be different for each individual will suffice.

Writing on birth control, Brunner declares that *nature* indicates that God intended sexual intercourse as a means of expressing love as well as being the method of procreation. He regards it as essential for the Christian ethic to stand for the independent significance of sex within marriage, not requiring procreation as its justification. This is, of course, the only grounds for a disagreement with the Roman Catholic position. If procreation is accepted as the primary purpose of sex, relegating affection to a secondary role, then birth control is unnatural. But if the two are placed on an equal plane, then artificial contraception is by no means contrary to the divine will. Brunner points out that planned families are of the utmost importance in an industrial age, when children no longer represent economic assets, but liabilities, when housing conditions are crowded. Under such circumstances, to leave things to chance is almost criminally irresponsible. As for 'birth control by self-control,' Brunner rightly replies that asceticism is not a virtue and is absolutely contradicted by the admonitions of the Bible. This is not to condemn such a practice; if some prefer it to the use of contraceptives that is their privilege. But they are not following any 'better way,' more pleasing in the sight of God. Considerations of space forbid any account of the extremely cogent observations which Brunner makes with respect to the current problems of sex and marriage, but the interested reader will find them worth the investment of some time.

Reinhold Niebuhr

Niebuhr views all of modern society from an historical perspective, against the background of the long course of western civilization, and current sexual mores and attitudes are no exception. He admits that the revolt of secular romanticism and naturalism against the sexual negativism of the Church, both Catholic and Protestant, is justified. Neither segment of Christianity has successfully related sexual life either to the total personality or to the total society. Catholicism's emphasis upon procreation must bear equal responsibility with Protestant Puritanism for the difficulties modern man encounters in his efforts to relate his sexual drives creatively to the whole of his life. Niebuhr endorses the secular attack upon the failure of the Church to deal positively and adequately with the fact of sex. The attitude of the modern mind toward sex contains a profound truth: it asserts that sex is natural and good. Niebuhr, however, discerns also in the attitude of modernity what he regards as a serious error: the belief that guilt, shame, and aberration can be dispelled by a program of education and enlightenment. He is not opposed to sex education, but he regards it as naïve to assume that sexual difficulties spring either solely or primarily from repression. They have their source rather in the same *fons et origo* as all other human derangement, namely, in freedom and sin.

Niebuhr brands several aspects of the modern attitude toward sex as naïve, unrealistic, and in some instances positively dangerous. He is disturbed not so much by the Kinsey reports themselves, which came as no devastating surprise, as by the presuppositions which underlie the whole project and the reception which was reflected in the reviews and notices. The sexual behavior of both male and female is approached entirely from a biological point of view, as though one were dealing with the coupling of animals, completely ignoring the fact that sexual relations in human beings have the profoundest psychological implications for the total personality. The Christian standards, so long dominant in western culture, are regarded as merely arbitrary, and whatever may have been normative about them has been rendered obsolete by the findings of the two reports. The assumption is that a new set of norms is to be produced by a statistical analysis of the prevailing practices. It would seem that society ought to define its norms in terms of what is typical. All that is needed in the future for moral standards is an accurate Gallup poll, indeed a triumph of scientific civilization! 'Here we have the modern sociological approach to the problem of norms reduced to its final absurdity. A learned doctor reviewing the (first) Kinsey report, asks the relevant question, whether the fact that most people have colds in the winter establishes colds as "normative." ' [8] However legalistic and self-righteous Christians may be, they do not make the mistake of regarding man as a slightly more complex animal, ignoring the dimensions of the personal. They know that the standards and norms by which life is governed are neither absolute and arbitrary nor solely produced by the flux of public opinion. Niebuhr regards the so-called 'scientific' attitude toward sex, as represented by the Kinsey reports and the reception accorded them, as the symptom of a disease far more serious than the sickness it seeks to cure.

For Niebuhr all ethical questions are rooted in anthropology, in the doctrine of man, and his own position is midway between the romanticists on the one side and the idealists on the other. He agrees with romanticism that man is more than pure mind or spirit, that his emotions and bodily impulses control him in powerful and important ways. But he agrees also with idealism in its contention that man transcends his purely physical being, though Niebuhr does not find the locus of this freedom in the reason, as do the idealists. Man is, for him, an animal, subject to the vicissitudes and necessities of nature, enjoying only a limited freedom from its organic forms. With such a point of view, nearly all of modern naturalistic philosophers would agree, but Niebuhr goes beyond this to the assertion that man is also 'a spirit who stands outside of nature, life, himself, his reason and the world,' and with this analysis the idealists agree. What is unique about what Niebuhr calls the Biblical doctrine of man is that it alone combines an awareness of man's affinities with nature with a recognition of his uniqueness, his freedom.

In the realm of sex, man is obviously an animal, sharing the conditions of impulse, and instinct, of copulation, conception, and birth with his fellow creatures. From this he can never escape. Niebuhr is critical at this point of some of the extremes of feminism for their tendency to ignore the limitations of bi-sexuality. He regards the fact that motherhood is a vocation while fatherhood is an avocation as rooted in biology, and while this can be reduced in effect so that alternative vocations become

8. Niebuhr, Reinhold, *Sex Standards in America*, in *Christianity and Crisis*, vol. VIII, no. 9, 24 May 1948.

available to women, it can never be completely overcome. Yet despite man's inescapable ties to the animal kingdom, the sexual impulse has far wider implications for him, because of his freedom. On the one hand, his libido can transcend mere procreation to ascend to the heights of love, family, and general creativity in art and religion, and on the other, it can 'become the perverse centre of man's existence, thereby devouring and corrupting other creative capacities.' The animal cannot know what it means to make sex the center of his life. His erotic impulses are controlled by timeless laws of instinct. Only man has freedom over his sexual drives, but his freedom is not absolute. He cannot escape the realm of nature; he can only channel its impulses.

In this connection, Niebuhr is sharply critical of Freud, who sought to base his theories in biology, to interpret human vitalities solely in organic terms. What he learned about the *id*, the source of the sexual impulses, however, came to him from the study of dreams, and this Niebuhr regards as eloquent testimony to his own understanding of man. For, he says, the dream, dwelling as it does in the twilight zone between consciousness and unconsciousness, reveals with remarkable clarity the blending of spirit and nature, animal impulse and spiritual freedom in human nature. The dream is rooted in biology, to be sure, but Niebuhr thinks Freud utterly failed to explain how physiological impulses are transformed into the complex spiritual phenomena which dreams represent. Niebuhr operates constantly from the base of the Biblical understanding of man as a psycho-physical unity, attacking both a too simple naturalism and a too idealistic rationalism. He rejects Bertrand Russell's contention that scientific contraception justifies sexual promiscuity, since it removes the danger of illicit offspring, on the grounds that such an opinion totally disregards the 'organic unity between physical impulses and the spiritual dimension of human personality.' All sexual relations are personal relations, and to engage in them without a personal sense of responsibility is degrading and destructive to both personalities.

Niebuhr does recognize serious shortcomings in the traditional Christian statements about sex. He admits that certain errors of idealism and mysticism very early made their way into Christian thought and continue to exert their influence. The attitudes engendered by Hellenistic dualism have given rise to the misconception that Christianity regards sex as the original sin. Niebuhr here places himself in the Biblical tradition, accepting sexuality as a fact of creation and identifying the original sin as pride, and he is able to document his position thoroughly from Paul and Augustine through Aquinas and Luther. All of them are agreed that concupiscence is an effect of the original sin and not its cause. Sensuality derives from the more primal emotion of self-love. But the explanations of the relationship between sensuality and pride have been notably unsatisfactory in historic Christian theology, partly because they have never been specific enough and partly because they contradict each other. The question of how self-love results in the further consequence of sensuality is not answered with sufficient psychological precision, or else the answers are involved in the strange contradiction of saying at one and the same time that the self no longer has control over the impulses of the body, and that the self's immoderate pleasure in these impulses is a further form of self-love.

This defect Niebuhr attempts to supply or at least to explore. He raises a series of probing questions. Does the sensualist go so far in his egoism that he loses all control of himself in his attempt to gratify a particular desire, or is a life among the fleshpots an attempt to escape from the self? Is sexual abandon the domination of another person by one's own self-love, or is it rather a kind of idolatry of the other person? Does sex make the self its god, or does it find its idol in another, since it is aware of the inadequacy of self-worship? Niebuhr believes that there is in all forms of sensuality and in sexuality in particular a mixture of self-love and escape from self into adoration of another. There is a bewildering confusion of elements in the sex life of sinful man. There is the creative discovery of self which results in the giving of the self to another in sex. There is the desire to dominate another and the impulse to give to another. 'The element of sin in the experience is not due to the fact that sex is in any sense sinful as such. But once sin is presupposed, that is, once the original harmony of nature is disturbed by man's self-love, the instincts of sex are particularly effective tools for both the assertion of self and the flight from the self.' [9]

It is in this soil that man's uneasiness about sex has its roots, for he knows how intimately related it is to sin. The active role of the male makes him especially prone to self-deification, while the passive female role flirts with idolatry, but both aspects are found in both sexes. There is one further purpose which may be served by sexual passion: it may be used as an anodyne, like alcohol. The ego, turning in disgust from the worship either of the self or the partner, uses sex as a means of escape. In prostitution, for example, the personal element is excluded as much as possible from sexual satisfaction. Here Niebuhr cites the novels of D. H. Lawrence, who seems to view sex as an escape, sometimes even identifying sexual desire and the desire for death. The recognition of the involvement of sex in sin is what gives rise to feelings of shame. Niebuhr refuses to agree with modern naturalism, which regards guilt and shame concerning sex as abnormal and unnecessary, the unfortunate result of civilization's repressions. He maintains that the sense of shame about sex came before the mores of civilized man, in exactly the same fashion that the inordinateness of sexual desire antedated and made necessary the taboos and disciplines of society rather than appearing as the results of those restraints. Yet Niebuhr has little patience, either, with Christian Puritanism or asceticism which has tried by undue repression to rid life of the sin in sex. He sees the whole problem as far more complex than either the dualist, who is inclined to regard sex as sinful *per se,* or the anti-ascetic, who thinks to remove all difficulties by relaxing all restraints. Fallen man sins in his sexuality by using it as the occasion for self-love, for idolatry, or for escape into unconsciousness.

Summary

This concludes the discussion of contemporary Protestantism. Weatherhead, it should be noted, would fall under the critical

9. Niebuhr, Reinhold, *The Nature and Destiny of Man,* Charles Scribner's Sons, New York, 1941, vol. I, p. 237.

eye of the other three, since he expects more to be accomplished
by wider education, greater freedom, and less prurience. Piper,
Brunner, and Niebuhr do not oppose such a program, but they
regard the infection in man's sex life as more deep-rooted, traceable to original sin, which is overcome only partially in this world
by divine grace, and only finally beyond history in the resurrection. Both Niebuhr and Brunner regard shame as intrinsic to
the human situation and explicitly deny that it springs from
cultural conditioning. Here they come perilously close to Catholic
natural-law theories, in their reluctance to maintain an openness
to the facts of anthropological research. Even if one admits that
shame is a product of civilization, it does not necessarily follow
that a return to primitive conditions is the solution. Not even
Freud believed that.

All four contemporary Protestants agree with Luther and Calvin
in their rejection of the Catholic preference for virginity and
celibacy. All of them look upon sex as a fact of creation, to be
accepted as good. They go back to the Bible, to the documents
which predate the Hellenistic corruption of Christianity. Perhaps
this is one of the real sources of the genius of Protestantism. Its return to Scripture makes possible a naturalism which Catholicism,
with its acceptance of tradition as of equal authority with Scripture, cannot embrace. The Old and New Testaments both reveal
an essentially positive attitude toward sex, where it is affirmed
as a divine blessing given man to be enjoyed, not a curse to be
escaped. The tradition, coming from the writings of the Fathers
of the Church, displays a considerable amount of Hellenistic
dualism, and Catholic dependence upon tradition is perhaps the
most important reason for a greater intransigence in interpretations of sex in Rome than in Protestantism. The Biblical outlook
provides also a strong antidote to legalism, and contemporary
Protestantism proves decidedly anti-legalistic in its attitudes toward divorce, birth control, and so forth. Sex is now affirmed once
more as a gift of God, as a good and natural impulse which
does not require the fact of procreation to justify it. Since man
is a sinner, seeking to make himself the center of life, he inevitably
misuses his God-given sexuality, degrading himself and his sexual

partner by the divorce of sex from personal love. Sex is again, as in the Bible, considered in terms of interpersonal relations instead of as a dark and mysterious power of evil. For this more positive attitude, contemporary Protestantism owes no small debt to secular sources, perhaps the chief of which is the school of psychoanalysis. A consideration of the psychoanalytic interpretations of sex is therefore in order.

TWO

Interpretations of Sex in Psychoanalysis

SIGMUND FREUD

IT IS ESSENTIAL to an understanding of the psychoanalytic interpretation of sex to realize that Freud did not begin with a full blown theory, or even with a well-worked-out hypothesis which he proceeded to demonstrate in his clinical practice. He began his career as a physician, specializing in nervous and mental disorders, and through his experience was gradually brought to the convictions about the nature of sexuality that have since characterized the movement known as psychoanalysis.

Freud himself, in his *History of the Psychoanalytic Movement*, written in 1914, recalls how far from his mind were any such theories of sex in his early years. Three casual comments by respected colleagues made little impression on him at the time and were recalled only in the light of his subsequent discoveries. Charcot, the great French neurologist, under whom Freud studied, in speaking of a case of hysteria, said 'Mais dans ces cas pareils, c'est toujours la chose genital, toujours, toujours, toujours!' Joseph Breuer, Freud's friend, physician, and early collaborator, remarked concerning a frustrated wife who was neurotic that such cases were always secrets of the conjugal bed. Chrobak, a medical lecturer at the University of Vienna, told Freud of a disturbed woman who was still a virgin after eighteen years of marriage, due to her husband's impotence, that the only prescription was one well known but impossible: *"Penis normalis dosim; Repe-*

tatur!" Freud's earliest writing reveals how unimpressed he was by these remarks. In some of his case histories, he stumbled quite by accident onto the sexual element in the life of the patient. He and Breuer, collaborating on *Studies in Hysteria*, found sex only one among a number of suppressed traumatic experiences buried in the unconscious. Breuer exhaustively acquainted himself with the minutest details of a Miss Anna O.'s life and never encountered a single thought or idea of a sexual nature. Freud's diagnosis of a Mrs. Emma von N. contained no thought of a sexual neurosis on an hysterical basis. He shared the view of Charcot and of his own patients that the connection of hysteria with sex was an insult. In 1894, however, he issued a paper on *The Defense Neuro-Psychoses* in which he observed: 'In all the cases I have analyzed, it was in the sexual life that a painful effect — of precisely the same quality as that attaching to the obsession — had originated. On theoretical grounds it is not impossible that this affect may arise in other spheres; I have merely to state that hitherto I have not discovered any other origin of it.' [1]

From this point on, Freud was a man with an hypothesis, applied to ever-widening areas of human experience, and he has been condemned as handicapped by a blind spot, ignoring all other phenomena in his effort to substantiate his theory. It was precisely on these grounds that Breuer broke with him, and Freud's tenacious adherence to his idea brought upon him a storm of criticism and abuse, even from his medical colleagues. If, however, Freud is to be condemned and disregarded for employing this method of working from an initial hypothesis, then a like treatment must be accorded every scientist who begins with a hunch based upon his original research and then proceeds to test his idea against the facts. Certainly, the evidence is that Freud maintained a high degree of flexibility in his theoretical formulations, constantly revising and adapting his ideas to conform to clinical experience. And there is much to be said for his own explanation of the violent reaction to his suggestions, namely

1. Freud, Sigmund, *Collected Papers*, The International Psychoanalytic Press, London, 1924, vol. 1, p. 66.

that it arises from the prudishness which inhabits the sexual realm and guards it zealously from any invading explorers who seek to find the facts.

In their early studies in hysteria Breuer and Freud experimented with the use of hypnosis on hysterical patients. (In medicine the term hysteria is used not in the popular sense of uncontrolled laughter or tears, but to refer to a physical symptom, for example a paralysis which seems to be of psychic origin, revealing no organic pathology.) They discovered that 'the hysteric suffers mostly from reminiscences.' In every case they found a series of traumatic experiences which had been forgotten by the patient, yet which returned under hypnosis, and it was these 'forgotten memories' which proved to be the cause of the illness. The two men were greatly surprised to find that the hysterical symptom disappeared when they awakened the memories of the repressed experience. This discovery led to the formulation of two concepts, both of which were to play major roles in the development of psychoanalysis: the unconscious and abreaction. The existence of the unconscious, a realm of the mind where are to be found memories and ideas not ordinarily accessible to conscious thought, was a conclusion forced upon Breuer and Freud by their clinical experience. Neither of them tried to locate the unconscious physiologically, in the brain or elsewhere, but they were convinced of its existence. The theory of abreaction likewise was the offspring of their medical practice. They found that traumatic experiences normally evoke a powerful emotional response. When a man is in a train wreck, he is seriously frightened, but if he feels his fear fully, if he relives the experience in his memory over a period of several days, he drains off the affects of the shock and no damage is done. He has reacted appropriately to the event; he has worked through the emotional tension successfully. But in some cases, the experience is too painful, too frightening, and it is pushed from consciousness, 'forgotten,' repressed. The memory continues to operate, however; it continues to affect the total organism, sometimes producing physical pain. The task of the physician in such a case is to resurrect the buried memory, to help the patient to discharge the emotional energy which has been bound and stored. This process of remembering and feeling is called abreaction.

Even Breuer found that the repressed memories and feelings which cause hysteria are very frequently sexual in character, but he was unwilling to follow Freud in finding a sexual element universally at the root of the neuroses. He preferred to speak also of such etiological factors as 'fright hysteria' and 'hypnoid states.' Freud, on the other hand, having begun with his hypothesis, was quite prepared to explore it further. He did not ignore all other elements in the histories of his patients. He knew that there are many factors contributing to the formation of a neurosis. He insisted frequently and vigorously that the origin of every nervous disorder is overdetermined, caused by a combination of agents. But he did believe that the most important determinant is sexual, not only in the majority of cases, as did Breuer, but in every case.

With this conviction as his starting point, Freud turned his attention to delineating four major types of nervous disorder: hysteria, obsessional neuroses, anxiety neuroses, and neurasthenia. In all of them, he believed that he found the primary etiological factor in the sex life of the patient. He found that hysterical patients uniformly reported a traumatic experience of sexual violation in childhood. They had reacted by 'forgetting' the event, repressing its memory, pushing it out of consciousness. With the attainment of puberty, however, attended by the awakening of sexuality, the old feelings of fear and horror which early became associated with sex were reawakened, and the hysterical symptom made its appearance, always revealing a direct connection with the original traumatic experience. The whole process was unconscious, running its course without any awareness on the part of the person concerned. Obsessional neuroses, whose chief symptoms are compulsive ideas or acts from which the individual is powerless to escape, such as compulsive cleanliness, the persistence of unnecessary hostility, or arithmomania, the necessity to count objects, Freud believed to originate also in childhood sexual experience. But where the hysteric reacted to his premature seduction or rape with fear and pain, the obsessional responded with pleasure, and his compulsions are reproaches which he makes to himself for that early enjoyment, reproaches disguised by the unconscious psychical processes of transformation and substitution. Freud linked hysteria and obsessions together as 'defense-neuroses,' defenses against memories of early childhood experiences with sex.

Anxiety neurosis and neurasthenia he labeled 'simple neuroses,' arising out of a current disturbance in mature sex life. Neurasthenia carries a symptom pattern of cranial pressure, tendency to weariness, indigestion, and general irritability. Anxiety neurosis characteristically presents a group of complaints, all of which are related to the one main symptom: anxiety. Restlessness, sleeplessness, vertigo, fear of catastrophe are the guises assumed by this underlying apprehension. These simple neuroses Freud traced to the sexual mechanism which he believed to be constantly building up tensions in the body. When the tension reaches a certain point, the entire nervous system is affected, through a complex process, in such a way that a discharge or orgasm occurs. This is the 'normal' pattern, but when some interference blocks the discharge, a nervous disorder ensues. Neurasthenia is caused by the substitution for normal coitus of some less satisfying form of relief, such as masturbation or spontaneous emission. Anxiety neurosis is produced by a blockage which prevents 'the somatic sexual excitation from being assimilated psychically.' Either some inhibition prevents the individual from even being aware of his sexual needs, or there is a progressive accumulation of tension due to enforced abstinence or frustrated excitation, as in *coitus interruptus*, relative impotence or frigidity, or the erotic play of engaged couples who stop short of intercourse. Neurasthenia springs from inappropriate or inadequate methods of attaining relief from sexual tension, anxiety neurosis from a hindrance to the psychical co-operation necessary if the nervous system is to discharge its accumulated pressure.

Freud did not regard these four types as mutually exclusive. He found hysteria and neurasthenia, as well as obsessions and anxiety neurosis, in frequent combination in the same individual.

What was fundamental in his theoretical formulations at this point in his career (1896) was his conviction, born out of his clinical experience, that the origin of the disease, the determinative factor in every neurosis and even in some of the psychoses, not only could but must be traced to the sexual life of the patient. The other side of the coin was Freud's own dictum that 'No neurosis is possible with a normal *vita sexualis.*' His whole theory of the etiology of neuroses received a rude and severe shock when he discovered to his consternation that many of the traumatic childhood seductions described to him by his patients were pure fabrications with no basis whatever in fact. It is a tribute to Freud's scientific devotion to truth that he made no effort to avoid the consequences of this disastrous disclosure. He admitted that he had been wrong, but he did not abandon his search for a theoretical framework which would do justice to the facts, as his first attempt had failed to do.

He had already begun to recognize the necessity for a psychology of normal mental and emotional processes. Even before his house came crashing about his ears, his opponents had voiced their skepticism, declaring that even if his claim had some validity for the mentally ill, which was doubtful, certainly his findings had no bearing whatever on normal human beings. This opposition, together with Freud's own scientific curiosity, led him to search for a more comprehensive psychology than the nineteenth century had thus far placed at his disposal. He anticipated such a constructive enterprise in a lecture on *The Aetiology of Hysteria,* delivered on 2 May 1896, before the Society of Psychiatry and Neurology in Vienna. He remarked concerning the question why an infantile memory of sexual impulses which was at the time unconscious and harmless should result in a pathological state, that it was 'purely a psychological problem, the solution of which may perhaps require certain assumptions about normal psychic processes, and the part played in them by consciousness.' Later in the same lecture he referred his audience to 'this psychology which has yet to meet our requirements — the future patho-psychology.'

The foundations for such a psychology were laid in two books, *The Interpretation of Dreams,* published in 1900, and *The Psy-*

chopathology of Everyday Life, in 1904. In the first work Freud developed a theory which came to him during his therapeutic work with patients. In collaboration with Breuer, he had begun using hypnosis in his early therapy, but he soon abandoned this technique for the free-association method, where the patient lay on a couch while Freud laid his hand upon the neurotic's forehead and commanded him to relate whatever came to mind. This process later underwent still further modification; the doctor refrained both from physical contact and from active command. The patient lay, completely relaxed, still on the couch, but now with Freud sitting behind where he could see without being seen; the patient allowed his thoughts free rein, reporting everything that came into consciousness. This is the method still used in psychoanalysis today. Freud found that frequently his patients would, during free association, tell him of their dreams, and he became convinced that dreams have a definite meaning. With this as his starting point, he worked out his theory, using his own dreams as his chief examples, thus avoiding the criticism that he was dealing with neurotic phenomena.

Freud divided every dream into two parts: the manifest dream content, what is remembered on awaking, and the latent dream thoughts, the emotional state which expresses itself in the dream. The latter is always an unfulfilled wish, as the so-called 'somatic dream' illustrates. The thirst of a sleeper is quenched by his dream of drinking cool, clear water, or the pressure of his bladder is relieved by his dream of urinating. The primary function of every dream is the preservation of sleep. When man lies down to rest, the doors to the outside world are closed, but his wishes, desires, and wants continue to exist. If they become too acute, he wakes up. The purpose of the dream is to satisfy these wants without disturbing the sleep. Only in the dreams of small children, however, do the wishes which produce the dream appear in undisguised form, do the latent dream thoughts come through clearly. In adults, a kind of censorship operates, distorting and disguising the latent dream thoughts into the manifest dream content, which often seems bizarre and meaningless, so that a dream remembered in the morning appears utterly absurd. Why does the transformation occur? Why the disguise? Why it is necessary for what Freud called the dream work to metamorphose the latent dream thoughts into such strange and unrecognized symbols? In the answers to these questions Freud found the beginning of his comprehensive psychology.

He believed that the unconscious, or at least that portion of it which he was later to call the 'id,' is a seething mass of primitive, anti-social drives. All men, not merely the neurotic, have wishes which cannot be fulfilled without danger to society and therefore danger to self. Some of these impulses are, of course, sexual, but by no means all of them. Some spring from ambition, the desire for prestige, hatred, or rage. In waking life these primitive strivings are subdued and repressed by a kind of unconscious censorship which turns them back, refusing them admittance even to the level of awareness, much less of action. During sleep, however, the quiescent state draws the barb from the danger of acting out such desires, so the censorship is able to relax. The gates to consciousness need not be guarded quite so zealously, and the watchdog can allow at least some of its hundred heads the luxury of rest. But some of the eyes remain open even in sleep, and the wishes fulfilled by the dream are disguised in symbolic form so that they bear little resemblance to their real nature. If the dream grows too bold in its granting of unconscious desires, without appropriate guise, the censor sounds the alarm, anxiety mobilizes its forces, and sleep is shattered into the pieces of wakefulness. Freud believed that by the free-association process he could translate the manifest dream content into the latent dream thoughts, an enterprise which gave him important insights into the emotional life of the dreamer. He found numerous symbols recurrent in the dreams of most people, symbols which abound also in mythology and folk tales, derived from the most primitive stages of humanity.

Freud did not maintain that every dream has a sexual element or meaning. He believed that the great majority contain some sexual material, but he recognized that many dreams are the harbingers of other desires. What is of particular interest is the psychology which his dream theory reveals: his interpretation of the unconscious as a reservoir of primitive and amoral impulses, dammed behind the floodgates of a censorship which allows outlet only in the disguised and harmless form of the manifest dream content. He called the censor a 'criticizing instance,' a sort of screen which lies between the unconscious and the system of consciousness. And he declared, 'I do not believe that psychoneurotics are to be sharply distinguished . . . from other persons who remain normal — that is, I do not believe that they are capable of creating something absolutely new and peculiar to themselves. . . . Psychoneurotics do no more than reveal to us, by magnification, something that occurs less markedly and intensively in the minds of children.' [2]

The Psychopathology of Everyday Life carried on the task of applying the psychology of the unconscious to further realms of normal life. Here Freud dealt with such common experiences as slips of the tongue, slips of the pen, mistakes in reading or hearing, errors of action, forgetting of names or things. He believed that there is always an unconscious motivation which lies behind such mistakes, that they never occur as the products of mere chance. Not only is a neurosis 'overdetermined,' but all psychic processes, even in normal human beings, follow a strict path of determination. Forgetting something invariably betrays the presence of a distaste or disinclination in the unconscious; a slip of the tongue reveals some repressed impulse which managed nonetheless to escape the repression. Freud here elaborated further his new psychology, describing mental and emotional structures which contain on the one hand desires, drives, and impulses contrary to the standards of social acceptability, and on the other a censor which strains constantly to keep such anti-social impulses out of consciousness as well as out of action.

Having constructed a preliminary psychology upon the foundations of his clinical experience, Freud applied it to his findings with respect to sexuality in such a way that his theory would be valid for all men and not only for psychoneurotics. In 1905 he wrote his *Three Contributions to the Theory of Sex,* calling the sexual instinct, which he regarded as analogous to hunger, the

2. *The Interpretation of Dreams,* in *The Basic Writings of Sigmund Freud,* Modern Library Giant, Random House, New York, 1938, p. 306f.

'libido.' Libido is the motor force of sexual life; it is a quantitative energy. The popular opinion of Freud's day held that libido does not make itself felt until puberty and that thereafter the aim of this energy, the satisfaction of this hunger, is to be found in a union of the genitals with a member of the opposite sex. The desire for such a union was understood to be instinctive and its purpose reproduction; sexual pleasure was merely an incentive to procreation. It was recognized that there are perverts who do not conform to this scheme, but such individuals are rare, and they are degenerates who alter in no way the facts of normal life. With this prevailing view Freud found himself in sharp disagreement. His experience led him to believe that the primary purpose of sex is not reproduction but pleasure, and sexual pleasure is a goal to which there are numerous roads. He pointed out that in the sexual aberrations there are variations from the so-called 'normal' instinct both in terms of object and of aim. The homosexual seeks his object in a member not of the opposite sex but of his own. Some perverts pursue their sexual objects in children, or animals, or in extreme cases, corpses. The object of sexual desire is by no means universally a person of the opposite sex. Nor is the libidinal aim always in the direction of a genital union. The *voyeur* and the exhibitionist derives his sexual pleasure from observing the sexual organs of others or from showing his own. There are those who ignore the genitals entirely and become fixated on other parts of the body: the anus, the mouth, the feet. Such people are not necessarily insane or degenerate, Freud insisted. Men and women who are 'normal' in every other respect as well as whole races or classes are found to deviate from the arbitrary sexual standards of heterosexual genital contact. Freud observed that the libido was the instinct least controlled by 'the higher psychic activities.' Any psychic or social abnormality will invariably affect the sex life of the individual, but sexual abnormalities often make themselves at home within thoroughly respectable and creative personalities, who have 'kept abreast of the human cultural development.'

This might appear as though Freud approved of the conventional standards of sexual morality, speaking of the control of sexual impulses by 'higher psychic activities' in the same breath with 'the human cultural development.' Actually, he was more than a little ambivalent about the restraints demanded by society. He believed that a certain inhibition of sexual activity is necessary if culture and civilization are to progress, but he was inclined to feel that the inhibitions demanded by western civilization were far too many. He looked with some nostalgia upon the ancients who placed their emphasis upon the sexual instinct itself and thought it ennobled base and mean objects, while modern man suspects the instinct and allows it expression only in the presence of a worthy object. In a somewhat later (1908) essay, *Civilized Sexual Morality and Modern Nervousness,* he discussed three stages in the development of sexual mores. In the first (and one cannot help wondering where Freud found such a society, even in antiquity) no restraint whatever was placed upon libidinal drives with respect either to object or aim. The second stage allowed all those forms of sexual activity which served to pro-create the species, and there are in fact numerous examples of this. In the third, and this represents modern western society, all forms of sex other than those which represent *legitimate* procreation are forbidden. Freud raised grave doubts whether sufficient compensation is offered in return for the sacrifices demanded, regarding such a rigid code as responsible for the alarming increase in nervous disorders and therefore endangering the culture itself.

To return to Freud's description of the character of the libido, he found from his study of sexual aberrations and of the sex life of children that the sexual instinct is made up of a number of component parts. He defined an instinct as the psychic manifestation of 'a continually flowing somatic source of stimulation' which is different from a stimulus, in that the latter represents an external excitation while the instinct operates internally. All instincts occupy the boundary between the psychic and the physical, and they derive their distinctive character from the particular bodily organs involved and from their aims. 'The source of the instinct is an exciting process in an organ, and the immediate aim of the instinct lies in the release of the organic stimulus.' [3] One

3. *Three Contributions to the Theory of Sex,* in *Basic Writings, op. cit.* p. 576.

might assume from this that Freud believed the libido to have its source in the genital organs and its aim in the relief from tension through orgasm, but such an assumption is mistaken. Freud found that sexual sensations are not confined to the genitals but are stimulated in numerous bodily areas which he labeled 'erogenous zones.' The mouth, the anus, the legs, the abdomen, almost any section of the body can be found to serve as the seat of erotic feelings, so that the libido is not confined to the genitals but is well-nigh ubiquitous. Even in normal sexual relations, various erogenous zones play significant roles in the preliminaries to coitus; kissing, touching, looking, fondling, even smelling all serve as 'prologues to the swelling act of the imperial theme.' The only distinction Freud made between the normal and the perverse in sex concentrated on the culmination of the sexual act. The stimulation of erogenous zones as preparation for the insertion of the penis into the vagina followed by orgasm is perfectly acceptable. Morbidity or perversion are characterized by a fixation on what are essentially preliminaries, and the achievement of orgasm by that means.

The importance of erogenous zones is evidenced not only by sexual aberrations and by the foreplay of normal coitus, but by the behavior of small children. The initial sexual experiences of all humans occur in infancy, and they are centered not in the genitals but in other parts of the body. The new-born babe discovers the meaning of pleasure first from sucking at his mother's breast. His primary concern is nourishment, but the universal phenomenon of non-nutritive sucking in infants, where fingers, toes, rattles, are vigorously attacked with pulling lips, indicates that pleasure is derived from the act of sucking itself, even when no milk flows into mouth and stomach. Freud called such pleasure libidinal, expanding the term to include all experiences productive of gratification not directly concerned with self-preservation. A sort of dualism between the primitive strivings of the unconscious and the censorship which repressed the dangerous urges had already manifested itself in Freud's thought. He elaborated this in his *Three Contributions* into a fully developed instinct theory, positing two sets of instincts: those having to do directly with the preservation and protection of the organism and those pursuing the goal of pleasure through the release of tension. The former he called the 'ego instincts,' the latter 'libido instincts.' 'The sexual activity leans first on one of the self-preservative functions and only later makes itself independent of it.' This relationship Freud called 'anaclitic' after the Latin verb *anaclino,* to lean on. The first libidinal experience of the infant is oral. The mouth, lips, and tongue are erogenous zones, sensitive to stimulation and pleasure quite apart from the needs of digestion. In this 'oral stage' through which all men must pass, Freud found what he regarded as the three essential characteristics of all infantile sexuality. 'It has its origin in an *anaclitic* relation to a physical function which is very important to life; it does not yet know any sexual object, that is, it is *auto-erotic;* and its sexual aim is under the control of an *erogenous zone.'* [4]

The next two stages of the child's psycho-sexual development, the anal and the genital, reveal these same three characteristics. Somewhere near the beginning of the second year of life, oral pleasure is supplemented by a new experience in connection with toilet training. The child discovers that withholding the fecal mass for a time until it passes through the anus with some violence of muscular contraction stimulates the mucous membranes pleasantly. Another anaclitic relationship brings to the fore another predestined erogenous zone in another auto-erotic experience. Somewhere in the vicinity of four years of age, the genitals are activated by the attention directed to urination and by parental provisions for the cleanliness of penis and vagina. A preliminary tickling sensation, Freud believed, is felt in the genitals during the nursing period, but this erogenous zone does not become prominent until the later stage when masturbation (used in the sense of playing with the genitals) begins. This infantile masturbation is, according to Freud, universal, but it is almost invariably forgotten in later life. He advanced the theory that the faint and indistinct character of most memories of early childhood is a result of the desire to repress the recollection of masturbation, and that such experiences as are recalled are simply

4. *Ibid.* p. 587.

displaced reminiscences of sexual activity. Seduction is frequently responsible for initiation into the mysteries of masturbation; the younger child is instructed by an older person. But an external agent is by no means necessary to Freud's theory. Inner tension within the genitals is quite sufficient to make the child begin to play with his sexual organs.

This new understanding of infantile sexuality provided Freud with a substitute for his previous formulations, which had been undermined by the discovery that many of the childhood sexual traumas recounted to him by his early patients were pure fabrications. His new etiology of the neuroses replaced infantile experiences of seduction or rape with the repression of childhood sexuality, whether of fact or fantasy. He recognized that many children engage in various types of sexual play without developing neuroses in later life. Even seduction and rape do not inevitably produce serious disturbance. Only where repression has occurred, where guilt feelings push childhood experiences or imaginings under the rug of the unconscious, do neuroses result. It is therefore in one sense irrelevant whether repressed memories of early sexual activity have any basis in fact. Guilt and repression may be set in motion by the activity of the child's imagination, by his entertainment of forbidden fantasies. It is the reaction to infantile sexuality which is decisive. If sexual acts or impulses are regarded with fear and horror, hysteria will result, while obsessional neuroses are reproaches directed by feelings of guilt against pleasurable experiences or desires. Without repression, no neurosis occurs.

In all infantile sexuality the composite character of the libido begins to make itself apparent. It attaches itself to the mouth, the anus, the genitals as *predestined* erogenous zones, but any other portion of the body may take on the quality of an erogenous zone, so that the quality of the stimulus is more important in the production of pleasure than the nature of the bodily reaction. What gives rise to the sexual impulse is a feeling of sensitivity, of itching or tension in a given zone, and this somewhat painful sensation demands relief by some external stimulus which removes the tension and produces a feeling of gratification. Freud regarded the sexual processes as essentially chemical and expressed the half-hope, half-conviction, that the growing knowledge of the chemistry of the body would one day render the libido theory obsolete. He had done considerable laboratory research in his early years and always clung to a strong biological orientation, but he never overlooked the importance of environment and cultural influences. Some of the contemporary 'cultural' analysts have accused him of a passion for biology which blinded him to social conditioning (see chapter VIII), but they are somewhat unfair to Freud. He insisted that neither the constitutional or hereditary factors of sexuality nor the cultural pressures could function alone. Both forces play an indispensable role in the normal libidinal development as well as in the production of a neurosis.

Under favorable circumstances, at least in civilized life, the genital stage is followed by a period of latency which lasts until the onset of puberty. Parental training and social conditioning build around the libido restraining walls of shame, loathing, and morality. The child suppresses his infantile libidinal drives and undergoes the two-fold process of 'reaction-formation' and 'sublimation.' In the first, he learns from observing his parents and other adults that what previously gave him great pleasure, playing with feces, masturbation, displaying himself, should fill him with disgust and shame. Accordingly, he begins to react to sexuality as do the important persons in his environment and gradually the whole process becomes automatic, a reaction-formation. In fact, he overcompensates for these earlier drives, reacting excessively against them.

In sublimation, he begins to direct his sexual energy elsewhere, notably into the learning process. Freud regarded sublimation as essential. Continual masturbation from the genital stage through puberty would, in his view, result in a weakening of the powers at the child's disposal for the all-important tasks of education. Freud never advocated completely unbridled sexual activity, for that, he believed, would result in the stultifying of all civilization and culture. Only primitive savages use up all of their libidinal energies in direct sexual behavior, and this is the very reason why they remain primitives. In the development both of the race and the individual child, Freud regarded sublimation of libido as absolutely essential to the accomplishment of higher ends. He saw the statesman, the artist, the poet, as well as the growing child, as all deflecting sexual energy into their tasks. The latency period is both normal and desirable in civilized life.

With the beginning of puberty, two tasks remain to be accomplished if the individual is to enjoy a normal sex life. Both have been started in infancy and now await completion: the establishment of the primacy of the genitals and the achievement of object-love. Childhood sexuality is under the control of erogenous zones which do not cease to function at puberty, but rather are subordinated to a preparatory role. They are stimulated in sexual foreplay as a prelude to the union of the genitals and ensuing orgasm. The pleasure they bestow becomes a means rather than an end in itself. The woman has a further task, the transition from preoccupation with the clitoris to vaginal sensations. Freud was, on the basis of this, to make the later observation that the anal stage in childhood is followed not directly by the genital stage but by an intervening phallic period, in which attention is centered by boys on the penis and by girls on the female counterpart, the clitoris. At puberty, however, the normal course of events moves toward the subordination of the clitoris to a preliminary function, acting as an erogenous zone, leading to the penetration of the vagina. The second task of puberty is the movement from auto-erotic sensuality to object-love, the detachment of the libido from the self and its transference to other persons. This process is begun during the genital stage of childhood by the Oedipus complex, in which the boy loves his mother and the girl her father. If all progresses normally, this love is suppressed by shame and morality together with the incest taboo, and when it is re-activated at puberty, it is attached to other members of the opposite sex.

It will readily be seen how tortuous a path the individual must follow in order to arrive at normal sexuality in adult life (see Table I). All of this represents the *normal* development of the libido which is accomplished in the maturing process. Freud regarded the whole process as organically conditioned, education playing only a secondary and assisting role. His tendency to emphasize the biological at the expense of the cultural manifested itself in his

TABLE I

The Stages of Psychosexual Development

STAGE OF DEVELOPMENT	CHARACTERISTICS
ORAL STAGE Birth to one year	Chief erogenous zone is mouth. Pleasure derived from sucking. Anaclitic, auto-erotic.
ANAL STAGE One year to three years	Chief erogenous zone is mucous membrane of anus. Pleasure derived from withholding and releasing feces. Anaclitic, auto-erotic.
PHALLIC STAGE— GENITAL STAGE Four years to six years	Chief erogenous zone is penis or clitoris. Pleasure derived from masturbation. Oedipus complex strong, but stage is still auto-erotic.
LATENT PERIOD Six years to twelve years	Libido held in check by forces of shame, loathing, and morality (reaction-formations). Sexual energy sublimated into processes of learning. Taboo against incest subdues Oedipus complex.
PUBERTY— MATURITY Twelve years on	Libido reasserts itself directly as sexual apparatus begins to mature. Primacy of genitals established and erogenous zones subordinated to foreplay (in woman clitoris gives way to vagina). Auto-erotic behavior abandoned for object-love in member of opposite sex.

further elaboration of his theory of the etiology of the neuroses. Sexual perversions, he believed, are caused by two factors. Either the erogenous zone on which the pervert's attention has become fixated is *constitutionally* overdeveloped, or he has regressed to an earlier stage of development. If, when a river leaves its bed to forge new channels, it meets with too great resistance, it will return to the old path already cleared. So when an individual encounters hardship or failure in his progress of sexual development, he will return to an earlier form of adaptation, one which he has already successfully mastered. This process of retreat Freud called regression. Sexual aberrations are as common as they are because everyone has in childhood experienced the pleasure derived from the non-genital erogenous zones. Homosexuality is a particularly easy path because all humans are basically and organically bisexual, carrying within themselves hormones and secretions from both parents. The childhood history of most individuals reveals a strong attachment to members of the same sex, in girlish 'crushes' and in boyish 'hero-worship.' Freud was later to make much of this latent homosexuality. He regarded sadism and masochism as two sides of one coin, the active and the passive, and both as universal phenomena. All children are 'polymorphous perverse.' They have an organic predisposition to the perversions and hence can easily be seduced into any form of sexual activity.

The normal person escapes the sexual perversions in adult life, but what of the neurotic who is not sexually perverse? What importance do these constitutional predispositions have for him? Here Freud maintained that the neurosis is the negative of the perversion. There is an abnormal repression of the libido in the neurotic, a strong reluctance to allow sexual-energy release. But no dam can hold back the tremendous power indefinitely; the libido must break through in one way or another, and by means of what Freud called 'conversion,' the sexual drive is transformed into symptoms, which frequently symbolize dramatically what has been repressed. It is not only normal libidinal urges that are repressed in neuroses, but also perverse desires. Freud believed that all neurotics display, under analysis, unconscious strivings toward homosexuality, and that many reveal repressed longings to use the mouth or anus in place of the genitals. The active-passive complex of looking-exhibiting, or sadism-masochism, is likewise widely encountered in the unconscious of hysterics and other psychoneurotics. The repression usually covers a vast reservoir of sexual hunger, which contains many forbidden yearnings. Freud originally called this repression a 'defense,' but he recognized that the appearance of symptoms represents a failure of the defense, for the libido has broken through in the symptomatology.

To sum up, then, the libido is like a mighty river, forging forward with enormous energy. The normal course of the stream flows through the stages enumerated to its goal in the sea of adult sexuality. But it may miss that goal under two circumstances: the development of either a perversion or a neurosis. In the former, it is lost in a side channel, whirling round and round without going forward. This occurs either because the side channel is unusually deep and captures the river, or because the stream has retreated to its old bed, finding the terrain ahead too resistant. In the neuroses, the stream is dammed up too tightly, but it seeps through the cracks, muddied and adulterated so that only the expert can recognize it for what it is. Only if the river is diverted or blocked do neuroses develop, which goes back to, 'no neurosis is possible with a normal *vita sexualis.*' [5]

With the *Three Contributions to the Theory of Sex,* published in 1905, Freud laid the foundation of his interpretation of sex, and for the most part this foundation remained unaltered for the rest of his career. He grew increasingly reluctant, however, to confine himself to the diagnosis and treatment of emotional disturbances. He had, as he confessed in his *Autobiography,* a strong theoretical inclination which he held in check in his early years, but the increasing acceptance of his ideas gave him the security he needed to expand their implications. Everywhere he looked, he found libido — in all cultural achievement, in art, in friendship, in religion. This last he developed in *Totem and Taboo,* which appeared in 1913. His interest in the Oedipus complex led him to the anthropologists' studies of primitive tribes and their discoveries of the savage's dread of incest. With typical German thoroughness, he went through all the literature available: J. B. Frazer, E. B. Tylor, R. R. Marrett, W. Robertson Smith. He discovered that totemism is found among primitive tribes scattered all over the world. Totemism is a type of religio-social organization in which the members of a tribe regard themselves as members

5. *Collected Papers,* vol. i, p. 276.

of one family group, descended from a totem object, usually some animal such as a wolf, a bear, or a turtle. Rigid taboos are set up, prohibiting sexual relations between two members of the same totem. Exogamy, the practice of marrying outside the group, is universally practiced in a totemic society. The savage displays an even greater fear and horror of incest than civilized man, building the most elaborate barriers to prevent it and even extending those barriers beyond actual consanguinity to fellow members of the tribe. Freud was strongly inclined to believe that probably membership in the totem originally descended through the mother, though he admitted that he could not substantiate his belief from the data he had. If matrilineal descent were the rule, a son could not have sexual relations with his mother or sister because they belonged to the same totem, and the father's exclusive right to the women would be protected. But if, as actually seems to be the case in many primitive societies, the descent is traced through the father, there is no totemic barrier to incest between mother and son, for the mother belongs to a different group. It is not difficult to understand Freud's preference for maternal descent, since this provided him with the origins of the Oedipus complex, where the father forbids the son to possess the wife-mother. Patrilineal practices were conveniently ignored.

Freud turned his attention next to the primitive's system of taboos, prohibitions attaching to various persons, places, and objects. Without laying too much stress on the point, and recognizing the obvious limitations of such a procedure, he compared primitive taboos with the phobias and compulsions of present-day obsessional neurotics. Freud believed that the situations and acts feared by the neurotic always, in analysis, betray a sexual origin. What the obsessional fears is the activation of some repressed sexual impulse, and the fear attaches itself, by a process of unconscious association, to things extremely remote from the original desire. If, by chance, the forbidden should be transgressed, then the neurotic has an elaborate ritual he goes through by way of penance in order to ward off the calamity which he is sure will follow. Freud called attention to the similarities to the savage's

complicated prohibitions and provisions for cleansing and atone-
ment following a violation of a taboo, raising the question whether
the taboos of both primitive man and modern obsessional man
might not spring from the fear of repressed impulses.

This preliminary exploration of aboriginal religion led Freud
to advance an ingenious theory about the origins of totem and
taboo. The problem which perplexed the anthropologists was
why such rigid prohibitions were set up to prevent the killing of
the totem animal and the incidence of incest and why both taboos
were relaxed on certain ceremonial occasions when the whole
tribe joined in a sacramental eating of their totemic ancestor,
culminating in an orgy of indulgence in forbidden sex. Freud's
solution was based on an hypothesis advanced by Darwin that the
earliest species of men lived in small herds dominated by a father-
chief. Freud posited the theory that this leader was extremely
jealous of his exclusive right to the females of the group, and as
the young males began to mature and to display sexual interest,
they were driven away from the herd. One day these exiled
brothers banded themselves together, hurled themselves on their
father and killed him, devouring his body, hoping thereby to gain
for themselves some of his power and strength. But this terrible
deed did not win for them the ends they sought. Since the brothers
were many, no one of them could take the father's place without
first defeating all the others. And feelings of shame and guilt
seized upon the patricides so that they atoned by denying themselves the very thing they had sought: the possession of their
father's women. In order to prevent a repetition of the bloody
event, they set up the totemic taboos, symbolizing their father in
the totem animal who was not to be killed and forbidding coitus
with the women of the tribe. The ceremonial ritual in which the
sacred animal is killed and eaten is a commemoration of the
original act, serving as a kind of catharsis. Freud admitted that this
was a long leap in the dark, referring to it in his *Autobiography*
as not so much his hypothesis as his 'vision,' but he felt that it
accounted for all the facts more adequately than any other theory
he had encountered. He found a predilection for totemism,

identifying the father with an animal, among modern children (cf. 'Analysis of a Phobia of a Five Year Old Boy,' *Collected Papers,* vol. III, no. 2) as well as among primitives. So religion seemed to him based on the Oedipus complex; man projects his male parent into an omnipotent Father-God who is both feared and loved. Freud later developed this theory still further in his *Future of an Illusion* (1928), tracing the operation of the libido in the religious impulse.

Up until 1914, Freud's theory of the instincts was relatively simple. He divided all human instincts into two classes: those of the ego, aiming at self-preservation, and those of the libido, striving after pleasure. In connection with his studies of primitive animism set forth in *Totem and Taboo,* Freud found certain modifications of that theory necessary. The animistic beliefs of savages see all natural objects inhabited by spirits and all natural processes, such as rain, the growth of crops, sickness, susceptible to influence by magic. This is the first stage of human cultural development and strikingly parallels the earliest consciousness of children. Both are characterized by what Freud called 'omnipotence of thought,' an attitude described in the popular song, 'Wishing Will Make It So.' The primitive uses magic to bring about his desires; the child uses his imagination; but both believe that their thoughts are effective causes for events. This stage in both the primitive and in the child is succeeded by a secondary one, when the omnipotence is projected onto the gods in the one case and onto the parents in the other. The illusion of one's own potency is abandoned, though not entirely, since the powerful ones can still occasionally be influenced. The final stage is achieved both in the culture and in the individual with the arrival of science and maturity, where all ideas of omnipotence are abandoned and man's fragile and finite state is accepted realistically. Society progresses from magic to religion to science; the individual moves from auto-erotism to narcissism to object-love. This middle stage of narcissism represented a new development in Freud's theory of sexual growth. He found that there is an intermediate step between auto-erotism and object-love, where the person has an object for his libidinal drives, but that object is none other than himself. 'For the purposes of analysis the ego impulses and the libidinous impulse cannot be separated from each other.' [6]

Freud did not altogether abandon the opposition between ego and libido, but he did modify his instinct theory to conform to the data provided by further clinical experience, and this modification he described in a paper published in 1914, *On Narcissism: An Introduction*. Narcissism is a sexual perversion where the individual 'treats his own body in the same way as otherwise the body of a sexual object is treated,' deriving his pleasure and orgasm from looking at and fondling his own self. This bears close resemblance to the psychotic state of paranoia and dementia praecox, where the person withdraws almost completely into himself, cutting off all contact with the outside world. He has no object of interest or concern except himself. In general, Freud believed that all perversions and most psychoses represented a regression to an earlier stage of development, and this is what he now asserted with respect to narcissism and megalomania, that there is in the normal process of growth a primary self-adoration to which the adult narcissist or megalomaniac simply returns. His preoccupation with the self is not a new state but an old one. The mental life of small children reveals the same overestimation of the power of thoughts and wishes which is characteristic of all megalomania. The small child believes that his desires and ideas are magic: they are effective causes of events. All of this leads to the conclusion that there must be an original investment of the libido in the self which is later exchanged for investment in others, in objects (as opposed to subject). At this early stage, it is impossible to distinguish between ego and libido, so closely are they bound together. During this narcissistic period, the ego instincts display a libidinal aspect, and the libido is attracted to the ego. Thus, Freud modified his earlier division of the instincts into ego and libido and further subdivided the latter into ego-libido and object-libido. The ego is a reservoir out of which the libido rises. In this earliest state, the ego is weak and insecure, requiring all of its libido for itself, but as the ego acquires strength and confidence, it can afford to extend its libido to others.

6. *Totem and Taboo* in *Basic Writings*, p. 876.

The first attachments or cathexes, as Freud called them, of the libido are anaclitic. The infant's relationship to the mother's breast is narcissistic; he thinks of it as a part of himself, making no distinction between himself and this important external object. This attitude extends to the whole person of the mother who takes care of him. He 'introjects' his mother into his own ego and loves her as he loves himself. Then he discovers, as he grows, that his mother is separate, that she is not subject but object. He continues to love her, and this is his first experience with object-libido, his first investment of the libido outside himself. His libido is to his ego as the pseudopodia are to the main body of a protozoan. The fluid mass of protoplasm can put forth a part of itself as a 'pseudo-foot' and then withdraw it again, resuming its original shape, if it can be said to have one! So the ego can invest its libido in objects, in persons other than the self, but it can also withdraw the libido back into itself. The libido is limited in its quantity and self-love impoverishes object-love, while love for others is purchased at the expense of love of the self. At one end of the scale is the megalomaniac, whose libido is wholly turned inward without concern for others, while at the other is the man in love, whose libido is so totally absorbed in his beloved that his own ego is humble, self-abasing, and self-forgetful. If his love is returned, his ego is nourished and warmed by the affection directed to him, but if he loves in vain, his ego becomes pauperized, and he will suffer feelings of inferiority and worthlessness.

This narcissistic ego-libido can be observed, Freud believed, not only in small children and in paraphrenics, but also in relatively normal adults. In sleep and in organic disease, the libidinal attachments to outer objects are withdrawn into the self. When men are ill or injured or think they are (hypochondria), there is very little libido to invest in others; the self demands it all. The reverse side of the coin is the person in love, but Freud declared that there is a narcissictic object-love as well, when the ego really loves itself in the beloved. A homosexual may love persons who seem to him to be like himself as he now is, or as he once was, or as he would like to be. Or, some individuals love in an anaclitic fashion, seeking libidinal objects among persons who remind them of their mother or father, but in any case the totality of one's libidinal energy is never wholly directed to others. There is always a residue which remains attached to the self.

The ego, whose concern is for self-preservation and adjustment to the real world, refuses untrammeled expression to the urges of the libido, whose concern is for pleasure, since the satisfaction of some libidinal urges would endanger the self. When the ego is so constituted that libidinal desires are not even permitted to attain consciousness, repression is taking place. Repression proceeds from the self-respect of the ego or from what Freud called the ego-ideal, a measuring rod by which a man judges himself, a self-portrait of himself as he would like to be. 'To this ideal ego is now directed the self-love which the real ego enjoyed in childhood. The narcissism seems now to be displaced on to this new ideal ego, which, like the infantile ego, deems itself the possessor of all perfections.' [7] This ego-ideal Freud was later to elaborate into the super-ego, but for the present he contented himself with the statement that it has the same characteristics as that called the 'conscience' with the function of watching the real self and measuring it according to the ideal. The ideal ego he regarded as the product of parental criticism and other environmental influences. This whole formulation plays a central role in Freud's theory of sex, for it is the ego-ideal which is the recipient of self-love, which represses libidinal drives unacceptable to it, and which in certain cases determines the object of the libido. The person who loves in a narcissistic way frequently seeks as his object someone who possesses excellences which he does not have but wants to get in order to attain his ideal.

This scheme of object-libido and ego-libido, Freud maintained between the years 1914 and 1920. In 1920, he modified his instinct theory once again, producing a third formulation which he held until his death. This final form found expression in his *Beyond the Pleasure Principle,* though certain anticipations of it are to be found in a paper entitled *The Instincts and Their Vicissitudes,* published in 1915. The 'pleasure principle,' Freud called the economic aspect of mental life, the strong tendency of the human

7. *Collected Papers,* vol. IV, p. 51.

organism to seek the maximum of pleasure and the minimum of pain. Pain, or 'unpleasure,' as he sometimes called it, results from an *increase* in excitation or stimulation, while pleasure results from an alleviation of the stimulus, a relief from excitation. Freud regarded the chief function of the nervous system as the reduction of stimulation to the lowest possible level, seeking in so far as possible to maintain the organism in an altogether quiescent condition. All the instincts have pleasure as their sole aim, but the pleasure principle is modified by other factors. The reality principle which prevents the direct expression of instinctive urges in such a way that the organism would be endangered, is under the control of the ego's concern for self-preservation. The pleasure principle is not entirely abandoned, but the reality principle insists on the postponement of certain satisfactions and the substitution of safer methods of attaining pleasure for less acceptable ones. The ego, charged as it is with adjustment to reality, knows that the direct and immediate fulfillment of certain desires for pleasure would cost a price not worth paying. Freud believed that the sexual instincts, however, are the least educable, the least tractable to control by the reality principle and frequently force activity 'to the detriment of the organism as a whole.' When the quest for pleasure becomes so imperious that the reality principle is overthrown, the action of the instincts results in pain, though their goal is pleasure. But the reality principle is in reality only a modification of the pleasure principle, since it seeks the well-being of the ego.

Freud had discovered, however, what seemed to be an exception to the pleasure principle, in certain childhood games and in the traumatic neuroses, a phenomenon which he called 'the compulsion to repeat.' This compulsion recovers from the past experiences which were decidedly unpleasant and which had no connection with instinctual drives. In the transference which takes place in psychoanalysis, where the patient transfers onto the therapist all of the emotional attitudes he felt toward his parents, many extremely painful childhood circumstances are re-enacted. The psychoneurotic's infantile sexuality has perished in an almost disastrous fashion. His sexual curiosity was left unsatisfied and he

felt increasingly helpless and unable to do for himself. His attachment to the parent of the opposite sex was disrupted, sometimes by
the arrival of another child, arousing jealousy and hostility. As
the demands made upon him increased with his advancing years,
he felt rejected and unloved and he carries into adult life a painful
scar on his ego's self-assurance. Yet all of these unwanted situations
and painful emotions are relived by the patient in his relationship
to the doctor. He feels once more unappreciated and uncared for;
he compulsively repeats the anguish of his infancy. Such an experience led Freud to the conviction that there exists in the mind
a compulsion to repeat which is 'beyond the pleasure principle,'
which is more primitive and more fundamental than that principle,
and which sets it aside.

'What follows,' Freud wrote, 'is speculation, often far-fetched
speculation,' [8] but he was determined to pursue the implications
of the repetition-compulsion. He theorized that the task of the
mental apparatus is the reception of stimuli from without and
instinctive impulses from within, attempting to protect the organism against too powerful or too dangerous quantities of either.
The primary process of mental life is its inner unconscious core
upon which is overlaid the comparatively thin veneer of consciousness. The higher strata of the mental apparatus (consciousness with its pre-conscious vestibule, containing those thoughts
and ideas which are potentially conscious) has the task of binding
the instinctual excitation which rises out of the unconscious. Until
that excitation has been bound and channeled, the pleasure principle cannot operate; all energy must be directed to lashing down the
highly dangerous energy which is loosed. This is the first significance of the compulsion to repeat: the ego is repeating its experience with an unbound instinct, unpleasant as that experience may
be, because it must bring that instinct under its control before
it can do anything else. The second and more important significance is that the repetition-compulsion represents an attempt to
return to an earlier stage of life, a stage when the unbound instinct
had not yet broken loose. Freud believed that 'an instinct is a

8. *Beyond the Pleasure Principle*, Liveright Publishing Co., New York, 1950,
p. 27.

compulsion inherent in organic life to restore an earlier state of things which the living entity has been obliged to abandon under the pressure of external disturbing forces.' He found a kind of inertia in all organic life, a tendency to maintain, and failing that an attempt to return to, an altogether undisturbed and unstimulated existence. If pain is defined as excitation and pleasure as the relief of that excitation, then the greatest pleasure of all is death. Freud advanced the thesis that there is a conservative tendency in all things living, a reluctance to change, and that what appears to be growth and development may be no more than a striving to return to the original state. The goal of life cannot, he thought, be anything other than a movement back to an initial state from which the organism has departed. Since inanimate matter existed before life put in its appearance, and since it is true, Freud believed, that all things living die because of *internal* reasons, then one is compelled to say that 'the goal of all life is death.'

But in certain forms of life this motion toward death can be interrupted, halted, and even reversed. The protista, a simple form of microscopic water animal, engages regularly in what is called 'conjugation,' in which two individuals coalesce for a time, after which they separate, still as two individuals. No cell division occurs, but the process has a rejuvenating effect on both individuals so that they go on living, whereas without conjugation they would die. This fusion, Freud thought, may be taken as typical of the effect produced by all sexual union. If the 'death instinct' leads to an equalization of chemical tensions within the body, reducing all activity to inactivity, then the introduction of fresh stimuli, the combination and re-grouping of living cells in higher, more complex forms prolongs the process of 'breaking down,' or 'living down,' those chemical tensions. The sexual instincts seek for life, and they can be called 'life instincts,' or even self-preservative instincts which are set against the inner impulse to death, the so-called Nirvana principle.

But what of the theory that *all* instincts are conservative, seeking a return to an earlier stage? Is this also true of the sexual instinct? This question confronted Freud with serious difficulties.

He experimented briefly with the theory that the embryo repeats the origins of organic life (ontogeny recapitulates phylogeny), but he could find no really significant scientific evidence to support such a theory. He retreated into myth — the legend of the androgynes, recounted by Aristophanes in Plato's *Symposium*. According to this myth, man was originally created double — two men, two women, and the man-woman androgynes. Zeus split them apart, and ever since the two halves have been striving to regain their original unity, a convenient explanation of sex and love whether heterosexual or homosexual. Freud asked, 'Shall we follow the hint given us by the poet-philosopher, and venture upon the hypothesis that living substance was at the time of its coming to life torn apart into small particles which have ever since endeavored to reunite through the sexual instinct?' [9] This was to move into the realm of utterly unbridled speculation, and Freud withdrew with the confession that he was dealing with pure hypothesis without the solid foundation of his two previous instinct theories. He did, however, in spite of his recognition of the purely theoretical character of his life and death instincts, continue to believe in them to the end of his career. He no longer saw the sexual or libidinal instincts as opposed to the ego or self-preservative drives. On the contrary, he found them unified in what he called eros — the impulse toward life, toward combination and development. Against the eros instincts are set those of thanatos — the movement toward death, toward the cessation of all stimulation and excitation, the breakdown of metabolic processes, and the re-establishment of inorganic matter. In the tension between these two sets of instincts, all of life is lived. The death instinct is never to be found in its pure form but always in association with the sexual instincts. The two most notable examples of this blending are sadism and masochism, but all of life is an ambivalence of affection and anger.

In 1923 Freud published a book entitled *The Ego and the Id,* containing what he was later to call 'The Anatomy of the Mental Personality.' He organized and reclassified material that had appeared in his previous writings, describing the mental apparatus

9. *Ibid.* p. 80.

in terms of the familiar 'ego, super-ego and id.' What was new in this formulation was the term super-ego, which he had previously called the ego-ideal, and the concept of the id, or literally 'it.' (The Latin *ego* is the equivalent of the German *Ich* and the English I, while the Latin *id* is rendered into German as *Es* and into English as it.) The reason for making this further differentiation was Freud's discovery that the 'unconscious' was far more complex than he had realized, comprising not only a dark reservoir of primitive instincts but also part of the ego-ideal, and even of the ego itself. Therefore, a sharper delineation within the unconscious became desirable if not necessary. Freud saw all human organisms entering life as pure id, pure instinctual drive. Gradually contact with the external world forces the beginnings of self-awareness, of the ego, which initiates the operation of the reality principle. These beginnings are characterized by the process of incorporation: whatever the ego needs, it identifies with itself, takes into itself, making little or no distinction between subject and object. When it becomes necessary to accept such a distinction, when, for example, the mother's breast is withdrawn, the child learns that the mother is 'other' than himself and is forced to an awareness of the distinction between his ego and other objects. 'The ego is that part of the id which has been modified by the direct influence of the external world.'

In its contact with the external world, the ego learns that certain instinctive desires of the id are socially unacceptable and dangerous. The impulses of the id, including the sexual instincts, know nothing of society, civilization, taboos, consequences. They are blind and seek expression in the pursuit of immediate gratification and pleasure. The ego has the task of mediating between these constant demands for pleasure and the demands of reality. The ego controls the gateway to action, and Freud used the metaphor of a horse and its rider to describe the relation of the id to the ego. The rider has to try to hold in check the horse who is really stronger than he is, often guiding his mount where it wants to go. 'So in the same way the ego constantly carries into action the wishes of the id as if they were its own.' The ego is caught between the very powerful instinctive drives of the id on the one hand and the equally powerful restrictions of society on the other.

As if the poor ego did not have enough problems, still another protagonist is added to the drama: the super-ego. As the ego begins to be aware of the distinction between itself and other objects, it also knows that it wants and needs some of those objects either for self-preservation or for pleasure. This need, or desire, Freud called an object-cathexis, which derives its energy from the id, and which has strong erotic overtones. When the ego forces the id to give up a sexual object, that same ego frequently 'introjects' the object into itself, modifying itself to resemble the desired object and thereby drawing closer to the id. 'When the ego assumes the features of the object, it forces itself, so to speak, on the id as a love-object and tries to make good the loss of the object by saying, "Look I am so like the object, you can as well love me." ' [10] This involves a desexualization, an abandonment of the sexual designs which the id had on the original object, and Freud suggests that this is the path followed by all sublimation: changing object-libido into narcissistic libido, and then giving the libidinal energy another, desexualized aim.

In the process of introjecting desired objects into the self and desexualizing them, the earliest identifications which the child makes are decisive, exercising a profound influence on his subsequent career. The first of these identifications is with the parents, more specifically with the mother, which is based in the first instance not on an object-cathexis but on an earlier, more primitive stage in which the child makes no differentiation at all between himself and his mother. The libidinal object-cathexis comes later and then is given up by means of the introjection just described. This process is complicated, Freud believed, by two factors: 'the triangular character of the Oedipus situation and the constitutional bisexuality of each individual.' The small boy begins with an object-cathexis toward his mother which is built on his earlier identification with her, through the breast. He has a similar identification with his father, based upon paternal ministering to his infantile needs. These two attitudes exist for a time side by side, identification with the father and object-cathexis with erotic over-

10. *The Ego and the Id,* The Hogarth Press, London, 1927, p. 37.

tones toward the mother. As his sexual wishes for his mother grow in strength, the boy finds his father a rival, and the Oedipus complex is established. Ambivalence toward the father begins to operate, feelings of hostility mingle with those of love and identification. A desire is born to get rid of the father and take his place with the mother. If the Oedipus complex is successfully resolved, the boy gives up his object-cathexis for his mother, replacing it by an intensified identification with either the mother or the father. From the previous discussion one would suspect that the identification would be with the mother, since it is the maternal object-cathexis that is abandoned. Actually, the normal expectation is just the reverse: the boy identifies strongly with the father, the girl with the mother. How is this to be explained? Freud answered by pointing to the fact of bisexuality. All humans are the products of both male and female characteristics, so that the Oedipus complex is really two-sided, positive and negative. A boy not only feels affectionate toward his mother and hostile to his father, but also has feminine desires for his father with corresponding hostility and jealousy toward his mother. The dissolution of the Oedipus complex, then, means that *both* parents are identified with the ego as a substitute for object-cathexes directed toward them. It is the relative strength of the masculine-feminine sexual disposition which determines which identification will prove the stronger. Men who are organically and constitutionally more masculine will identify more powerfully with the father and mature heterosexually, while those with a more predominant feminine bias will lean toward the mother and become homosexual, in inclination and desire if not in fact.

The result of all this is the creation of the super-ego, which is not only a deposit left by the earliest object-cathexes of the id, but also a reaction-formation against those choices. It says to the ego both 'You ought to be like your father (or mother) in such a way as this' and 'You ought not to be like your father (or mother) in such a way as that.' The super-ego is the end-product of taking into the self objects toward which sexual desire was once directed. Parental commands and prohibitions become the demands and taboos of the super-ego, which serves as the agent of morality, of culture, of all that is high and lofty and ideal. It is the censor in the form of conscience that oversees all thoughts and deeds. It measures the actual accomplishments of the ego and either praises or blames as the ego falls short of or lives up to the ideals demanded. The severity of the super-ego depends, in some measure, upon the strictness of the parents, since the super-ego is made in the image of the parents, or more exactly in the image of the parents' super-egos. But in some cases the super-ego is harsh and relentless even where parents have been gentle and kind, keeping threats and punishments to a minimum. It is the function of the super-ego to set up high ideals, to watch over conduct, and to punish failure to live up to those ideals with feelings of guilt. The super-ego is the important agent of repression, refusing to allow thoughts which are inconsistent with its ideals to rise into consciousness.

The poor ego, then, is beset on three sides: by the instincts in the id which demand release, by external reality which insists that its restrictions be observed, and by the super-ego, which constantly holds up a high and lofty ideal to which it commands conformity. The id is entirely unconscious, only projecting its desires into consciousness in the form of thoughts or images; the super-ego is largely unconscious, while the ego is partly conscious, partly pre-conscious, and partly unconscious. Freud always insisted that this was a dynamic and not a topographical description of the human personality. He referred to it as the mythology of psychoanalysis, recognizing the impossibility of assigning any place in the brain or nervous system to any of these structures.

It will be noted that in most of the foregoing discussion of the various stages of sexual development, the masculine gender has been used, a usage neither altogether accidental nor entirely a bow to common parlance where the male pushes the woman behind him. Freud believed that there is a special process which applies to the sexual development of women. In addition to passing through the oral, anal, phallic (clitoris), and genital stages, which she has in common with her brothers, as she does the Oedipus complex, the latency period, and puberty, she must perform two tasks peculiar to her sex if she is to arrive at full maturity. She must make a transition both in her own genital pleasure, from clitoris to vagina, and in her choice of sexual object, from mother to father. Neither of these applies to the boy, who once having discovered the penis can enjoy it for the rest of his life and who can maintain his infantile attachment to the mother in the form of his subsequent sexual pursuit of women. The girl has 'to change both her erotogenic zone and her object, while the boy keeps both of them unchanged.' [11]

The mother is the primary object of attachment and identification for both son and daughter, for it is she who breast-feeds, bathes, and dresses the infants. The daughter must substitute for this primal cathexis an interest in and desire for the opposite sex, symbolized by the father. Freud rejected any simple idea of a basic heterosexuality as explanation for the change, convinced that it was far more complex than that. He pointed to the frequent metamorphosis of a girl's love for her mother into hatred with the accompanying complaints that the mother weaned her too soon or deserted her for another sibling or deprived her of pleasure by forbidding erotic play. The mother robs the child of the three most important things in life: food, affection, and pleasure. Yet all of these thefts are characteristic of the mother-son relationship as well, and they engender hostility and resentment in the boy also, but they do not overcome the tender feelings toward the mother. What is different in the girl's case? The difference, said Freud, is to be found in the castration complex.

This experience plays the strongest role in the resolution of the Oedipus complex in the boy. He sees the female genitals and is aware of the lack of a penis, a lack which he relates to threats made or phantasied in connection with earlier masturbation. He fears that if he pursues his desire to eliminate the father and possess the mother, he, too, will lose his penis. He suffers castration anxiety, which is strong enough to dissolve the Oedipus complex, indeed to submerge all sexual activity, and the latency period begins. The castration complex begins in the girl in the identical way — with the sight of the genital organs of the op-

11. *New Introductory Lectures on Psychoanalysis,* W. W. Norton and Company, Inc., New York, 1933, p. 162.

posite sex. She reacts with envy, wishing that she too had something like that. The important point in the experience is that she
blames her mother for her unhappy lack and turns instead to her
father who possesses the desired penis. So it goes in normal development, but when the castration complex is severely traumatic, the girl may respond by either giving up sex altogether
(frigidity) or by acting as though she did have a penis (homosexuality). Under normal circumstances, the desire for the penis
is replaced by the desire for a child, a child begotten by the
father, and this ushers the girl into the Oedipus complex. Notice
that the boy terminates the Oedipus complex by way of castration anxiety, while for the girl the castration complex is the gateway into the Oedipal triangle. This has two important results:
first, the boy replaces the attachment to his mother and father
with the construction of a severe super-ego, while the girl never
entirely gives up her attachment to her father; and second, this
attachment means that the female super-ego 'cannot attain the
strength and independence which gives it its cultural importance.' Women do not have the same capacity for cultural creativity as men because their Oedipus complex is resolved in a
different, less complete fashion. Further, women are apt to be
more narcissistic than men, attempting to compensate for their
deficiency, and hence being loved is to them more important
than loving. Freud capped his deprecation of the female sex by
declaring that although the libido is neither masculine nor feminine, 'more violence is done to the libido when it is forced into
the service of the female function,' since nature seems to have
paid more attention to the demands of masculine sexuality than
to those of femininity. Indeed, said Freud, speaking teleologi-
cally, there is a sense in which 'the achievement of the biological
aim is entrusted to the aggressiveness of the male, and is to some
extent independent of the co-operation of the female.' [12] Male
arrogance, it would seem, is an affliction not peculiar to theologians.

The work of Freud's last years did not substantially alter the
interpretation of sex presented in the foregoing pages. His last

12. *Ibid.* p. 179–80.

book, *An Outline of Psychoanalysis,* published posthumously in 1949, revealed no major shifts in viewpoint. In the final decades of his long life, he turned increasingly to the application of libidinal concepts to cultural and social problems, as in his *Group Psychology and the Analysis of the Ego,* a study of mass or mob psychology, or in his *Civilization and Its Discontents,* a rather pessimistic portrait of culture purchased only at the price of instinctual pleasure. But he refused to play the role of prophet, reformer, or social planner. He merely observed and reported what he saw, convinced that in the end all value judgments are 'immediately determined by . . . desires for happiness; in other words . . . these judgments are attempts to prop up . . . illusion with arguments.' [13] Yet the 'House That Freud Built' was built upon the foundation of therapy, an intimate and immediate concern for diagnosing and treating patients who were emotionally or mentally disturbed. This was Freud's primary interest; his theories were always secondary to his role as physician and healer.

In summary, Freud described man's 'mental apparatus' dynamically as divided into three parts. The id contains the primitive, animal instincts which are subdivided into two main groups: the *eros* or libidinal urges, striving toward growth, combination, development, and the *thanatos* or destructive instincts seeking to return to the simple, inorganic state from which all life came. The super-ego is composed of the introjected personalities once sought by the id as sexual objects, and functions as a censor, conscience, ideal, measuring stick. The ego has the thankless task of acting as arbiter among the conflicting demands of the id, the super-ego, and reality. The whole human organism is dominated by the pleasure-principle and its modification in the reality-principle. The child's sexual development passes through oral, anal, and phallic-genital stages, enters on the Oedipus complex, gives way to the latency period, and then comes to life again at puberty. If all goes well, the various components of the sexual

13. *Civilization and Its Discontents,* Jonathan Cape and Harrison Smith, New York, 1930, p. 143.

drive will be synthesized in adult, heterosexual, genital behavior. But any one of the component drives, oral, anal, homosexual, or part of the destructive instincts (as in sadism-masochism) may be too constitutionally strong to be properly synthesized, and a fixation at that level will result. Or, one may regress to a previous stage if difficulties are encountered in maturing. This is the etiological explanation of the perversions. When, however, the super-ego refuses to allow the perverse desires even to rise into consciousness, repression creates a neurosis, in which those desires find expression through the symptoms. When health and maturity are achieved, certain parts of the libido's energies are sublimated into desexualized activities and interests. This sublimated libido is responsible for culture, civilization, creativity. Only a part of the libido's urges can be sublimated, however; some of them must be allowed direct expression. Therefore, society must be warned that too prohibitive sexual codes will exact an enormous price in increased mental illness. But Freud did not, as is often popularly supposed, declare that sexual abstinence invariably produces neurosis, that free sexual expression guarantees or even assists mental and emotional health. The human organism is much more complex than that; what is important in health and disease is the state of the unconscious, the nature of motivation, of attitude, of inner feeling. These are far more decisive than any act. It is not *what* one does sexually that is of central concern, but *why* one does whatever he does. Freud specifically stated that 'only a minority of pathogenic situations due to frustration and the subsequent accumulation of libido thereby induced can be relieved by the kind of sexual intercourse that is procurable without any difficulty.' [14]

Freud saw man as a totality, with sex as one part, perhaps the most important part of his nature. He proclaimed that sex was natural, that procreation was secondary to pleasure, and he cautioned society against too severe restrictions on sexual instincts. But Freud was still a Victorian. He was not the romanticist he

14. *A General Introduction to Psychoanalysis,* Garden City Publishing Co., 1943, p. 337.

has sometimes been called. Rather, he was a rationalist who approved of the stern conscience, who sought to bring the irrational, primitive side of human nature under the disciplined control of the reason. When sex plays its proper, ordered role in the total pattern of the personality, it can contribute to growth, development, and physical and emotional health. This was Freud's goal.

VIII

CONTEMPORARY PSYCHOANALYSIS

FREUD WAS handicapped in his declining years by a painful cancer which seriously curtailed his theoretical and literary productivity. In 1938 his native Vienna became Nazi territory, and as a Jew, he was in serious peril. His followers arranged an escape to England, and there he died in the following year, 1939, when he was over eighty years of age. Psychoanalysis has come, if not of age, then at least to be accepted by the medical profession as a member of the family. It may still wear knee pants, but it is no longer a foundling wailing on the doorstep. The majority of practicing psychoanalysts today are Freudians, following 'the master,' as A. A. Brill called him, on broad theoretical lines if not in minute detail. Their present position is perhaps best expressed in a work by Otto Fenichel entitled *The Psychoanalytic Theory of Neurosis,* an expansion and elaboration of essentially Freudian theories with few major deviations. The observer or historian is more interested in the more dramatic modifications of 'the master's' thought, while recognizing that these are 'splinter' movements, in the sense that they do not represent the main beam of psychoanalysis. It is beyond the scope of this book to examine all of the modifications and rejections which have occurred since the beginning of psychoanalysis. That has been done elsewhere.[1] Nor is it feasible in one chapter to discuss all of the

1. Cf. Clara Thompson and Patrick Mullahy, *Psychoanalysis: Evolution and*

varying psychoanalytic interpretations of sex, the central concern of Part Two of this book. Obviously, all that is possible is a cursory look at two or three representative figures in the field. No pretense is made at a comprehensive coverage. Each analyst chosen speaks, in some degree, only for himself, yet each represents the point of view of many others. These are of interest because they modify and in some instances reject Freud's formulations, but it should be emphasized again that the largest number of contemporary psychoanalysts is conservative, far more 'orthodox' than the deviants discussed here.

In this connection, Freud's own words are of interest. He described psychoanalytic theory as the attempt to explain two experiences, the facts of resistance and of transference. 'Every investigation,' he said, 'which recognizes these two facts and makes them the starting point of its work may call itself psychoanalysis, *even if it leads to results other than my own.'* [2] It would seem that Freud regarded his method as decisive, maintaining an openness and flexibility concerning the theories and hypotheses built around the clinical data which the method yields. No efforts have been made by the various Psychoanalytic Associations to prevent the deviants from orthodox theories from using the magic name. A proper vigilance is exercised against unauthorized and untrained charlatans and their use of the term 'psychoanalyst,' but that is an entirely different matter from the theoretical differences between the members of the profession.

Karen Horney

Dr. Karen Horney began her career as a psychoanalyst in Europe and for some fifteen years followed the orthodox Freudian 'party line,' but after emigrating to the United States, where she settled in New York City, she was compelled to break with Freud at many points. She and several colleagues felt stultified in the American Psychoanalytic Association as well as in the Interna-

---

Development, Hermitage House, New York, 1950; and Patrick Mullahy, *Oedipus: Myth and Complex,* Hermitage House, New York, 1948.

2. *History of the Psychoanalytic Movement,* in *Basic Writings,* p. 939. Italics added.

tional Association, and together they staged a 'walk-out,' forming their own Association for the Advancement of Psychoanalysis. Horney was, as long as she lived, the dominant figure in the new group, and her influence is still manifest. These 'cultural analysts,' as they are sometimes called, were not alone in deviating from 'the master,' as this chapter will indicate, but other analysts felt no compulsion to withdraw and found a new 'school.' Franz Alexander and Sandor Rado, for example, are still respected members of the original Psychoanalytic Association, although they are, to some rigid Freudians, dangerous heretics. Why did Karen Horney find it necessary to make so dramatic a break?

She herself explained her action by her complete rejection of Freud's instinct theories and the substitution for his biological, constitutional bias of a cultural, an environmental orientation. 'My conviction, expressed in a nutshell,' she wrote, 'is that psychoanalysis should outgrow the limitations set by its being an instinctive and a genetic psychology.' She sought to overcome those limitations by a new emphasis 'on the life conditions molding the character,' on 'the environmental factors responsible for creating neurotic conflicts.' [3] She felt that Freud's interest in the genesis of neuroses and the character structure in infancy and early childhood was less productive than her own concern with the present state of the personality, and she preferred what she called a 'prevailingly sociological orientation' to a 'prevailingly anatomical-physiological one.' The Oedipus complex is not, as Freud had maintained, the kernel of every neurosis, nor are the so-called polymorphous perverse drives of childhood the keys to the understanding of neurotic disturbances. Rather, one must look for a general atmosphere which is threatening and rejecting, evoking in the child feelings of being unwanted and unloved, of helplessness and worthlessness. In response to such an environment, the individual perforce develops certain 'neurotic trends' which are actually devices by means of which he seeks to cope with a hostile world. It is the cultural, sociological situation that is of primary importance.

3. Horney, Karen, *New Ways in Psychoanalysis*, W. W. Norton & Co., New York, 1939, p. 9.

Horney accused Freud of one-sidedness in his analysis of the character structure of both normalcy and neurosis, of placing all his eggs in the basket of instinct, of biology, to the grievous neglect of the environment, the culture. There is some truth in this accusation, for Freud's early years in the laboratory biased him strongly in favor of physical-chemical categories of understanding, but there is less truth than Horney maintained. Freud recognized that there were many neurotics who would never have succumbed to illness without the impetus of adverse life situations. He never regarded all neuroses as constitutionally inevitable. His recognition of the role of the environment was illustrated in one well-known passage in which he pictured the childhood erotic play of two little girls, one the child of an upper-middle-class apartment dweller, the other the daughter of the apartment-house janitor. The former will be taught as she grows that sex games are evil and disgusting, and the memories of her transgressions will give birth to feelings of guilt which will in turn produce neurosis in later life. The janitor's daughter, on the other hand, will grow up without any such inhibitions and prove barren of guilt and neurosis, though probably extremely fertile of sexual pleasure.[4] Such a description scarcely sounds like a man who wholly averts his gaze from the influences of the environment, so fixed is his attention on instinct. Horney herself seems at times to go to the other extreme, filling her own basket with the eggs of culture at the expense of biology, but allowances must always be made for polemics. Eagerness to state a point sometimes transforms emphasis into overemphasis.

Horney did express her appreciation of a number of Freud's findings, and she accepted with grateful acknowledgment many of his theories. His interpretation of sex, however, was not one of them. She criticized the entire concept of the libido on three grounds. First, she refused to accept the idea that all bodily sensations of a pleasurable nature are sexual in character, a statement which she called a 'basic contention' of the libido theory, though she admitted that Freud nowhere made such an explicit assertion. It is true that in childhood there are erotic sensations

4. Freud, S., *A General Introduction to Psychoanalysis*, p. 208f.

experienced in connection with sucking, toilet training, et cetera, and that these same sensations seem to play an important part in later perversions, where the mouth or anus are used as sexual orifices. But, said Horney, the ultimate satisfaction in all such situations rests with the genitals. The stimulation of the mucous membrane of the mouth in fellatio is in no way comparable to the stimulation of the vagina in coitus, considered from the point of view of the sensations aroused. 'Oral activity is merely a condition for genital satisfaction, just as there may be a condition for genital excitement in being beaten, in exhibiting oneself or seeing the naked body. . . . Freud recognized this objection but did not consider it evidence against his theory.' [5] Horney agreed that Freud has greatly increased man's knowledge of the kinds of stimuli which may lead to a sexual response, but she denied that those stimuli are in themselves sexual. The sadist may derive sexual satisfaction from cruelty, but this does not mean that cruelty can be regarded as an integral part of the sexual instinct.

Horney looked on the whole libido theory and its accompanying delineation of erogenous zones as unproven and highly doubtful. Her chief objection was not, however, to Freud's discussion of infantile pleasure strivings or the perversions but to his assumption that the majority of character traits are attributable to transformed libido. She examined Freud's data in considerable detail, turning first to the so-called aim-inhibited strivings. She recognized Freud's contribution of valuable clinical findings, conceding that some expressions of affection and tenderness may result from aim-inhibition. The object of the libidinal urge remains unchanged, but the direct, sexual aim is inhibited and transformed into a desexualized feeling of attachment. Similarly, the desire to dominate and control others may be a transformed sadism, although whether sadism is essentially a sexual phenomenon is another question. But this does not mean, Horney insisted, that all affectionate impulses and all strivings for power are aim-inhibited instincts. Affection may be an expression of maternal love or simply a means to allay anxiety, having nothing to do with sex, even though it may have an

5. Horney, *op. cit.* p. 51.

erotic appearance. A struggle for power may be related to strength and leadership, or to devotion to a cause, rather than to weakness and a sadistic thirst for revenge.

Horney subjected to a similarly critical analysis Freud's theory of sublimation, which regards curiosity and a thirst for knowledge as sublimated desires for sexual information, and interprets many habits and character traits as the products of deflected libidinal energy. Horney thought it perfectly natural for an instinct theorist, finding organic conditions in combination with similar psychic attitudes, to assume that there is a causal nexus between the two. She, however, rejected the instinct theory and regarded both the physical condition and the psychological attitude as manifestations of the same general structure. Constipation and greed are frequently found as partners, but the character trait is not an effect of the peristaltic disorder. Both are symptoms of the person's underlying character, which has one goal, 'to hold on to what he has and never give away anything, be it money, love or any kind of spontaneous feelings.' There are certain similarities between one's general attitude and his sexual behavior, and it is the value of the theory of sublimation that this connection has been revealed, but Horney insisted that it is a serious error to assume that the one is caused by the other, an assumption that led Freud to the mistaken conviction that a normal sex life precludes the possibility of neurosis. Horney contended that there are many persons suffering from severe emotional disturbances, so that their work is adversely affected, persons who are in agonies of anxiety or who display typical compulsive or schizoid trends, but who nonetheless derive complete satisfaction from sexual intercourse. She conceded that there are psychic disturbances with the sexual partner in every neurosis, because all interpersonal relations, sexual or nonsexual, are disrupted, but this does not mean that the capacity of the neurotic to achieve a fully satisfactory orgasm is necessarily impaired, nor that it is this incapacity, where it does exist, which is responsible for the neurosis. Horney implied that the chief difference between herself and Freud in this respect was her belief that sexual disturbances are the effects of neurosis, while he thought of them as the cause.

One more aspect of Freud's theory of libidinal character traits which Horney tried and found wanting was the concept of reaction-formation, the building of walls of guilt, shame, and loathing against certain sexual drives. Here again, she admitted that overkindliness may be a compensation for sadistic trends, that generosity may be a reaction-formation against an instinctive greed, but she refused to accept the theory as a sweeping generalization, applicable to every character trait. Kindness may arise out of a positive attitude toward other persons, and generosity may be the spontaneous reaction of a warm and affectionate nature.

Freud's theory of frustration she attacked at several points. Frustration does not invariably give rise to hostility; healthy children and healthy adults can endure frustration in considerable quantity without rage or hatred. Its constancy in neuroses springs not from its etiological character but from its derivative relationship to anxiety. The neurotic's anxiety makes the satisfaction of his demands imperative to his security, and frustration of those demands represents to him a threat. Neurotic anxiety does not result from the frustration of basic instinctual drives as the ego's response to the growing tension produced by frustration, but from 'conflicting trends within the personality.' It is somewhat difficult to see the essential difference between 'conflicting trends within the personality' and the conflict Freud portrayed between the ego, super-ego, and id in their interplay with the conditions of reality. But Horney chose to regard her inner conflicts as occurring between culturally conditioned trends in the personality rather than between the instincts themselves on the one hand and between the instincts and society on the other.

Having denied the validity of the erogenous zones, and, at least to her own satisfaction, refuted the libidinal theories of character formation by attacking in turn the concepts of aim-inhibition, sublimation, reaction-formation, and frustration, Horney summed up: 'The libido then in all its contentions is unsubstantiated.' [6] The lack of substantiating evidence for erogenous zones and character types formed only two grounds of her rejection of Freud's libido theory. Her third objection was based on her conviction that the whole assumption on which the theory rests is dangerous. That assumption is 'that man is driven to fulfill certain primary, biologically given needs, and that these are powerful enough to exert a decisive influence on his personality and thus on his life as a whole.' [7] One would have thought that such an 'assumption' was almost in the category of natural law, so self-evident as to require no demonstration, but Horney found it dangerous for three reasons. First, she thought it distorted the true picture of the ego, of the neuroses, and of character in general, since it ignored the role of culture. Second, the assumption leads to the attempt to understand a complex mechanism by analyzing only one of its parts instead of taking the more comprehensive view of the whole. Third, the instinct theory sets to therapy final limits which do not really exist. Freud was convinced that analysis could go no farther than the constitutional structure of the patient permitted. Horney, interpreting the character as largely the product of the environment, believed that the additional environmental influence of the analysis itself could bring about more fundamental changes.

Having rejected the libido theory and raised serious questions about the place of instinct in human life, what did Horney substitute for the Freudian formulations? Her criticism of those formulations create in the reader the impression that she came perilously close to regarding sex as a learned desire, a drive created by the culture and the environment rather than a biological need with which all men are born. Horney offered two alternatives to Freud's psychology. First, she presented a different interpretation of the *power* of the so-called instinctual drives which Freud saw as so imperious as to be irresistible. The basic needs were for him such that they demanded satisfaction in one way or another; the instincts will not be denied. Horney admitted that such a characterization is valid for neurotics, and

6. *Ibid.* p. 68.
7. *Ibid.* p. 70.

she conceded that Freud also distinguished the neurotic from the healthy at this point, describing the latter as operating on the basis of the reality principle, possessing considerable ability to postpone the satisfaction of instinctual needs or to deflect their force into other channels, while the neurotic lives by the pleasure principle, determined to achieve immediate and direct satisfaction regardless of the consequences. Freud, according to Horney, found the difference between the two in the strength of the instinct. The neurotic lives closer to infantile life and is ruled more directly by the pleasure principle or by instinct. Horney, on the other hand, insisted that man is not ruled by the pleasure principle alone but by two guiding principles — safety and satisfaction. Again one is somewhat at a loss to understand how the dual drives of safety and satisfaction differ from the motive force of the pleasure principle and the reality principle. Horney persisted in her assertion that what placed the neurotic under the dominance of an instinctual drive is *not,* as she understood Freud to claim, the desire for pleasure at all, but the search for safety. So long as pleasure is the only goal, healthy persons can renounce food, sex, money for the sake of some other goals, but when they are in the grasp of anxiety, when the sacrifice of these things represents a threat to safety, then the renunciation becomes impossible. What gives the neurotic's strivings after pleasure their peculiar power and urgency is not the irresistibility of the libidinal drive but the frantic search for security, for escape from anxiety.

This introduces Horney's substitute for libido. The creator of the character structure was, for her, what she called 'basic anxiety.' A child develops this basic anxiety not so much, as Freud maintained, because he fears castration or loss of love as a punishment for satisfying his intinctual drives, but because the environment is feared *as a whole,* seen as unreliable, threatening, unfair, unloving. It is not only the satisfaction of forbidden drives which produces anxiety, but also the fulfilment of his 'most legitimate wishes and strivings.' This general anxiety, elicited as a response to a hostile environment, is the seed from which neurosis grows in a child, who perforce searches everywhere and always for security, for safety from the hostile world in which he lives. It is the frantic need for safety which gives power and urgency to his strivings. What the particular strivings turn out to be depends in large measure upon the kind of environment in which he finds himself. They are strivings which he uses for coping with the world in his incessant search for security. These strategies, or 'neurotic trends' as Horney preferred to call them, she elaborated into three basic types of character: moving toward people, moving away from people, and moving against people.[8] The dynamics of human behavior are determined not by inner instinctual drives but by the need to escape anxiety, the striving for safety. Sexuality becomes a tool in the service of this all-important struggle for security. Horney admitted that sexuality in the normal sense is not a neurotic trend but an instinct. She was insistent, however, that sexual drives frequently become in effect neurotic trends when their satisfaction becomes a means of allaying anxiety.

Her first alternative to Freud's instinct theory, then, was her assertion that it is anxiety and the imperative need to escape it, not the irresistibility of the instincts involved, which gives the strivings of neurotics their intensity. Her second alternative has already been partially foreshadowed; she regarded the various drives which Freud called instinctive as products of the environment. Freud recognized the importance of cultural factors in molding character, as Horney admits, but he limited their influence to the mere modification of instinctive patterns. Horney, on the other hand, stressed the cultural determinants of personality at the expense of the biological.

In general, one gets the impression that Horney was unclear about the relation between normal and neurotic behavior. She explicitly stated that 'it is impossible to distinguish clearly between neurotic and normal,' and pointed out that the same environmental factors which produce neurotics also affect the normal person. Yet the former reveals a far greater power and intensity in his strivings than the latter, and clinical findings

8. Horney, Karen, *Our Inner Conflicts*, W. W. Norton & Co., New York, 1945.

based upon experience with neurotics are not to be applied to the normal. In dealing with Freud's concepts of feminine psychology, for example, Horney reported that he believed women to be more masochistic than men. 'But,' she rejoined, 'it must be remembered that the available data concern only neurotic women,' a statement which sounds less like a psychoanalyst than a lay opponent who refuses to take the findings of analysis seriously because they are based upon people who are disturbed. Granted that there are differences between the normal and the neurotic, it is largely a matter of degree, as Horney herself seemed to realize on occasion. But when her polemical purposes were served, she had a convenient lapse of memory at that point; she was never altogether clear about the role of sex in normal development. Quite obviously the neurotic's sex life is colored by his neurotic trends, as the entire first half of *The Neurotic Personality of Our Time* makes abundantly clear, showing how sex is used as a means of getting attention or affection in order to escape anxiety, while the second half describes sex as a weapon in aggression, in the struggle for power or prestige, and also as a means of allaying anxiety. As goes the neurotic trend, so goes the sex life. But is this also true of the normal person? Horney answered in the affirmative, as might be expected. In *Our Inner Conflicts* she came closest to a psychology of normal life and here she asserted that all men have neurotic trends. The distinction between the normal and the neurotic lies primarily in the *quantity* of anxiety, though Horney recognized that there are qualitative differences as well. The normal person responds genuinely to threatening situations with appropriate anxiety without being paralyzed by it; he can deal with his problems as they arise without disproportionate difficulty. The neurotic, on the other hand, is anxious about persons, places, or things which do not really threaten him, and he responds even to actual danger out of all proportion to the reality. His acts take on a compulsive, frantic character because he is trying desperately to escape his anxiety.

So far as sex is concerned, however, Horney insisted that it is possible for the neurotic to enjoy a normal and satisfactory sex life. The anxiety of a neurotic is not ubiquitous, that is, it does not necessarily affect all aspects of his life. But what determines which factors are impaired and which left undamaged, and why do some people become neurotic while others remain normal? Horney found the answer to both questions in the culture, the environment, which was what she accused Freud of making of instinct. Even if one grants that Freud was one-sided in his biological emphasis, certainly the antidote lies in a greater recognition of both the instinct and the environment, and not in Horney's equally one-sided emphasis on the cultural factors in the development of personality. It is clear that Karen Horney made a genuine contribution to psychoanalysis. She was correct in her contention that Freud was overly anxious to base his findings in the 'pure science' of biology, a solicitude which led him to mistake certain cultural manifestations for instinctive phenomena. If he had known more about anthropology, for example, he would have recognized that the Oedipus complex, at least in its western form, is by no means universal. Horney was probably right also in her contention that some features of Freud's feminine psychology were the products of cultural conditioning rather than of instinctual necessity, but there is serious question whether she was justified in the extremes she adopted in her rejection of the instinct theory in its entirety and in her belief that she was developing new concepts where in actuality she was simply using different terms to say the same thing. In her interpretation of sex, Horney was in no serious conflict with Freud when she asserted that the need for safety and security is at least equal in strength with the sexual urge, though she made it appear as though Freud denied that assertion, and in her polemical desire to sharpen the quarrel, she went so far as to create the impression that sexuality is almost a product of the environment. Freud never denied that sex is frequently used as a means of allaying anxiety, nor was he blind to the fact that sex is often coupled with the striving for power and prestige, but in all of its vicissitudes, the sexual urge remains a powerful instinct, a biological drive whose demands are difficult to deny. What Horney did was to fall into the very pit she accused Freud of tumbling into. She developed valuable insights into the way in which the environment can mold and modify the sexual drives, but she became so preoccupied with those insights that she overlooked the sexual instinct itself. She was quite right when she said, 'Just as all is not gold that glitters, so all is not sexuality that looks like it,' but Freud was equally right in his contention that sexuality can masquerade in many costumes.

One word more needs to be said concerning Horney's criticism of Freud's psychology of women. It will be recalled that Freud placed great emphasis on penis-envy, the form taken by the castration complex in little girls. Horney reviewed the evidence for Freud's theory, pointing out that it was based mainly upon three observations: the voiced wish of small girls for a penis, the acting out of those wishes in 'tomboy' behavior, and dreams of adult women which sometimes endow them with the desired organ. Horney interpreted all three of these from a point of view sharply at variance with Freud's and arrived at different conclusions. Little girls' wishes for penises have no more significance, she declared, than their desire for matured breasts; their boyish behavior may represent a rebellion or unhappiness at not being attractive; and penis-possessing dreams are not universal, visiting only neurotic women. All of these phenomena can be interpreted from a different point of view. The wish to be a man may be no more than the desire to possess those character traits which society regards as masculine: strength, courage, achievement, independence. Penis-envy as a dream-symbol, however, Horney recognized as the result of repression, since symbolic expression is necessary only to repressed desires, and there is no necessity to drive wishes for masculine character traits out of awareness. The analyst, in seeking to discover the true nature of the repressed drives which express themselves in symbolic form, must refuse to accept the explanation that a woman's inferiority feelings spring from the fact that she is a woman. As with members of minority groups, such an excuse is merely a form of resistance to facing the real sources of the inferiority. One of these real sources is the failure to live up to the excessive demands of the ego-ideal, the grandiose ideas of the self. Another 'real' source of the desire to be a man may be repressed ambition, containing elements of egocentricity and destructive aggression. Horney believed that to allow a female patient to hide such factors in her personality behind the facade of penis-envy is positively harmful to the therapy. Once those factors have been faced, the wish to be a man vanishes from the patient's associations.

Horney disposed not only of Freud's theory of penis-envy but also of his contention that women are intrinsically masochistic. She conceded that many neurotic women have masochistic wishes, but denied that this fact had any important implications for normal feminine psychology. She did not regard either sadism or masochism as essentially sexual phenomena, but as the result of conflicts in interpersonal relations, and neither as an exclusively feminine characteristic. If masochism is defined as the 'attempt to gain safety and satisfaction in life through inconspicuousness and dependency,' then Horney was prepared to concede that western civilization contains cultural factors fostering such attitudes among women. The prevailing ideas of the weakness of the female sex, of her dependence on the male, of her lack of fulfillment without a home and children do not in themselves produce masochism, since many women have found happiness and satisfaction in those terms, but such an atmosphere does tend to develop masochistic trends in women if and when they become neurotic.

Finally, Horney agreed with Freud that woman fears most of all the loss of love, but again she insisted that this is culturally conditioned, rather than instinctive. For centuries, woman's place has been in the home; outside activities have been limited sharply. It is not therefore surprising that her relations to husband and children should assume paramount importance. Fatherhood is only an avocation; if a man loses his family, he still has his work. But motherhood is a vocation, and a deserted wife is desolate. Women do, under these conditions, tend to overvalue love, and Horney pointed out ways in which contemporary civilization has aggravated that tendency. Prior to the modern 'gadget-age,' homemaking was a large task with real responsibilities, with children an economic asset, for they were additional workers in the home-industry or farm which preceded the industrial revolution. Large families were desirable and profitable, and the wife had an important function in economic life, providing her with a sound basis for self-esteem. Modern life restricts the number of children and minimizes the status of homemaking, magnifying the woman's role as a courtesan whose main task is to please the man, to win and hold his love.[9] Horney saw all of this as cultural, with nothing biological about it at all. She agreed with Freud 'that differences in sexual constitution and functions influence mental life. But it seems unconstructive to speculate on the exact nature of the difference.'[10] Her shrinking from this extremely important enterprise, the exploration of the relationship between instinct and culture, makes one wonder whether Freud's theory of resistance applied to feminine penis-envy is so farfetched after all.

Franz Alexander

Another contemporary analyst who has also modified Freudian theory at several important points, but without finding it necessary to organize a new 'school' outside the American Psychoanalytic Association, is Dr. Franz Alexander, the director of the Chicago Institute for Psychoanalysis. Alexander shares the concern of Horney and her colleagues for cultural factors in the development of character and in the etiology of the neuroses; in fact, he has sometimes been described as one of the new 'cultural' analysts, the Neo-Freudians. Yet Alexander is a more orthodox Freudian than the members of the Association for the Advancement of Psychoanalysis, for, as he puts it, 'I cannot agree with those who maintain that ambition, competitiveness, and the urge for accomplishment are imposed upon the individual by external cultural conditions. Cultural conditions may encourage and strengthen one attitude rather than another, but culture does not introduce anything into the organism that is not already

9. For further discussion of this whole problem, cf. *Modern Woman The Lost Sex,* by Ferdinand Lundberg and Marynia Farnham, Harper & Brothers, New York, 1947; and *The Second Sex,* by Simone de Beauvoir, Alfred A. Knopf, New York, 1952.

10. Horney, *New Ways in Psychoanalysis,* p. 119.

there. It plays with all the possibilities of human nature as with a fine instrument, but it does not create anything fundamentally new.' [11] Alexander also criticizes the Neo-Freudians for what he calls their 'ethnological bias.' He admits that many of their assertions are valid and that they have contributed valuable insights to psychoanalysis, but he warns against their too heavy reliance on anthropological data, the study of primitive societies. In these tribal cultures, one finds an extremely static situation, where the same codes, mores, and taboos have been in force for centuries, where all of life is prescribed by tradition and custom, and to draw from this type of society conclusions that are supposed to be relevant to the dynamic culture of the modern west, which is constantly in a state of flux, the younger generation constantly in rebellion against the elder, is a highly questionable process.

Alexander remains closer to Freud than Horney and her school. He regards psychology as essentially a biological science; mental activities are adaptive mechanisms, as fully physiological in basis as breathing and digestion and will one day be described in terms of physics and chemistry. He accepts Freud's interpretation of the purpose of the nervous system: the maintenance of an equilibrium between the stimuli of the external world and the needs and demands of the internal organism. Whenever energy is consumed, it must be replaced. This is to be understood by the application of two principles: stability and inertia. The principle of stability is 'the tendency of living organisms to preserve internal conditions like temperature and the concentration of body fluids at a constant level.' [12] This is the physiological basis of the stability principle. Its psychological basis rests upon the tendency of the ego to protect the organism as a whole from excessive stimulation both from without and within. This principle applies equally to all instincts and emotions: all of them obey its law, which is in essence the law of self-preservation, striv-

11. Alexander, Franz, *Our Age of Unreason*, J. A. Lippincott Co., New York, 1942, p. 230.
12. Alexander, Franz, *Fundamentals of Psychoanalysis*, W. W. Norton & Co., New York, 1948, p. 35.

ing toward the best possible conditions under which life can function.

The principle of inertia is the 'tendency of the organism to replace adjustment requiring effort in experimentation by effortless automatic behavior.' Alexander distinguishes between automatic functions which are unconditioned and unlearned, such as breathing, digestion, and circulation of the blood, and those functions which must be learned through trial and error. The learning process begins with a groping experimentation and then proceeds to a repetition of useful, workable patterns which the experimentation discovered. The aim of the learning process is the gratification of needs with the minimum expenditure of energy, which is another way of stating the principle of inertia. The relationship of this to the principle of stability is readily apparent, for the organism must experiment to satisfy its internal needs and reduce tensions, and the activities proven successful are consolidated by repetition. These two principles together constitute the basic psycho-dynamics of life. There are, however, certain disadvantages to these dynamics, for life is in a constant state of flux, continuously confronted by growth and change, both internally and externally. This requires flexibility, adaptability, but the inertia principle seeks to cling to the old ways already learned and established, since that requires a smaller expenditure of energy. Freud called this indolence on the part of an organism under the dominance of its inertia *fixation*. He also pointed out that when changing conditions become too complex, making adaptation too difficult, *regression* ensues, the return to earlier, already mastered patterns of behavior. Life is a constant struggle between the demands of the external world for growth and change and the internal demands of stability and inertia.

All of this is pure Freud, expressed in some new language to be sure, but still Freud. His theory of the conservative nature of the instincts together with his belief in a 'compulsion to repeat' led Freud to his final formulation of the life and death impulses, eros and thanatos. Alexander does not share Freud's concept of a death instinct, which he characterizes as not a description of instinctual forces but 'a philosophical abstraction.' He regards death as the *result* rather than the *aim* of certain disintegrative factors operating in living creatures. Biology shows a dualism of anabolic construction and catabolic destruction of biomolecules, but it does not show any conscious, purposeful instinct whose aim is to reduce all organic matter to inorganic. On the contrary, all living cells seek to preserve their lives, but in the complex, multi-cellular organisms, this individualism with the disinclination of each cell to sacrifice its autonomy operates as a destructive force. Where a highly particularized specialization of cells has developed, a part severed from the body will die. But it is not death which the living cells seek; rather they aim at their own, independent life. This process can be seen in social behavior, where men will co-operate to meet a common foe but return to their individual self-centeredness once the danger is past. It can also be seen in the psychology of individuals. Maturity implies the integration of a person's various drives and needs, and so long as the integration is maintained — with the individual component urges subordinated to the dominant goal of life — the person functions successfully. But if one need is accentuated, owing, perhaps, to a change in the environment, its demands may become so imperious that the integration is destroyed and the person breaks down. Whenever external conditions become so complex that the organism is unable to adapt to them, it regresses to that which it has already learned, and so fails to master the new situation. 'What Freud called the death instinct is a tendency not toward death but toward old and worn patterns of life.'

Alexander returns to Freud's first instinct theory, which drew a distinction between libidinal drives and the urge toward self-preservation. The latter instinct expresses itself in terms of the combined inertia-stability principle, but in order to understand growth and propagation, the forces which foster adaptation and change, Alexander turns to the instinct of eros, or what he calls the principle of surplus energy. Growth is inescapable. No matter how hard the child may struggle to maintain the *status quo,* to avoid expending energy in growing up, he finds himself developing nonetheless. He moves through the various stages predetermined by his phylogeny. Despite minor variations, all men learn at approximately the same age to creep, to walk, to talk. The sex glands mature in everyone at about the same time, and shortly thereafter, physical growth ceases. Progressively, the child becomes increasingly independent of his parents, but he resists the process at every step. Under the dominance of inertia-stability he does not want to change, to grow. This is not, however, the whole story. There is another force at work, another psychological drive which not only accepts growth as inevitable but also speeds the movement toward adaptability and independence. This is the principle of surplus energy, or the instinct eros, the name the Greeks gave to the god of both love and play, always described as a child. Alexander regards eros as an altogether appropriate symbol, because he brings together under this instinct all activities and impulses of the organism bound not to self-preservation but to the sole pursuit of pleasure. Almost everything which the child learns begins as playful experimentation, moving hands and feet, focusing the eyes, creeping. None of these is utilitarian when first attempted. There is no connection with self-preservation, no desire to get something for the self. All of these activities are purely pleasurable, carried on as play. The fact that they later prove useful and important in the independence and adaptability of the growing child is purely fortuitous. No such intention exists. The child plays only because it amuses him. These playful exercises were called by Freud libidinal; Alexander calls them erotic.

Activities governed by the erotic principle, carried on for the sake of pleasure alone, are not subject to the principle of inertia. They are meant to expend energy, not to conserve it. They are dynamic and creative; they are responsible for growth and propagation. They drain off surplus energy not required either for the preservation of homeostatic stability or for survival. Excess energy disturbs homeostatic equilibrium and results in internal excitation, and the stability principle requires that it be discharged. Now whence comes the surplus energy? Alexander interprets life as the interplay of three drives: first, the organism *takes in* the energy it requires through eating and breathing; next, it *retains* such energy as it needs for growth; and finally, it *expends* the remaining energy in the process of living, discharging energy in the form of bodily heat, waste products, and erotic activities. For the child, these erotic activities consist largely in play, in exploration of the body. The child has this surplus energy to 'spend' because his parents supply all of his wants. He requires large quantities of energy for growth, using up most of his energy in that enterprise. Intake and retention far outweigh elimination. That is why the child grows so rapidly, but apart from growth, the child has to use little energy for self-preservation and has a surplus of energy which must be discharged if stability is to be maintained. In unicellular organisms, absorbed energy is used for growth and the maintenance of life, but when a surplus is accumulated, it is expended in propagation. The organism divides. Seen from this point of view, propagation is simply growth, a continuation of the development process outside the organism, that is, in its offspring. All energy not required for growth or the preservation of life, then, is surplus, erotic, discharged by the child in playful experimentation and by the adult in biological procreation or in sublimated creative activities.

It will readily be apparent that this dualism between self-preservative drives and erotic drives corresponds almost exactly to Freud's early formulation of ego and libido instincts. Alexander's theory corresponds to still another of Freud's ideas, that sex is quantitative in character rather than qualitative. Freud described the various phenomena of infantile sexuality, the erogenous zones whose stimulation provides pleasure not only to the immediate area but produces excitation in the genitals, and he noted that sexuality attaches itself to all intense emotional experiences, not only love but hate. 'These wide variations,' says Alexander, 'indicate that the sexual impulse does not have one specific content, but that any emotion can become sexualized. On the basis of these observations Freud originally concluded that sexuality is not dependent on a special emotional quality, but must have a quantitative basis. Unfortunately he did not elaborate this irrefutable contention.' [13] This elaboration Alexander proceeds to supply. His contention is that 'sexuality discharges any excitation, regardless of its quality.'

As evidence of this statement he turns first to unicellular life, where cell division follows this principle of surplus energy. When the cell reaches the limit of growth, it must divide. Surplus organic matter which cannot be incorporated into the parent organism must be eliminated, and the result is a new organism. This principle, says Alexander, rules all propagation. Further evidence is elicited from the perversions, which are obviously forms of surplus excitation which cannot be integrated into the total personality. Sexual sadists, for example, are on the whole very timid, retiring people who have serious difficulty in expressing their hostility and aggression in ordinary life. They have repressed these drives, which find outlet in sexual activity where the primary desire is to hurt and torture. Masochists suffer from feelings of guilt and need punishment, which they find in sexuality. Yet their sex lives frequently present a sharp contrast to their general egotism. And if their sexual suffering, which compensates for their self-centeredness, is blocked for one reason or another, they will substitute 'moral masochism,' courting suffering in other ways. A third area to which Alexander turns for evidence of his theory of the erotic principle is the process of growth. The child engages in erotic play throughout his development. For the infant this play is pre-genital or extra-genital with centers of pleasure in the mouth, anus, and other erogenous zones. In the latency period, the intellect functions erotically in the form of curiosity, expending surplus energy not needed for survival or growth. At puberty, competition — proving one's self — becomes an eroticized aim, but when the growth cycle is completed at maturity, the genito-urinary tract, which has been gradually moving in this direction all along, assumes the function of draining off not only waste material but surplus excitation as well. Almost all surplus energy not required for self-preservation is discharged through this tract, which brings Alexander to the formulation, 'Every gratification intrinsically has an erotic char-

13. *Ibid.* p. 76.

acter, which is satisfaction of a tendency for its own sake and not subservient to the needs of the total organism.' [14]

Alexander's theory of eros is identical with Freud's first theory of libido, and both broaden sexuality to include all pleasurable activities not directly concerned with self-preservation. Creative, artistic activities are erotic with the function of relieving the tension of surplus energy. Pleasure associated with eating is not erotic, since it is self-preservative, but thumb-sucking is erotic. Curiosity which is related to orientation in the environment is preservative; purely pleasurable exploration is erotic. Rage or anger necessary to self-preservation are not erotic, but all other aggressive impulses are. 'Sadism is destructiveness for its own sake.' Surplus energy accumulated beyond pragmatic requirements is released in erotic forms, but during the process of development, this principle is reversed. Activities begin as erotic and then become useful in maintaining life, losing their erotic quality.

Alexander follows Freud closely in his delineation of the path from infancy to maturity. In each of the various stages, the psychological development follows the underlying biological growth. In the first, or oral, stage the infant concentrates all his attention on the incorporation of energy and its retention for purposes of growth. The surplus excitation is minimal, but the infant does engage in non-nutritive sucking, which is erotic, discharging whatever surplus there is. There are certain emotional attitudes related to the act of feeding, feelings of security which are associated with the relief of hunger and sensations of being cared for which are linked with oral pleasure. The pleasure derived from stimulation of the mouth's mucous membrane in non-nutritive sucking springs from a primarily passive orientation, marked by dependent, receptive, demanding attitudes. But there is an active side to oral assimilation, for the child will sometimes bite the nipple if the milk does not flow freely and easily, encouraging an aggressive attitude which takes by force what is not given. Still another oral attitude is envy, aroused in the child when he is put away from the breast and replaced by a younger sibling.

14. *Ibid.* p. 79.

Next, or to some extent simultaneously, comes the anal stage, in which the child learns that excremental functions also provide pleasurable sensations. The erotic aspect is to be found in the child's interest in these functions and their products beyond the necessities of elimination. Most children display pronounced coprophilia (fascination with excrement), playing with feces, experimenting with urination, asking endless questions and making endless jokes about their eliminatory organs. They discover that both ends of the alimentary canal can produce pleasure and experiment in withholding the fecal mass, enjoying the sensations of pressure in the mucous membranes of the anus. The pleasure of anal retention proves the chief obstacle in toilet training. Certain emotional traits, such as stubbornness and greed, are also related to this stage. Excrement is the small child's first possession to withhold or give to his parents as he chooses, and his early attitudes can have a decisive effect on his later attitudes toward other possessions. In general, it is customary for toilet training to follow weaning, and in his first few years the infant is confronted with two serious interferences with his biological functioning. This may give rise to hostility, to biting the nipple or excreting as defiance of parents. When such discharge of energy is not related to the elimination of obstacles interfering with the satisfaction of needs, it is sadism, or erotic aggression, the desire to hurt for its own sake.

As the child's physical independence increases, as he learns to walk and talk and feed himself, his erotic gratification begins increasingly to center on his genitals. Sexual impulses and erotic drives do not exactly parallel the other aspects of mental and physical growth; they rush ahead, outstripping the rest. In the Oedipus complex, the typical emotional triangle of the phallic-genital stage, the child foreshadows his later sexual development. He subsequently forgets his early attraction to the parent of the opposite sex and his concurrent jealousy and hostility to the parent of the same sex, a repression made necessary by the discrepancy between the development of the ego and the development of the instincts. Together with the Oedipus complex, rivalry between siblings develops, as they compete first for the mother's love and then for the privileges that come with grow-ing up, staying up later at night, going out alone, and so on. Alexander calls this progressive rivalry as over against the earlier, regressive rivalry which responds to the threat of a new baby by a new outburst of infantile behavior. The repression of the Oedipus complex brings about the gradual disappearance of the child's sexual curiosity, which is replaced by curiosity about the world. This is the latency period.

At puberty, the growth process produces organic changes which direct the sexual impulses into mature forms of behavior. Bio-logically, the adolescent is now an adult, ready to reproduce. Emotionally, however, he has still to adjust himself to his new status; he feels insecure, torn between two competing impulses, procreative genital sexuality and the regressive, dependent tend-ency, a tension which will last throughout his life. The adoles-cent wants on the one hand to forge ahead into adulthood, while on the other, he wishes he could return to his childhood depend-ency. The former drive manifests itself in competition, in the attempt to measure up to others, to prove himself, and even his sexuality is highly competitive. Not until he feels fully secure in full maturity does mature love make its appearance. In adoles-cence the sexual object serves the ego, while in maturity, some-thing genuinely new in sexual development occurs, when love becomes generous, outgoing, giving, showing that the person is now possessed of strength and energy which are surplus. He no longer requires them for his own self and can give them to others. Alexander regards genital sexuality, the term both he and Freud give to mature behavior, as more than the summation and mix-ture of all the pre-genital trends. Mature sexuality does include early erotic activities in foreplay preceding coitus, looking, touch-ing, kissing, but something new has been added — the ability to give out of one's own abundance. This is the psychological counterpart to the biological production of sperm and ova. The organism reaches beyond concern for its own growth to concern for the growth of others. The chief difference between mature love and pre-genital sexuality is the outgoing productivity of the former and the narcissism of the latter. The narrow preoccupation with one's own development gives way to genital sexuality and reproduction, the overflow of surplus energy which produces new life.

There are several points of especial interest in Alexander's discussions of normal sexuality and its development. First, he agrees with Horney and the Neo-Freudians that the Oedipus complex is not a universal biological phenomenon as Freud believed. There are cultural variations so that among the Marquesans, for example, the mother's hostile attitude drives the children from her. Alexander believes, however, that there is always a possessive attachment to the adult on whom the child is dependent, be it mother, father, aunt, uncle, or grandparent, and jealousy coupled with hostility against rivals. Cultural conditions determine which members of the family constellation play which roles, but the complex is always there in some form, biologically predetermined by the prolonged dependence of the human child upon some kind of adult care. Second, Alexander has an interesting theory concerning the castration complex in boys, declaring that this fear is preceded by earlier experiences in which the child loves something which he considers a part of himself, with a resultant loss of pleasure. In being weaned, he loses the breast (which he at first regarded as a part of himself), and in toilet training he must give up holding his feces as a source of pleasure, learning to evacuate his bowels regularly. 'In both cases, erotic pleasure is followed by the loss of something pleasurable.' It is not surprising, then, that early masturbation arouses fear of losing the penis. This represents an ingenious explanation of the origins of the castration complex, even in boys who have been subjected to no actual threats at all. A third point of interest is Alexander's view of feminine development. He is inclined to agree with Horney that it is the environment rather than any deep biological instincts which molds the attitudes of the growing girl. Horney regarded the turning of the daughter from her mother to her father as the result not of penis-envy or castration complex but of her natural femininity which is attracted by a male. Alexander believes with Freud in physiological and psychological bisexuality, but he agrees with Horney that the particular parent or adult to whom the child turns for satisfaction and security is determined by environmental circumstances and not by biological factors.

Alexander sees all sexual perversions as either fixations on or regressions to early, immature forms of sexuality, and he regards the former as more significant, for even in cases of regression some element of fixation must be assumed. In general, what causes a fixation and subsequent regression is the emotional involvement of the family in the Oedipus complex. Because of attachments to certain types of pre-genital activity and fears of certain others, the child develops a fixation on a particular form of sexual gratification. 'In the child the desire for mastery (sadism), painful striving (masochism), curiosity (voyeurism), showing off and getting attention (exhibitionism) are all sources of erotic pleasure. In perversion, these early erotic strivings continue to appeal because normal and mature sexual release is blocked.' [15] This is true not only of all the foregoing perversions where the *quality* of the sexual strivings is distorted but also of those where the *object* of the urge is abnormal, as in homosexuality, pedophilia (desire for children as sexual partners), and zoophilia (desire for animals as sexual partners).

Perversions cannot, according to Alexander, be regarded as the disintegration of the mature sexual instinct into its constituent parts, for mature love contains something unique, not present in the pre-genital drives. In perversion the integration of the various pre-genital drives into mature sexuality has never taken place. Perversions are therefore not simply the regression of adult sexuality to an earlier level; adult sexuality has never been reached at all. The emotional factors which cause such arrested development are many. Strong hostility in the Oedipal situation will produce sadism; fixation to a dependent, submissive attitude brought about by anxiety and guilt over the hostility will result in masochism or homosexuality. The latter may be caused in one of two ways: either the child avoids competition and rivalry with the parent of the same sex by assuming a seductive attitude (in which case the homosexual interest is usually in older persons, as

15. *Ibid.* p. 260.

parent substitutes) or else the child identifies itself with the parent of the opposite sex (in which case the homosexual interest is in younger persons to whom the homosexual can give the kind of parental love he wanted and thus gain vicarious satisfaction). All perversions result from fixation on early forms of erotic release; once a child has learned a sexual pattern, he tends to repeat it, in accordance with the inertia principle. But perversions develop only in persons whose normal sexual development is blocked by insoluble emotional problems created by early family situations.

In summary, it is clear that Alexander is far more Freudian than Horney, yet he does modify and alter psychoanalytic theories wherever he feels the clinical evidence requires it. He regards sex as a quantitative discharge of surplus energy or tension, regardless of the source of that surplus. His eros, like Freud's libido, is broadened to the extent that it is not exclusively a theory of sex but of pleasure. Mature sexuality is characterized by the capacity for love, for giving; sex which seeks its own, based on strivings for prestige or self-assurance, is adolescent. Like Freud, Alexander is a dualist. He sees life as a constant tension between the inertia-stability principle on the one hand and the principle of eros, of growth, development, and propagation on the other. Even within the sex instinct itself, there is a struggle between the progressive drive toward adult, mature love and the regressive urge toward previous, pre-genital modes of gratification. Like Freud, Alexander places strong emphasis on biology, on instinct, but like Horney, he also sees the importance of culture and environment.

Sandor Rado

The Director of the New York Psychoanalytic Institute, Dr. Sandor Rado has been in the United States since 1931. In that year he left the directorship of the Berlin Psychoanalytic Institute to assume his present position, the first of its kind in this country. He has been one of the leaders in analytical circles for over thirty years, and although his pen has not been so prolific as that of Horney or Alexander or Menninger, so that he is not so well-known to the public, Rado is nonetheless widely respected in the profession. Abram Kardiner has popularized some of his theories, but his own writings have been confined to articles in psychoanalytic journals with restricted circulation. He has made several significant contributions to the interpretation of sex and for that reason is included in the present chapter.

Rado has modified many of Freud's theories, regarding such a modification as an obligation not only to science but to Freud himself, who left to his followers 'not a creed but an instrument of research.' All of Freud's early work was occupied with the libidinal factors in neuroses. The later years of his life were devoted to his instinct theories, his 'mythology' as he called it, and to the exploration of the ego. Almost all subsequent analysis has continued to enlarge the role of the ego at the expense of sexuality both in character and in neuroses. Rado points out that Freud himself abandoned the theory that sexual disturbance lies at the root of all neuroses and substituted anxiety as the decisive factor in the etiology of psychic pathology, but from this shift in emphasis Freud drew no conclusions for the therapy he was practicing. He was so engrossed with his theoretical formulations that he drew away from clinical data and moved into the realm of speculative generalities. This has left his successors with the task of sifting out the facts from their metaphysical milieu, and, says Rado, the further enterprise of constructing a new 'frame of reference that would rest on our established biological knowledge of man and suit our medical needs.' [16] Rado seeks to provide this new framework with what he refers to as an *egology*, dealing with the dynamics of mental processes in terms of the integrative functions of the ego. Neuroses are seen as a disturbance of the total personality, and great stress is laid on anxiety and its crippling effects. It is unnecessary to present any detailed consideration of this egology, which is mentioned merely as an example of Rado's departure from orthodox Freudian theory. Yet Rado,

16. Rado, Sandor, 'Developments in the Psychoanalytic Conception and Treatment of Neuroses,' *Psychoanalytic Quarterly*, vol. 8, no. 4, October 1939, p. 429.

like Alexander, remains in the American Psychoanalytic Association. His more traditionally oriented colleagues there evidently do not stultify him.

Rado has also modified Freud's sexual theories, rejecting the whole idea of bisexuality completely. He begins by going back to biology, to the sources of sexuality in evolution. In the most primitive forms of life, the unicellular creatures, propagation is asexual, occurring as binary fission. Evidently the first instance of the co-operation of cells in protean life came in the formation of devourer colonies around a common enemy. By exchanging certain digestive functions and by going in for specialization, the digestive processes of the colony were increased in efficiency. A later stage among the protozoans produced new hereditary possibilities by fusing the nuclei of two individuals, and all subsequent evolutionary development was characterized by the union of a pair of germ cells, differentiated into male and female. Except, then, for the most primitive forms of life, sex as a reproductive mechanism can never be understood on the level of the individual. There must always be the male-female pair: two sets of sexual organs and systems, carrying sperm and egg. The differentiation of male and female seems to follow what Rado calls a push-pull principle. The male germ cell probes toward the egg; the penis penetrates the vagina, pushes in and out and shoots its semen; the male individual, as the bearer of penis and sperm, aggressively pursues the female. On the other hand, the egg attracts the sperm cells, pulling them toward it; the vagina receives the penis, acts as a suction pump, draws the semen into the uterus; the female individual attracts the male, enticing him to her side. The male pushes, the female pulls; the result is reproduction. This is the physiological description of sexuality.

On the psychological level, Rado indicates that in the 'higher animals' on the evolutionary scale, mammals with a large development of the cerebral cortex, sexual behavior undergoes a gradual change. 'Stereotyped inherited forms, organized at lower levels, have broken down, and the pattern has become increasingly modifiable and dependent for its completion upon the animal's individual experience.' [17] Man remains an animal, subject to certain basic laws which govern all mammals, but his greater cerebral development gives him a higher degree of flexibility, a further development of individuality. His variability is limited, however, by the cultural and environmental patterns imposed upon him, so that his sexuality is always a combination of culture and instinct. Man's relative freedom from the rigid bondage of instinct enables him to separate sexuality from reproduction and to seek for pleasure. He is capable of conscious motivation, of a deliberate quest for orgasm which is different in degree if not in kind from the instinctive character of animal sexuality. From the psychological point of view, Rado regards this desire for orgasm and its accompanying pleasure as the dominant aspect of sexuality. Reproductive intentions may or may not be combined with this motivation. Women who are pregnant or past the menopause continue to have orgastic desires, and what they want is pleasure. The physiological aspect of sexuality is the reproductive pair; the psychological aspect is the pleasure pair.

Rado believes that Freud's libido theory tried to include so many experiences that it ceased to be a theory of sex and became a theory of pleasure. Therefore it is important to define what is meant by the term 'sexual,' which Rado confines to orgasm itself, occurring either as a surprise or as the result of behavior motivated by the search for orgastic pleasure. The only form of libido, then, which is genuinely sexual is genital libido. Oral libido is pleasure of the mouth, narcissistic libido is pleasure in loving one's self, and so on. Rado agrees with Horney that even the sexual pleasure of active fellatio or passive pederasty is centered in the genitals and not in the mouth or anus. As the stimulation of the so-called erogenous zones leads to genital excitation, the pleasure is sexual. The whole body can become a single instrument of sexual expression, but this must not be confused with sensual pleasures which have no connection with sex. The most significant aspect of Freud's theory of erogenous zones,

17. Rado, Sandor, 'An Adaptational View of Sexual Behaviour,' in *Psychosexual Development in Health and Disease,* Hoch and Zubin, eds. Grune & Stratton, New York, 1949, p. 162.

Rado believes, was his recognition that the meaning of any psychological event is to be found in its motivation. He who would understand behavior must ask the question why. What purpose was served? What did the person seek to gain? In these terms it is essential to distinguish between bodily sensations which form a part of the highly complicated mechanism of sexual arousal and those which are pleasures of another sort. The pleasure mechanism of the body can be of service to a variety of purposes, nutrition, creative, artistic work, release from tension, strivings for prestige. What is decisive is the motivational context.

The 'standard coital pattern' as Rado calls it, follows the anatomical indications. The male penis penetrates the female vagina and orgasm ensues. This pattern is motivated by the desire for pleasure, but it also forms the condition of reproduction. The physiology of sexual arousal is far from clear, but it is presumed that certain humoral factors make a direct impact upon the brain. Psychologically, this internal stimulation must be translated into awareness and elaborated into the state where the individual consciously desires sexual activity. The degree of the internal excitation is enormously varied from person to person, and even within the same person it is subject to many vicissitudes. One man may encourage sexual desire so that it becomes the center of his existence, while another may divert some of his energies into other channels, but there is a certain minimum of orgastic requirements which cannot be satisfied in any other way except direct sexual release. Sublimation, in other words, has its limits.

Having defined his terms, Rado turns to his criticism of the concept of bisexuality. He attributes the origin of the myth to the fact that sexual partners envy each other in their capacity for sexual enjoyment, which 'may have inspired one Hindu mystic of antiquity to invent the doctrine of bisexuality; to be both male and female, a pair by oneself, is a perfect dream; it leaves nothing to be envied and nothing to be feared.' [18] The widespread popularity of the legend is due to the ubiquity of emotional conflict connected with the discovery of the difference

18. *Ibid.* p. 169.

between the sexes. Powerful support was given to the myth in the nineteenth century when it was discovered that the urogenital systems of the two sexes came from a common embryonic origin. When cellular material of both male and female gonads were found in the embryo, it seemed conclusive that bisexuality was established as a fact of nature — which provided a convenient explanation for homosexuality. If all persons are the products of male and female cells, then in some the balance is less equitable than in others. Krafft-Ebing, the famous Viennese psychiatrist and author of *Psychopathia Sexualis,* believed that since the peripheral sexual apparatus is bisexually predisposed, as the embryos revealed, then this must apply to the central part also. The cerebrum must contain male and female centers which determine the individual's sex behavior. Homosexuality is the result of the strength of the wrong center. Krafft-Ebing recognized that hermaphroditism or other abnormalities of the genitals almost never accompanied homosexuality, and this led him to assume that the central part of the sexual system is autonomous, independent of anatomical structure, and subject to developmental disturbances apart from the development of the sexual organs themselves. Rado points out that there was not in the last decade of the nineteenth century and never has been any neurological evidence to support such an assumption. But the absence of other hypotheses resulted in the almost universal acceptance of Krafft-Ebing's.

Freud followed Krafft-Ebing's lead, describing the central as well as the peripheral part of the sexual apparatus as bisexual. He knew, however, that such a theory had not been physiologically substantiated, and that only biological research could substantiate it. He accepted it as one of his assumptions, borrowed from an outside source, and always recognized it for what it was, never confusing the assumption with established fact. Some of his followers, however, were not so discerning and regarded bisexuality as an established fact rather than as an hypothesis. They did not realize, as Freud did, that bisexuality cannot be proved or refuted by psychoanalysis, that such confirmation can come only from biology. Rado points out that contemporary biology renders the inescapable verdict that there is no such thing as bisexuality in man or any of the higher vertebrates. The double embryological origin of the genital system does not produce any physiological duality in reproductive function. There are individuals who possess parts of the genital organs of the opposite sex, semi-hermaphrodites, but this results in the impairment of sexual activity — sometimes rendering any activity impossible — not in a double reproductive capacity. Physiologically, there are only two sexes, male and female. The rare occurrence of hermaphroditism does not produce a third sex, but either no sex at all or else one or the other with some peripheral appurtenances of the opposite sex. The highly publicized 'transformations of sex' by operation are either simply the castration of a male, who nonetheless remains a male, even without his genitals, or else the establishment of the truly dominant reproductive system, obscured and confused by physical anomalies. But there is always one sex or the other, never both.

The question remains, however, whether psychology follows physiology. To apply the motivational test to sexual pleasure, what is the purpose of that behavior, regardless of its aim or object? Rado answers that the purpose is orgastic pleasure which is always centered in the genitals, so that a man always has a male orgasm no matter how much he may pretend to be a woman, and a woman always has a female orgasm, no matter how desperately she tries to be a man. All perversions represent abnormality of sexual stimulation, but whatever the means of stimulation, the physiological orgasm reflex remains unchanged. This principle applies to deviations both of aim and of object in the sexual act. Exploration and stimulation of the anus, mouth, and other parts of the body may be said to serve as tributaries to sexuality in so far as they contribute to tumescence in the genitals and orgasm, but if orgastic pleasure is not the motive of such activities, they are not sexual but alimentary or attached to some other basic biological system.

On the basis of this evidence, Rado finds six major flaws in the classical psychoanalytic theory of bisexuality, with its assumption that masculine and feminine components are to be found universally in both sexes. (1) The only certain designation of masculinity or femininity can be assigned to fantasies or wishes expressing the desire to possess the opposite type of genital equipment or to serve the opposite function in reproduction, and such fantasies are relatively rare. (2) No distinction has been made between the fantasies of adults and children: a wish which in an adult may be clearly masculine or feminine may in a child be the result of ignorance or misunderstanding. (3) There is no evidence whatever for the contention that masculine or feminine manifestations in the personality are the results of constitutional components of the opposite sex. Fantasies are primarily environmental in the origin of their contents, and they may or may not be indications of constitutional factors. Man has wanted to fly like the birds since earliest times, but this does not mean that he is constitutionally predisposed to fly. (4) There has been no consistent clarity in the discussion of constitutional components. Homosexuality is supposed to be the result of the female disposition in the man and the masculine disposition in the woman, yet in some forms of homosexuality there is no relation to the behavior pattern of the opposite sex. (5) The term homosexual has been extended to cover so many relationships that it has become almost meaningless. Any friendship or affectionate feelings between two persons of the same sex is traced to covert homosexuality. As Rado has already confined the term sexuality to deliberate or accidental orgasm and behavior leading to it, he demands a similar restriction of the term homosexuality. (6) The assumption of a homosexual component has not served to stimulate research on the source and nature of such a component. Rather, its existence has been assumed as if research had already established it.

If the source of sexual abnormalities is not to be found in constitutional predisposition, then what is the cause of perversions? What impels people to apply aberrant forms of stimulation to their standard coital equipment? Rado's answer is fear. He points out how children frequently discover the 'facts of life' in a highly charged emotional atmosphere. Boys and girls are ordered to give up their early masturbation under threat of injury and loss. The cultural pattern is extremely powerful, and the attitude toward sex as fearful and evil may be communicated even to the children of enlightened parents through playmates, servants, or teachers. The little boy is very often frightened by his first awareness that girls are without the penis, and he concludes that they are victims of the mutilation with which he has been threatened. He may be driven completely away from the dangerous vagina, or he may suffer from premature ejaculation, caused by his eagerness to escape that fearful place as soon as possible. The timid little girl sees the penis as a weapon which will penetrate her violently and painfully, and she may develop frigidity as a defense against being violated. Rado speaks of 'fears of genital diminution' and shows how incapacitation for sexual intercourse, starvation, and exclusion from the group have been social punishments from primitive times, punishments which are still threatened in the nursery. The fears of sexual damage are reinforced by fears of the loss of nourishment or love.

All of these fears are magnified when the child's dependence upon his parents is invaded by his orgastic desires. Unconsciously most mothers tend to stimulate their sons, as do most fathers their daughters. The attachment to the parent of the opposite sex creates hostility toward the parent of the same sex, and the Oedipus complex is born. What happens in the child's relations with his family group, mother and father and siblings, will determine in large measure his later attitudes in life. This is the seedbed in which he grows his attitudes toward co-operation and competition, toward authority, toward submission or domination. Here he nurtures his hopes, his fears, and his feelings about sex. If his early experiences are colored by fears that he will lose love or nourishment, that his genitals will be damaged, then sexual activity becomes a threat rather than a promise. His fears exercise an inhibiting effect on his sexual behavior, predisposing him to a failure which reinforces his fears.

Any one or all of the various parts of sexual activity may be inhibited in such a way that the standard coital pattern is replaced by modified patterns, in which the penis is not inserted into the vagina and orgasm is achieved by a different kind of stimulation. Such stimulation may be applied to the genitals or to other parts of the body, or it may be purely mental. The difference in outward behavior in modified coital patterns suffices to distinguish them from normal sexuality, but psychoanalysis seeks to understand inner motivation as well as outer act. From the standpoint of motivation, the modified patterns can be divided into three groups: reparative, situational, and variational.

Reparative patterns are the result of early fears which act as inhibitors on normal sexual functioning. Reparative acts are attempts, for the most part unconscious, to repair damage done to the individual's self-esteem by his sexual failure. He discovers that although the standard coital pattern is blocked, he can still gain orgastic pleasure by means of some modified form of sexual activity. These modified forms are rigid and inflexible, because they are essential to sexual gratification. Situational patterns spring from the lack of opportunity for normal sexual outlets, and in such circumstances even healthy persons are sometimes forced to seek satisfaction in a modified coital pattern, but these activities are adopted as the result of conscious choice rather than unconscious necessity, and generally they are abandoned as soon as the situation changes so as to permit normal coitus again. Variational patterns are based on the old adage that 'variety is the spice of life.' The healthy individual may seek a new type of experience, but he is not bound to do so, nor is he compulsively attracted to any one modified coital pattern. The external behavior of all three types may be identical, but the motivation is quite different. Reparative behavior is exclusive and necessary, while situational and variational activity is neither. The great majority of Kinsey's incidents of modified behavior were probably motivated either situationally or variationally rather than reparatively, but Dr. Kinsey takes no notice of motivation. Rado believes that legal codes which punish sex deviants are not only futile but positively harmful, since modified patterns, carried on with a willing partner, harm no one, and the laws create an atmosphere of guilt and fear where blackmail and real crimes flourish.

In discussing some of the specific forms of modified sexual patterns, Rado rejects the theory of any sadistic-masochistic instinct, cutting through the confusion of the complex theoretical formulations to observe that those who rely for sexual pleasure upon pain are not pursuing death or self-destruction colored with sex; they are simply paying what they regard as the necessary price of their pleasure in advance, the price of punishment. Because of the strong fears of sex aroused early in life, these individuals can enjoy orgasm only if pain accompanies the pleasure, but pleasure is their primary goal. In this connection Rado disposes of Freud's death instinct, asserting that there is no inner drive toward destruction and death. Rather, death is simply the result of failure of adaptation. Where adaptive powers are not over-taxed, life can go on indefinitely as in the microscopic metazoa where life has been preserved for approximately one billion years. 'The battle of Eros and Death, as unfolded by Freud is a moving spectacle, filled with suspense, agony and hope. The scientific observer quietly reduces this Olympean drama to the observation that pleasure is the source and fulfilment of life, and death is its problem.' [19]

Of special interest, since he has rejected bisexuality, is Rado's discussion of homosexuality. He points out that the male-female sex pattern is indicated not only by the anatomical structure of human beings but also by the cultural conditioning of the marital and parental pair. The power of this bio-social structure is such that even those who seek a mate of their own sex are striving to approximate the pattern. The early childhood desires of homosexuals always reveal normal elements. These desires may be driven underground by fears of the opposite sex, but their strength cannot be broken by any force except complete schizophrenic disorganization. All homosexual activity is characterized by the desire to act out the male-female pattern, achieving the illusion of having or being a member of the opposite sex. Homosexuals seek out their opposites: the masculine woman is attracted to her feminine counterpart and vice versa.

The fear basis of all homosexuality is indicated by the fact that male pairs come together because each finds in the other the reassuring penis, while female pairs look in each other for the anxiety-allaying absence of the male organ. In the one case it is

19. *Ibid.* p. 179.

the vagina that is feared; yet the she-male tries to make his mouth or anus serve the vaginal function, even in the latter case assuming the standard coital position, lying on his back with his legs drawn up and spread apart. In the other case, the penis is avoided; yet the he-female will express strong desires to penetrate and even to impregnate her partner, sometimes using an ingeniously contrived fake penis to approximate genuine coitus more closely. Rado classifies homosexuals as he-males, she-males, he-females, and she-females, according to their motivation. Each of the four types reveals a different developmental history. The he-male is in most respects forceful and masculine, but he retreats from the mutilated and dangerous female, seeking a partner who is soft and feminine but who lacks the fearful vagina. The she-male has lost his 'push' completely, but he has learned to experience orgastic pleasure through the stimulation of the mucous membranes of his anus, which 'by variational richness of innervation may have been anatomically predisposed to this vicarious function.' He vaginalizes his anus and pictures himself in the 'pull' role. The he-female is at once frightened and fascinated by the threat of penetration, and she develops an illusory penis, pretending that she is penetrator rather than penetrated. The she-female accepts from the harmless female sexual advances and stimulation which she fears from the dangerous male. Where mouth-genital contact is practiced, it is the equivalent of a kind of magic-love which sometimes exists in a normal male-female pair, resembling the infant sucking at the breast. The motivational pattern is the desire to recapture the alimentary, child-parent dependency relationship, where the baby has its needs supplied instantly, as if it possessed a magic control over its environment. It cries and presto! — food is forthcoming, or the painful pin removed. Rado concludes that there is no innate desire for the same sex and that all homosexual behavior is motivated reparatively, situationally, or variationally. 'Accordingly, the fear voiced by many patients that their constitution includes a "homosexual component" has no foundation in fact.' [20]

Rado characterizes his theoretical orientation as adaptational

20. *Ibid.* p. 187.

or functional, a point of view fundamental to modern biology, where the interest is increasingly in a dynamic rather than a structural approach, when the investigator is no longer content merely to describe what is; he also wants to know why. This does not mean that the scientist has turned theologian, seeking a teleology, for the 'why' which is sought is merely mechanistic and not ultimate in character. Adaptation and mechanism are closely related. Behavior is seen adaptively as means and ends, mechanistically as cause and effect, but the two go together. Adaptational research is the 'reconnaissance arm' of biological inquiry, searching for means and ends. Causal analysis is the 'task force' which lands and demonstrates that the relationship is one of cause and effect. Practically speaking, this means that the psychoanalytic investigator always looks for the motivational force behind all behavior. He is concerned to know *why* a given act is performed much more than *what* the act was or *how* it was done. For Rado, all sexual behavior can be understood only as the underlying motive is discerned.

It is clear that Rado's approach is bio-social, a combination of instinct and culture. He is not so 'constitutionally' biased as Freud, nor is he so 'culturally' oriented as Horney. He seeks to weigh both factors on the scales of the evidence without tilting the balance with his own theoretical prejudices. His rejection of bisexuality and his consequent explanation of homosexuality as the result of an environmentally conditioned fear of the opposite sex is not accepted by many of the contemporary psychoanalysts, who prefer to cling to the traditional theory, claiming that at least *some* homosexuals are congenitally predisposed. In general, however, Rado's interpretation of sex seems remarkably sane and balanced, containing a minimum of speculation. Where the clinical evidence is insufficient, he is silent, speaking only on the basis of what he regards as well-established facts.

Summary

These three contemporary psychoanalysts, Horney, Alexander, and Rado, have departed from Freud, severing the umbilical cord which bound them to the master. They have all wandered farther from the parental home than most of their colleagues, although all three of them have had ample company on their journey. Freud's theory of a death instinct has been widely abandoned by modern analysts, though some, like Karl Menninger, still adhere to it. Horney's cultural orientation was shared by Harry Stack Sullivan and the generation of analysts trained and influenced by him, and although the majority of the profession remains closer to Freud's instinctual formulations, they are increasingly appreciative of environmental influence in the development of character and neurosis. Horney and Rado have both rejected the libido theory for different reasons. Rado accepts it as valuable to the therapist in searching for pleasure patterns but denies that it is a theory of sex. Horney was suspicious of and hostile to the entire instinctual bias of Freud, while Alexander accepts the instinctual emphasis but goes back to Freud's first scheme of libido drives and ego drives. In the realm of sex, Freud himself gave up the notion that sexual traumas are the root cause of most neuroses, substituting anxiety as the decisive etiological factor, and anxiety continues to be the ubiquitous infection discovered by the probing of the contemporary analysts. The origin of psychic disturbances is seen increasingly to lie in a general atmosphere of rejection and lovelessness, arousing fears and anxieties in the child. It is in such an environment that sexual discoveries are made and sexual attitudes formed so that the neurosis attacks and disturbs sexual activity as well as all other interpersonal relations. Rado and Alexander, in the company of most modern analysts, find the sexuality of patients a more reliable 'window' through which to view the psychodynamics of the personality than did Horney. They also weight constitutional factors more heavily than she. The attitude toward the Freudian character types, oral, anal, phallic, and so on, and the interpretation of such activities as smoking, painting, surgery, and writing as sexual, is mixed, with many analysts still using these categories and others modifying them. Alexander calls the activities erotic and Rado would agree that they are libidinal, but neither of them would mean by those terms 'sexual.' The whole trend in contemporary psychoanalysis, which was actually begun by Freud himself, is to focus increasing attention on the ego, with the result that the ubiquitous character of sexuality becomes less important.

In analytical circles, a growing interest is manifest in cultural problems, seeking to discover and to correct those social ills which produce neurosis. All analysts would agree that a less legalistic, moralistic attitude toward sex is an extremely important goal in the quest for increased mental and emotional hygiene. Not all of them share Freud's view that culture requires sexual repression and sublimation, nor would they all take as essentially pessimistic an outlook on the inevitable tensions between the individual's instinctive needs and society's demands as he did. But they would urge a transformation in the prevailingly dualistic, negative approach to sex, replacing the impression that it is evil and fearful with a more naturalistic appreciation which accepts sexuality as a source of pleasure and increased community between persons. Sex is not a threat but a promise, and children should learn that fact from their earliest infancy, not simply from their parents' words but from the whole emotional tone of the family constellation. The contemporary analysts do not pose as moralists, trying to impose any preconceived standards either on their individual patients or on society as a whole. They do not seek to play God. But as citizens, they too are concerned for the welfare of the commonwealth of which they are a part, and they labor unceasingly to relieve individuals and society of the false guilt feelings which are rooted in a faulty understanding of the nature and function of sex. In this enterprise the Christian forces of the community not only can but must co-operate fully, the more especially because they bear a large share of the responsibility for preserving, if not for creating, the negative fear of sex in western civilization.

THREE

A Critical Reconstruction

of Christian Interpretations of Sex

RECONSTRUCTION

The Contemporary Situation

THE TASK of reconstruction is a perennial one. Like Sisyphus, laboriously pushing his wheel to the top of the hill only to have it roll back down again, every age must create a fresh point of view. It is impossible to construct a universal history, since the prejudices and presuppositions of the period in which it was produced will inevitably influence the interpretation, and succeeding generations will detect the bias. It is equally impossible to erect a universally valid system of ethics, one which will be viable in all times and places. Christianity's recognition of that fact has in no small measure been responsible for its survival as a cultural influence, through all the vicissitudes of western civilization. Any statement of Christian Faith, if it is to be heard and heeded, must be made, to some extent at least, from the perspective and in the language of the period in which it is spoken. Any reconstruction of a Christian interpretation of sex in the mid-twentieth century, therefore, must begin with an attempt to understand the state of the nation with respect to sexual mores.

There are at least three factors in contemporary sexual attitudes and practices which demand special attention. The first is the revolution which has resulted in the sexual emancipation of women, a rebellion successfully accomplished in the space of a few decades. In the nineteenth century, the 'good' woman was almost completely denied the experience of erotic pleasure. Western civilization as a whole permitted the uninhibited enjoyment of coitus to the prostitute, the mistress, or the loose chambermaid but not to the wife and mother, for whom sex was a burden to be borne, a necessary evil to be endured for the sake of one's duty to posterity. The divine curse upon Eve was extended so that women not only brought forth their children in sorrow but conceived them in sorrow as well. If a wife discovered by accident that sexual pleasure was not an exclusively male phenomenon, she jeopardized her standing in her husband's eyes if she betrayed her discovery. Within the space of two generations, all of this has been radically changed. Women are now permitted and even expected to enjoy sex, relishing all the delights of pre-coital preparation and joining the male in orgasm. All of the modern marriage manuals provide detailed instructions on the approved methods of initiating women into the once all-male fraternity of erotic pleasure. The deletion of the segregation clause in the charter has not been an unmixed blessing, however. In previous generations, the husband could proceed directly to orgasm, blithely unconcerned about his wife's response; he was not expected to arouse her. As a result, there were few anxieties about masculine potency and even fewer about feminine frigidity. Women experienced frustration in varying degrees, but since that frustration was contained within a socially accepted pattern, little emotional damage was done. The new situation imposes demands upon both sexual partners, transforming a prosaic physical function into an art. Any difficulty in awakening the woman's sleeping passion produces anxiety on both sides of the bed. Doubts about the man's skill in the arts of love mingle with fears about the woman's frigidity, and the mixture evicts the spontaneity and relaxation which are essential to satisfactory coitus. Reassurance about one's sexual prowess is as common a goal of marital infidelity as passion. Sexual incompatibility, a prevailing fear of the young anticipating marriage, is almost always emotional rather than physical. Thus the sexual liberation of women with its attending pleasures and problems is a dominating factor in the present scene.

The second aspect calling
measure out of the first. Th
resulted in the withering a
morality. Formerly, men w
fields of youth scattering th
to the plowing of the acre
experienced in the labors
refuge from the chill of h
of prostitute or mistress,
lady, however, who prov
marital relations gravely
a wife and mother. Her
hanced, but she was alm

unblemished purity and innocence. Anyone who has had any close contact with the youth of today realizes that they no longer see double. Petting is almost the rule rather than the exception; many a married couple looks back upon at least one incident of sexual intercourse during their engagement, and a prolonged period of coitus before marriage is by no means rare. The young man of the present is far less concerned about the virginity of his prospective bride than was his grandfather, or even his father. He does not want a wife who has been promiscuous, but he is extremely tolerant of a previous love affair which has been sexually consummated, especially since he may himself have been similarly involved. It is no longer true that men lose their respect for a girl who is willing, and parents find it increasingly difficult to frighten their daughters out of the primrose path.

The third factor which must be recognized, closely related to the previous two, is the very high percentage of deviation from the 'accepted' moral standards of society, as revealed by the Kinsey reports. One cannot know to what extent similar deviations characterized previous eras, but however frequent they may have been, it seems clear that complete sexual abstinence before marriage followed by monogamous fidelity until death is a pattern found with increasing rarity on the contemporary scene. The traditional standards of sexual behavior, resting on the fundamental premise that sex must be confined to the bonds of monogamous

matrimony, are hono
servance, then at le
came first, the th
it would be di
result of th
tionship
for bel
mor

ed if not more in the breach than the ob-
st in a manner rapidly approaching it. Which
eoretical skepticism or the practical violation,
ficult to say. Some regard the new freedom as the
destruction of the old taboos; others see the rela-
eversed, the rejection of the ideals as a rationalization
avior. But both in theory and in action, modern sexual
ality is confused and chaotic.

A suggestion popular in many circles is the theory that moral
standards should conform to actualities. Dr. Kinsey brings evidence of what the actualities are, and his case is strengthened by
the data offered by animal psychologists and anthropologists
about the sexual behavior of other species and other cultures.
All of the deviations from the traditional standards which Kinsey
discovers in American life are to be found among primitive tribes
scattered all over the world and among the various species of
mammals from white rats to anthropoid apes.[1] Throughout the
animal kingdom and throughout human societies, the observer
encounters not only pre-marital and extra-marital intercourse,
but also masturbation, homosexuality, mouth-genital contacts,
even sexual relations across the line of species, 'bestiality,' as men
call it. On the basis of such evidence, many are insisting that anything in the realm of sex is perfectly 'natural.' Further ammuni-
tion is provided for the barrage against society's conventional
moral standards by the prevailing belief that psychoanalysis
shows emotional disorders to be the inevitable price of sexual
abstinence. The weapons forged by scholarly research are eagerly
seized by willing hands, though the minds behind the hands do
not understand the nature of the munitions they use. The reports of Dr. Kinsey and his associates, the writings of Freud and
other psychoanalysts, and the conclusions of the anthropologists
and sexologists are talked about rather than read by the general
public,[2] producing considerable misunderstanding and misinfor-

1. Cf. Clellan S. Ford and Frank A. Beach, *Patterns of Sexual Behavior*,
Harper & Bros., New York, 1951.

2. This statement is made despite the fact that the first Kinsey report
proved to be a best seller. One has the distinct impression that most people

mation in the current thinking about sex. Part of the ferocity of the attack upon moral standards is certainly traceable to rationalization, the attempt to justify behavior that violates those standards; but there is also a large measure of sincere conviction that a new set of norms is needed, which will genuinely direct rather than simply excuse present practice. That conviction profoundly challenges the sexual mores which have been so long dominant in western culture.

In such a time as this, when women have been emancipated and many of them are taking full advantage of their new-found freedom, when the double standard moves toward the realm of recollection, when traditional standards are violated and attacked, it seems to many that the religious elements of society stand as the guardians of the sexual Bastille, which must be stormed and captured by the forces of the new revolution. It must be confessed that there is much not worth defending in the interpretations of sex found in Augustine and Aquinas, in Luther and Calvin. The Church has been guilty of preserving and preaching a point of view not generic to Christian faith, an attitude which originated in Hellenistic dualism and which is not only un-Biblical but also anti-Biblical. The perennial error of defending reaction against the right must not be continued. As the young zealots of today are quick to point out, Galileo was forced to recant, Bruno was burned at the stake, Darwin was vilified and slandered, and once more the Church manifests its typical social inertia. This means that Christianity is confronted with the serious responsibility of re-examining its traditional interpretation of sex in full awareness of the present situation, raising the question whether the new 'science' may not be right, as Galileo and Darwin were right, unpleasant though such an admission may prove. This is not to say that Christians must give ground simply because pressure is exerted. When they are sure that the word they speak has been given them by God, then

---

bought the book expecting a series of case-histories, after the manner of Krafft-Ebing, and quickly laid it aside when they discovered its real character. As one wit remarked, 'It is the most widely bought and least widely read book of our generation!'

'neither persecution nor peril, nor famine nor nakedness nor sword' can stop their mouths, but Christians must always take care lest they confuse the word of man with the word of God. History has demonstrated repeatedly that time makes ancient good uncouth, and while men of faith are assured that there is in Christianity a truth which is in some sense eternal, beyond all the vicissitudes of the temporal order, they must recognize the perennial necessity for the reinterpretation and restatement of that truth.

Christianity and the Facts of Life

This raises the pregnant problem of the relationship between Christianity and the scientific or semi-scientific disciplines which concern themselves with sexual behavior: biology, psychology, sociology, anthropology, and psychoanalysis. What are the points of contact and conflict? There is a sense in which one deals here with two disparate realms of discourse. The claim of these other observers is that they are not concerned with rendering moral judgments but with presenting the facts. In so far as this is true, the Christian can only be grateful for their diligent service, for Christian Faith involves the conviction that all truth is of God and that nothing is to be feared from the facts, regardless of their source. Gold remains gold, wherever and by whomever it is found. There are few Christians today who would defend the obscurantism or the obstinate fear with which some sections of the Church regarded scientific research in days gone by. The facts in any area of life are to be welcomed. That is why psychoanalysis must be of such interest to anyone concerned with the realm of sex, because it has produced such a wealth of clinical data. A similar interest, of course, applies to other disciplines which offer relevant findings. But facts very rarely exist in a vacuum. They are almost always presented in the context of an interpretation, and interpretations are quite different from the facts themselves. Subjectivity can never be ignored, and the closer the approach to matters directly affecting the observer himself, the more difficult objectivity becomes. The 'purity' of science moves in a descending spiral from mathematics and physics through astronomy, chemistry, and geology, to biology and psychology, and it almost vanishes in the so-called social sciences. The farther from man, from the scientist, the greater the objectivity possible. So long as science confines itself to its proper sphere — the description of uniformities in nature — no friction is possible between Christianity and science. But when implications for human behavior are derived from those uniformities, either implicitly or explicitly, then Christianity is not a disparate realm of discourse but a coincident one. The facts are set in a context of meaning and value, and this is precisely the concern of Christian Faith.

Professors Ford and Beach of Yale in their book *Patterns of Sexual Behavior* make the following assertion: 'We consistently eschewed any discussion of the rightness or wrongness of a particular type of sexual behavior. Moral evaluations form no part of this book.'[3] This would appear to be a strictly scientific approach, rendering disagreement impossible. To be sure, it is of great value as the authors suggest, to be able to compare the sexual behavior and standards of one's own society with those of other men and other species of animals, inquiring into the similarities and differences to be found. Such a study must be approached with extreme caution, however, for there is a constant temptation for both author and reader to draw inferences from the anthropological and biological data. Those inferences are usually covert rather than overt, but close inspection usually discovers them.

That such a temptation is not only encountered but also yielded to can be demonstrated by referring to the published account of a symposium held by the American Psychopathological Association. Dr. Kinsey opened the proceedings, presenting the substance of his findings about the sexual behavior of the American male. He was followed by Professors Ford and Beach, each of whom read a paper which described, in somewhat abbreviated form, the biological and anthropological studies they later expanded into book form. All three of those reports, of course, detailed widespread deviation from the sexual norms of western

3. Ford and Beach, *op. cit.* p. 14.

civilization not only among American males but also among primitive tribes and among animals. Abram Kardiner, a psycho-analyst with training and experience in sociology and anthro-pology, was responsible for leading the discussion on these three papers.[4] He opened that discussion by saying:

This is one of the most remarkable meetings I have ever attended. The speakers all acted as if they were in collusion to put over a certain point. . . . This entire array of evidence is presented in a way as to render it entirely misleading. The picture Dr. Kinsey sees of human sexuality by his particular method of study, is the product of a particular set of social conditions prevailing in Western culture. Dr. Beach's evidence is en-tirely untrustworthy. How can anyone compare the manifestations of homosexuality in animals as having even the remotest resemblance to the same phenomenon in man, where it is a highly conditioned choice to the exclusion of heterosexual activity? And Mr. Ford's method only proves that from this particular method of cross-cultural study, in the domain of sex anything can happen, and usually does. And from this method we learn precisely nothing. What Mr. Ford has done is to tear sexual behavior out of the entire social context and give us only the end products. No, human sexuality cannot be studied in this way. If we are to know anything about the relation of sexual mores to the total adapta-tion of a society, then Mr. Ford's technic is very misleading.

Kardiner is extremely suspicious of this comparative approach because the implication is strong that what society regards as perversions are traceable to phylogeny, rooted in the biological nature of man. This is precisely what Dr. Kinsey maintains, in-sisting that modified patterns of sexual behavior are both normal and natural and that they must be accepted. Moral standards must be altered so that what are now regarded as sexual ab-normalities are no longer condemned because they are not really abnormal. Kardiner, on the other hand, believes that sexual be-havior in human beings is highly conditioned by their environ-ment and that at least 85 per cent of sexual perversions are the result of a cultural conditioning which arouses fears of normal sexuality in the young, driving them into deviation. Change the cultural atmosphere and most of the abnormalities will disap-pear. He concedes that there may be a small number of perverts who are constitutionally predisposed, but he is reluctant to call

4. *Psychosexual Development in Health and Disease*, p. 85f.

their sexual patterns either normal or natural. It is of the utmost importance to uncover the motivation behind sexual behavior, both individually and collectively, because only then can it be seen in its true perspective. Therefore little is to be learned from a study of the sexual mores of a primitive tribe without reference to the role these mores play in the total life of the society. Yet Professor Ford persists in precisely that approach in the book which he and Beach co-authored, and Beach continues to present his evidence of animal sexuality as though there were not important limitations on this sort of material. It is almost inevitable that the reader will draw conclusions from the book about the sex life of his own culture, and despite their explicit denial, the authors give the impression that they have themselves drawn similar conclusions.

This is the danger which besets all presentations of anthropological data. The facts are set in a context of meaning. The alternative is not to abstain from such studies or such reports but rather to face openly the realities, admitting that presuppositions and valuations do exist and clarifying what they are. The scientific observer is often unaware that his bias is showing, and the remedy does not consist in the futile effort to eradicate such a bias but in the frank admission of it. No author can help allowing his own attitudes to color his presentation. That is a part of being human. No man is ever entirely neutral about the central issues of life. He has values which he seeks to preserve and propagate, fears and anxieties which trouble him, enemies against whom he strives. He may be entirely unaware of such feelings and attitudes, but they are an essential part of his psychodynamics nonetheless. Whether one calls it a *Weltanschauung,* or a philosophy of life, or a religious faith, some sort of total orientation, of integration of life into a meaningful whole is an inescapable consequence of being human. Richard Niebuhr has made the distinction between what he calls internal history and external history. In the latter, an attitude of detachment, impersonality, and objectivity is pursued; the quest is for the facts as they are, however painful and unpleasant they may be. But man can never stop there. He must always go on to ask what those facts imply, how they affect him as a person, and this is the realm of internal history, the realm of concern, of valuation, of passionate attachment. Two historians approach the data of American history; by personal conviction one of them is a liberal, the other a conservative. Both will present the same events, the same dates, treaties, battles, personages, and each will insist that he is being 'objective'; yet their students will derive from the two courses an entirely different understanding of the American past, because the two mentors have a different internal history. This duality of internal and external characterizes the approach to every set of facts. The quest for the ultimate meaning of all facts, for the significance of life as a whole, is an inextricable aspect of the human situation. Erich Fromm has pointed out that 'the need for a system of orientation and devotion is an intrinsic part of human existence. . . . Indeed, there is no other more powerful source of energy in man. Man is not free to choose between having or not having "ideals." . . . All men are "idealists" and are striving for something beyond the attainment of physical satisfaction.' [5] It is Fromm's virtue that he frankly admits that his own system of values is humanistic. Freud was unaware of the extent to which his thinking had been influenced by the mechanistic determinism of the nineteenth century, and Karen Horney has shown how many of his formulations were colored by that influence. Yet she herself was not altogether conscious of the way in which the naturalistic humanism of her own times impressed itself on her thought patterns.

The question of life's meaning is of concern to all men, whether the question is explicitly asked and answered or not. Fromm is reluctant to call this basic human thirst for meaning 'religious' because of the overtones of that term, but whatever the terminology, the reality is recognizable. The search for *complete* objectivity is a futile one, since even the natural scientist begins with certain convictions and presuppositions about the nature of reality. His own subjective interests lead him to select this field of inquiry rather than that as the object of his research.

5. Erich Fromm, *Man For Himself*, Rinehart & Co., Inc., New York, 1947, p. 49.

Psychoanalysis itself rests upon underlying ontological assumptions. The metaphysical question cannot be avoided; the facts of life must always be related to the meaning of life. The two elements can never be entirely separated, so that the facts cannot be left to science and their interpretation to religion. It is not so simple as that. What must be sought is a harmonious relation between the two, so that the scientist recognizes that he is not a robot but a man, facing and admitting his presuppositions and prejudices, and the theologian is impelled to find meaning in terms of the facts as they actually are and not as he thinks they ought to be. Certain elements of natural-law theory in Roman Catholicism are out of joint with the findings of biology and anthropology, and serious questions can be raised about Emil Brunner's understanding of monogamy as an 'order of creation,' divinely ordained for all men. In this type of reasoning, there is always the danger that the facts will be tailored to fit a theory. A particular view of meaning becomes a Procrustean bed into which all facts are forced, whether they fit or not. There have been and undoubtedly will continue to be errors and oversights on the part of both theologians and scientists, but the situation will not be greatly ameliorated by hurling recriminations back and forth. The common cause of understanding the difficult problems of this highly complex area of human sex relations will best be served by co-operation and mutual understanding.

Certainly all possible data must be gathered from every source, recognizing that there is disagreement even about the facts themselves. As the editors of *Psychosexual Development in Health and Disease* have confessed, 'even though we have amassed a great quantity of observations, we still lack a comprehensive understanding of sexual behavior.' [6] This ought to lend a note of humility to any and all discussions about sex. Far too little is known as yet about the bodily chemistry of the sexual processes. No clear understanding has emerged of the relation between instinctual and constitutional factors on the one hand and the influence of culture and environment on the other. In the face of limited knowledge, it is the better part of wisdom not to attempt to

6. *Loc. cit.* p. v.

venture too far beyond that knowledge, not to pretend that one has the final and definitive word. But an attempt must be made on the basis of present understanding to organize those facts which are available into the framework of a total outlook on life and its meaning and purpose. The question of motivation must, on both Biblical and psychoanalytic grounds, be kept constantly in the foreground, in the quest to discover the goals and aims of individuals and of society as a whole. Any integrative orientation ought to be kept in harmony with the facts, but some kind of orientation is unavoidable. Christianity must rely for its facts upon the other disciplines, but it has both the right and the responsibility to interpret those facts in the light of its convictions about the ultimate meaning of reality. Psychoanalysis or any other scientific or semi-scientific school has, of course, an equal right and responsibility, but conflicts that arise between their interpretations and those of Christianity must be seen for what they are: not a quarrel between science and religion or between facts and their interpretations, but between two metaphysical systems, two valuational sets of presuppositions.

The Implications of Three Classic Christian Doctrines for the Interpretation of Sex

It goes without saying that the interpretation of sex presented in this volume is illumined by Christian Faith, of Protestant persuasion. Two basic principles underlie the following reconstruction: the conviction that Christian Faith offers the most adequate synoptic view of life available (the eternal truth of the Gospel) and the belief that that faith must be reinterpreted and restated in every age so that it speaks in accents which can be understood (the timely truth of the Gospel, or what Tillich calls the 'method of correlation'). There is nothing more irrelevant than answers to questions not asked. Also involved in the second principle is the conviction that Christian Faith must be adequate to the facts of experience from whatever source these facts may come. One does not become a Christian by way of empirical analysis; he does not derive his faith from experience; it is given to him. But once having entered the circle of faith, he can and must subject it to the constant corrective of the appeal to experience. A doctrine is to be maintained only so long as it continues to present an adequate view of reality. The idea of a double truth, that something can be true for faith but false for reason, is characteristic of decadence. The great souls of the Church have always seen the truth as one, taking as their motto, *Fides quaerens intellectum,* faith seeking understanding.

The first classic Christian doctrine with significant implications for an interpretation of sex is the belief in creation. Reference has already been made to William Temple's assertion that Christianity is the most materialistic of the great religions of the world. The theological centrality of the Incarnation and the liturgical importance of the Eucharist bear witness to the truth of that statement, as does the historical concern of the Church for men's physical welfare, but fundamental to all of these is the doctrine of creation *ex nihilo.* In the Orient the world is regarded as illusory and evil; in Greek thought matter was looked upon as eternal, co-existing with the forms from the beginning. Matter was called literally 'stuff,' pliable, capable of being molded and formed in infinite variety, but also with a certain intractability, a resistance to form. In some types of Hellenistic thought, the entire material world was described as evil, but whether this extreme was reached or not, physical substance was never looked upon as containing any organic connection with ultimate reality. The Judao-Christian tradition stands in dramatic contrast to all of this in its affirmation of the material world as having been created out of nothing by God himself. The Bible begins with the divine spirit, brooding over the void, and when God finished his work he looked upon everything that he had made, and behold, it was very good. Despite later intrusions of Hellenistic dualism into Christian thought, the creation idea retains its basic importance, whether in the East, which is highly mystical and sacramentarian in its view of every creature as a vessel containing the spirit of God, or in the medieval West, with the appealing charm of St. Francis' love for all of nature, or in the Reformation, where Luther sees the world as a gown which God wears and Calvin finds the work of God on every hand. The essential strand of Christianity is joyfully positive in its acceptance of the material world as the gift of God. 'All things are yours,' says St. Paul. The ascetic denial of things of the flesh derives from a dualistic attitude, which seeks salvation outside the world, removed from the mundane sordidness of material existence, in the things of the 'spirit.' But this is a denial of the faith in creation, a Hellenistic-Oriental attempt to escape from an evil and illusory world. The dualist cannot believe that the ultimate reality is in the world or that salvation is to be found there. Both must be sought outside the physical-temporal order. Biblical religion knows nothing of God or of salvation apart from history, from the activity of God in time. God is not some remote Absolute, removed from and indifferent to life, but he who speaks and acts in the world he has made. 'Every bush is aflame with fire, but only he who has eyes to see takes off his shoes.' The contrast between the mystical ascetic, who withdraws into a temple of contemplation and self-denial, and the Biblical man of faith, who is fully aware of the holiness of the given and is drawn into a life of activity in the world, is strikingly illustrated in the poetry of T. S. Eliot and W. H. Auden. Eliot finds 'the garden' in separation, while Auden sees it all about him.[7] The recovery of the doctrine of creation with its sense of the hallowed character of all things great and small is the most pressing need of modern Christendom, and it is indispensable to an adequate interpretation of sex.

A serious acceptance of the fact of creation demands a positive attitude toward the human body and all of its parts and functions. Any point of view which seeks to drive a wedge between body and soul, between flesh and spirit, describing the one as evil and the other as good must be rejected as anti-Christian. In Biblical anthropology, man is always a psychosomatic unity, flesh and spirit inextricably related to each other. The Old Testament knows nothing of asceticism, of disciplining the flesh for the sake of the spirit. On the contrary, it rejoices in the life of the body, in sensual pleasure of all kinds, sweet savors, rich feasts, eye-

7. I am indebted for this illustration to Professor Stanley Romaine Hopper of Drew University.

filling delights, enchanting sounds, and the joys of love. The
song of Solomon, allegorized and emasculated though it may be,
bears eternal witness to the appreciation of sensuality in Hebrew
thought. Jesus was no monk; he was called a 'winebibber and
publican.' The Son of man came eating and drinking, and his
sharpest rebukes were directed to those who scrupulously fasted
and held themselves aloof from the things of the world. Such
asceticism as Paul carried within his soul was apocalyptic and
not dualistic, based on climactic expectation, not world denial.
The body is to be used, not abused, to be enjoyed, not punished.
It is a temple wherein to sing the praise of God. There is nothing
shameful or indecent about it. Aesthetically speaking, certain
functions are more decorously performed in private than in public, especially the evacuative ones, but this is a question of taste,
not of morals. Aesthetic considerations apply equally to nudism,
since few individuals could pose as models for Greek sculpture.
Rare is the person who does not look better with some clothes
on. But this again, has nothing to do with decency or morality.
Primitive tribes who eschew the hindrance of garments are in
many respects more moral and certainly less erotically curious
than their more civilized brethren, a fact that has encouraged the
cult of nudism, which seems a trifle self-conscious, but which has
certainly produced no sexual orgies.

The literature on shame and modesty is impressively extensive,
the bulk of it produced by Christian theologians and anthropologists, and it is difficult to know where the truth lies. Recent
studies in child behavior coupled with reports on primitive tribes
render theories of innate shame as the result of original sin or
concupiscence increasingly difficult to maintain. There are several aboriginal societies where all sexual acts are public without
any secretiveness whatever, and the modern nursery school has
dissipated the notion that small children are constitutionally
modest. Pre-school boys and girls accompany one another to the
toilet and continue conversation with complete nonchalance
while they evacuate bowels or bladder. Children raised in such
an atmosphere seldom reveal any morbid curiosity about the
anatomy of the opposite sex, or any shame about their own

bodies. A kind of modesty may develop as adolescence draws near, but it is impossible to ascertain whether this is the result of social conditioning or the flowering of some innate tendency. The latter remains a possibility of course, but all theories of instinctive shame become increasingly tenuous and insecure.

What has been said about the body and its organs applies with equal force to the sexual act itself, which the Bible interprets as a divine command, a gift and not a problem. The whole question of the primary purpose of sex, whether procreation or pleasure, has produced a plethora of polemics. Roman Catholicism insists that natural law indicates the primacy of procreation; Freud placed himself on the side of pleasure. Biology confesses its ignorance when faced with such a teleological question. The unhappy fact seems to be that no one really knows, which leaves the field wide open for contending theories in the absence of conquering evidence. Speculation seems unfruitful. Who knows whether Nature offers the orgasm as an incentive to reproduction or whether conception is the fortuitous result of the alluring rites of Aphrodite? So long as it is recognized that all theories are merely theories, anyone is free to think what he likes, but a firm *caveat* must be entered against any dogmatic assertion of one point of view. It is impossible, on the basis of the existing evidence, to say, as Rome does, that natural law demands that sex for pleasure must never be performed in such a way as to block the possibility of conception. If that dictum is made a matter of revealed truth, a special divine command, men can disagree with the conclusion but not with Rome's right to such a belief. Protestantism is happily neutral on the question and therefore judges sexual relations on other grounds. Birth control is not banned because there is no strong conviction about the primary purpose of sex. The absence of natural-law theory in Protestantism liberates it to focus concern on sex as an interpersonal relationship, where the important motivational question deals with the attitude toward the sexual partner and not with reproduction.

Speaking purely from the point of view of personal motivation, without presuming to render any judgment on the teleology of Nature as a whole, the purpose of sex in man is the achievement of what the Bible calls 'one flesh.' Every sexual act, however casual or even commercial, at least points toward the most intimately personal relationship possible between two human beings. The creation faith asserts that man is made in the image of God. Every man is a 'Thou' and not an 'It.' As one of the characters in Richard Llewellyn's *None But the Lonely Heart* observes: 'I was out walking one day and in the distance I saw an animal. I came up closer and saw it was a man. I came up closer still and saw it was my brother!' To treat a person as though he were an animal or a thing is to violate not only his integrity but one's own as well. Sexual relations which are motivated by purely selfish lust, without regard for the partner as a person, a brother carrying the image of a common creator, are like a two-edged sword, dealing destruction on both sides. Sex at its best, that is when it fulfills its inner essence and purpose, is the union not simply of two bodies but of two persons. A sacrament is defined as the outward and visible sign of an inner and invisible state, and in that sense sex is sacramental, symbolizing in dramatic form the blending of two into one. Psychoanalysis recognizes that promiscuous sexual behavior springs from a disturbed personality, though exceptions are made in the case of the exploratory adolescent phase of development, which marks the transition between infantile and mature love. But maturity demands sexual behavior that is motivated by respect for persons, even in psychoanalytic terms, a significant testimony to the purpose of sex as it is rooted in the nature of man, which is in turn grounded in the reality of creation. Seen in this light, sex can be affirmed as one of God's greatest gifts to man, the key which unlocks the door to community. The fact that it is misused and diverted from its intended course no more renders it evil than any other aspect of the created world which may also be distorted and mishandled. The doctrine of creation, therefore, is compatible only with a glad and grateful acceptance of sex and of the human body and the organs that render coitus possible. Anything less than this is a denial of God's handiwork.

The second Christian doctrine illuminating the darkness of human sexuality is the belief in original sin, expressed in the myth of the fall of man. This involves the conviction, expressed in all of the religious and most of the philosophical traditions of the world, that there is a tragic contradiction between man as he was created (his essence) and man as he is (his existence). From the Christian point of view, one of the chief shortcomings of Freud was his failure to recognize such a contradiction. For him, man was entirely existence. The inner intuition that one is somehow more than and better than the anguished conflicts and tragic missteps out of which the fabric of daily life is woven were ascribed by Freud either to illusion or to the work of an inflated super-ego. In this respect, at least, Jung and some of the contemporary analysts who recognize the presence of positive and creative strivings in the human psyche are closer to Christianity than Freud. Man's essential nature is to fulfill himself, to realize his potentialities for love and community and creativity. This is expressed in the statement that he is made in the image of God and in the commandment to love God wholly and the neighbor as the self. Man's existence, however, is characterized by the failure of fulfillment, the lack of love, by separation and estrangement. He is at once a child of God (his essence) and a sinner (his existence).

It should be perfectly clear by now that the doctrine of original sin has nothing to do with sex between Adam and Eve. This has been made manifest in Part One where Catholic and Protestant theologians have united in insisting that original sin does not refer to moral misdemeanors, sexual or otherwise, but to a state in which man finds himself. Because the term sin almost always conveys to the modern mind the picture of some immoral act, Paul Tillich has suggested abandoning the word, at least for a time, and substituting the word 'estrangement,' which is what the Church has always meant by original sin. The myth in Genesis shows Eve tempted by the serpent, who according to later tradition was really Lucifer in disguise. He had previously attempted to make himself God, and having failed in his own effort, he prompted man to rebel, speaking to Eve the words of promise, 'That ye may be as God.' She and Adam were unable to resist the impulse to make themselves the center of the universe, and they became estranged from God, an estate passed on to all of their descendants. This produced estrangement from neighbor. Genuine community is no longer possible; there is an element of strangeness, even in the most intimate of human relations. No one can wholly know another, nor can he fully reveal himself to another. Only fragments of the totality are communicable. And the estrangement involved the very core of personality itself so that man is at war with himself. He is confused about his essential nature, wondering with the idealists whether it is reason, or with the romanticists whether it is emotion, and he cannot overcome the split within him which impels him to do what he hates and hate what he does.

Now whence comes this estrangement, this inner division? Is it pure neurosis, or does it have its seat in something innately evil in human nature? Reinhold Niebuhr in his Gifford Lectures, *The Nature and Destiny of Man,* offers a significant answer. Man, he says, is a child of nature, rooted and grounded in all of its limitations and finitudes, but he is also more than that. He is able to stand outside of himself, to transcend himself and his world. He possesses a degree of freedom over his natural impulses unknown to the animal, for whom it is impossible to make sex or the acquisitive impulse the center of its existence since its life is regulated by the timeless laws of instinct. Man, however, can make sex the center of his life; he can live to eat; he can worship mammon. This freedom, with its accompanying sense of responsibility gives rise to anxiety. Man grows dizzy in his position of suspension, as an animal yet more than an animal, as a spirit and yet a finite spirit. From anxiety, there are two avenues of escape. One is the way of trust, which leads to a creative relationship to God and neighbor; the other is the way of retreat, the attempt to find security in the only thing one is sure of, himself. The latter is no escape, since it only ends in further anxiety, but it is a broad highway on which all men walk, even the psychoanalyzed and the redeemed. In so far as they are able to take the other fork of the crossroads with which ubiquitous anxiety confronts them at every step, to enter in at the strait gate of trust, they find that their faith in existence itself, in their neighbors and in them-

selves enables them to transcend their anxiety and to fulfill themselves.

Anxiety is the root of sin, which is a statement strikingly parallel to the psychoanalytical understanding of anxiety as the
seedbed of neurosis. In the increasing communication between
theologians and psychoanalysts, the most popular topic of conversation is this emotional state which the Germans call *Angst*.
Both groups agree that there is in all men a basic, existential
anxiety, which is a part of the human situation, springing ultimately from man's knowledge that he must die. Both also recognize the reality of neurotic anxiety, which is created by a special
set of circumstances. The individual grows up in an atmosphere
which is hostile and rejecting so that he believes himself to be
not only unloved but unlovable. Filled with anxiety about himself, he is fearful of much in life that is in fact harmless and
blind to threats that are genuinely menacing, and he adopts all
kinds of strategies to ward off his anxiety. Neurotic anxiety can
be resolved by therapeutic techniques. Working largely through
the device of the transfer of the patient's emotional attitudes
onto himself, the psychoanalyst gradually helps the analysand to
realize that people can be trusted, that his fears are illusory, that
he does have many positive qualities which make him lovable.
The Christian can only be grateful to the healing power of the
analyst for the restoration of many a broken soul. No conflict is
possible on this ground. Tensions arise when Christians begin
to assert that religious faith can dispel neurotic anxiety or when
psychoanalysts suggest that existential anxiety is neurotic, soluble
in a therapeutic solution. Tillich has maintained that existential
anxiety is not the concern of the physician as physician, though
he can communicate courage and faith, and that neurotic anxiety
is not the province of the minister as minister, though he must
be fully aware of it. Each can in a measure approximate the function of the other, but neither can be replaced. Psychoanalysis has
a legitimate and essential role to play in dealing with neurotic
anxiety. The fact that an individual suffers from an anxiety neurosis is no more a reflection on his religious faith than cancer.
Both are diseases to be diagnosed and treated by a competent

medical practitioner. But after the analyst has delivered the patient from his neurotic fears, which are illusory, the analyst and patient alike must face their existential anxiety, which is genuine. Tillich describes this in three categories: the anxiety of fate and death, the anxiety of emptiness and meaninglessness, and the anxiety of guilt and condemnation. Absolute security is an illusion. All men are anxious about death, and all men are fearful of meaninglessness. The kind of anxiety centering around one's goals in life, the values which he cherishes and the truths he believes, the source of his ultimate concern, raises what is ultimately a religious question and demands a religious answer. It can be faced and accepted only with what Tillich calls 'courage,' which represents a profound religious trust, in however secular and anti-religious terms it may clothe itself.

Both Christianity and psychoanalysis agree that sexuality is to be affirmed, the one on the basis of the doctrine of creation, the other on purely naturalistic grounds, and both see anxiety as the central problem of the human situation, though Christianity focuses attention on existential anxiety, while psychoanalysis concerns itself with neurotic anxiety. Regardless of the varying stresses and emphases, however, there is a common understanding of human behavior as symptomatic, a recognition that a preoccupation with symptoms is both futile and mistaken. Any adequate analysis must penetrate the outer layers of activity to their meaning and motivation in the core of the personality. Sexual deviations are seen as symptoms of a disturbance which has anxiety at its roots, not as iniquities to be condemned. Such an understanding, which springs from the Christian doctrine of original sin no less than from theories of psychodynamics will contribute to the adoption of a therapeutic rather than a moralistic attitude toward sexual deviants. The difficulty with many Christians, both clerical and lay, is that they lack either a sound theology or psychological information, which leads them into one of two errors in their approach to persons involved in sexual irregularities. One kind of Christian will earnestly wish to be of help and will devote hours to the discussion of symptoms with the deviant, which may provide a warm and sympathetic empathy but will accomplish nothing in really dealing with the problem. The other type will urge the exertion of will power to subdue the evil demon within, ignorant of the fact that will power is precisely what the individual lacks. If that could help him, he would have used it himself long ago. The difficulty, whatever it is, must be traced to its source in the personality and understood. Insight cannot be attained, however, in an atmosphere of moralistic condemnation, be it ever so feeble, for even unconscious moral judgment in the helper somehow communicates itself to the person seeking help. This is the significance of the 'permissive' attitude of the psychoanalyst. The patient condemns himself and is constantly projecting his self-recriminations onto others, and it is only gradually and tortuously that the analyst is able to persuade him that he is genuinely accepted. Many ministers are unable to function effectively as counselors because of their essential moralism, which is sometimes unconscious. Perhaps the secret of Jesus' ministry of healing lay in the therapeutic attitude revealed by his words, 'Neither do I condemn thee.'

One of the problems presenting itself at this point is the question of what really constitutes a sexual deviation. The Church is apt to frown upon any sexual activity that transgresses the moral norm: abstinence until marriage followed by monogamous fidelity, and there is a tendency to be critical of the greater measure of tolerance evident in psychoanalysis. This, however, is nothing more than Pharisaism, as has already been pointed out in chapter 1. This is to judge in terms of an external law, and psychoanalysis is closer to Jesus than much of Christianity when it confines its own judgment to motivation. Most psychoanalysts would regard a good deal of what passes for perfectly moral marital sexuality as neurotic and disturbed and contrariwise would accept much of what is generally condemned as wicked and perverse with considerable equanimity. The Church is constrained by its own theology, no less than by scientific sexology, to engage in some hard rethinking of its position. Christianity and psychoanalysis can agree that Rado's standard coital pattern, the insertion of the penis into the vagina prior to orgasm represents the measure of 'normal' sexuality. There is nothing either perverse or wicked about any behavior which precedes that union and its climax, providing only that it is directed by mutual respect and mature love. In much of sexual foreplay, there are many varieties of stimulation both in fact and fantasy. When cunnilingus or fellatio are used as preludes to coitus or as variational patterns, they are perfectly natural and normal. There is even a normal sort of sadism-masochism in the so-called 'love-bite.' An activity does not become a perversion until it is used compulsively as a substitute for the standard coital pattern. A pervert is one whose access to normal sexual relations is blocked by his anxieties in such a way that he must seek 'reparative patterns.' Such an individual can achieve orgasm only reparatively, and he is a problem to himself and to society, as well as to the psychoanalyst and the Christian, but moral condemnation or legal prohibition will accomplish nothing. What is required is the recognition that his behavior is only a symptom of his estrangement, his inability to relate himself to his fellow human beings except in a distorted manner. An awareness that what is out of joint is his total orientation and not simply his overt sexual behavior will give rise to a therapeutic attitude toward him, a desire to help him achieve the kind of inner integrity which will make his aberrant sexual patterns no longer necessary. This is the only kind of therapy that will be effective with sexual deviants, the kind that goes to the root of the problem in the core of the personality. Any moral condemnation of the pervert will only drive him deeper into self-hatred, and stern demands for self-discipline will only increase his sense of weakness and failure. The Christian must confess that the kind of understanding and acceptance essential to a ministry of reconciliation to sexual perverts is far more prevalent among psychoanalysts than among pastors.

A wider measure of tolerance for perversion is demanded both by an understanding of the Christian doctrine of sin and by a knowledge of psychodynamics, but what of other, less bizarre forms of deviation from the sexual norms of society, i.e., premarital intercourse, adultery, and so on? Here again, motivation is the decisive factor rather than external legal codes. The philanderer, whether married or not, is driven to his promiscuity by inner anxiety. Psychoanalysis speaks of a Don Juan type, haunted by fears about his masculinity, his potency, who must constantly reassure himself. He is incapable of entering into any mature relationship with another person, unable to experience the satisfaction of coitus with a permanent partner, a person with whom he has become one flesh. His reparative pattern is quantitatively rather than qualitatively different from the norm, but the considerations applied to the pervert are equally relevant to him. Denunciation and the counsels of self-control will be of little avail. He needs to be helped to insight into the origin of his problem, the sources of his reparative pattern, and when the underlying anxiety has been recognized and dispelled, he will no longer find it necessary to pursue the kind of frantic reassurance which has been the real goal of his promiscuity. That is what must be understood about both the pervert and the philanderer: they are not seeking sexual satisfaction primarily but are using sex as a means to the end of allaying anxiety.

It would appear that a proper grasp of the implications of the doctrine of original sin requires the Christian to join the psychoanalyst in his tolerance and understanding, no less than in his therapeutic attitude toward deviations from the sexual norm. But what of the pre-marital or adulterous relationship which is neither perverse nor promiscuous? What is the Church to say to a young couple for whom marriage is for practical reasons impossible for a period of months or years and who choose to consummate their love for one another sexually, or to the married man who finds himself in love with another woman? From the psychoanalytic point of view, there is nothing reparative about such a relationship, and the reluctance of the analyst to dictate moral standards produces a highly permissive atmosphere. The individual is left free to act as his own conscience directs. Christianity has no such reluctance, nor should it have, for it has the altogether legitimate function of molding the conscience after the fashion of the law of love. No other law can be made binding, and there is a sense in which no generalizations can be made. Each case must be judged on its own merits, but Christianity and

psychoanalysis can quite properly point out that there is a difference between infantile love, which demands immediate gratification regardless of the consequences and mature love, which is
able to forswear immediate satisfaction for the sake of greater
goods. Any unmarried couple engaging in sexual intercourse runs
the risk of conception, of exposure and social censure, and any
married person has definite responsibilities to his mate and children. The phrase, 'But we love each other!' often overlooks the
fact that mature love is neither exclusive nor irresponsible. One
also loves parents and friends, husband or wife and children, and
one has responsibilities to them. The creation of one flesh in the
Biblical sense involves the joining of two total existences, economically, spiritually, and psychologically, and not just the union of two bodies. To attempt the one without the other is
dangerous to the entire relationship. Sexuality cannot be separated from the rest of life and made a thing in itself. It is always
organically related to the whole personality, the whole structure
of life. However, the Christian must recall that he is not to judge
lest he be judged, and he is wise to keep in mind the words
'There but for the grace of God go I.' The violation of the sexual
mores of convention is, seen through the eyes of Jesus, a comparatively minor misdemeanor.

The importance of a therapeutic rather than a punitive attitude toward sexual irregularities points to the third classic Christian doctrine which is essential to an adequate interpretation of
sex, the doctrine of redemption. If the decisive word in understanding the meaning of sin is 'estrangement,' the central term
in the concept of redemption is 'reconciliation.' When a man is
reconciled, he is no longer separated from God, cut off from his
neighbor, and divided within himself. His anxiety is not dispelled, but he is enabled to live with it, to go on in spite of it.
He gives up his efforts to make himself God, regarding himself
as the navel of the universe, and learns to trust him who is the
true source of his being. The fragmentation of his life is replaced
by an inner integrity, a wholeness, a recovery of his essence,
which is obscured and distorted by his existence. This is the significance of the New Testament's reference to Jesus as the second

Adam, the new man, the new being, in which all men are called upon to participate. The language of Gospels and Epistles abounds in words like reconciliation, reunion, resurrection, all of which have meaning for the psychoanalyst, who reads the neurotic predicament as a story of estrangement and anxiety and interprets the cure in terms of overcoming the separation which divides and of restoring genuine relatedness. Even the term resurrection is not altogether alien to psychotherapy, since many patients, at the end of analysis, speak of their experience as being born again or risen from the dead.

The inner transformation of redemption, the restoration of personal integrity is the goal toward which all of the teachings of Jesus point. He was not concerned with mere outer morality, with conformity to an external legal code. He did not set aside the Law of the Old Testament, but he did radicalize its understanding. Obedience to a law which is given simply because the law demands it, lacks the kind of inner affirmative response which Jesus sought, because such an orientation means that men do only that which is commanded and would do something else if that something else were required. The demand stands in purely formal and external relationship to man without his having made it his own. The fulfillment of an ethical command in such a spirit is to fall far short of the divine will, for God looks into the heart. This is the meaning of Jesus' statement that he came not to destroy the Law but to fulfill it; i.e. to fill it fuller. He knew that it is possible to appear outwardly righteous while inwardly one seethes with unclean desires. His sayings make this abundantly clear. He spoke of those who polish the outside of the cup while inside it is sticky with grime, about the whited sepulchres which look clean and shining to the eye but cover the decay of rotting bones and putrid flesh. He used the term hypocrite, which means in the Greek 'play-actor,' one whose behavior is dictated by his desire to win the approval of the spectators not by his own inner convictions. Jesus evidently did not regard it as any special virtue to refrain from adultery while inwardly filled with lustful desires and lascivious glances. He was no moralist, urging a wrestling match between reason and impure physical desire, with the bout always 'fixed,' so that virtue triumphs. It was not enough for him that will power should pin the shoulders of lust to the mat. He sought rather a transformation of inner attitude so that the conflict was at an end, the struggle finished between what one wants and what one does. His chief concern was for inner integrity, for singleness of heart, for oneness of mind. He did not interpret the human situation as a dualistic warfare between spirit and flesh, a pervasive split in the personality. 'A house divided against itself cannot stand.' 'No man can serve two masters.' 'If thine eye be single . . .' Jesus pointed to purity of heart, to singleness of purpose. As Tennyson put it, 'that mind and heart, according well, may make one music as before.'

Genuine inner integrity, with the accompanying ability to take existential anxiety into the self in full awareness and yet to go on in spite of it, can be achieved, from the Christian point of view, only on the basis of trust and love, the *sine qua non* of redemption. But these are not to be acquired by effort; they are given from beyond the self. Man learns to trust and to love only as he encounters acceptance and affection in his environment, whether as a child or as an adult. If in infancy he is rejected, finding himself in an atmosphere which is hostile and menacing, he is unable to love himself or anyone else, and he is beset by powerful anxieties. If, however, he discovers in later life, through religious conversion or therapeutic insight that he is accepted, then he is empowered to live in love and with his anxiety. Self-acceptance, which is absolutely indispensable to loving others ('Love thy neighbor *as thyself*'), is possible only through being accepted. This is the significance both of the Gospel which announces that God loves men while they are yet sinners and of the psychoanalytic acceptance of the patient. The neurotic on the couch has grown up believing that no one can love him as he is, that he must constantly conform to the wishes and expectations of others if he is to win their approval, and he bitterly resents the demands made of him. He tries desperately to impress and to win the analyst, discovering only gradually and painfully that such tactics are both futile and unnecessary. This was the problem of the Pharisees, at least as they are portrayed in the New Testament, whatever may have been true of them historically; they thought they had to earn the divine love and acceptance by being good. Rejecting themselves as they actually were, they set up an ideal image of themselves as they believed they ought to be and then attempted to prove to themselves and everyone else that they were actually conforming to that ideal image. The Apostle Paul experienced the failure of such an effort and learned, as the analysand must learn, that acceptance and love are gifts, not payments for services rendered.

Love casts out fear. When a man is able to accept himself because he is accepted from beyond himself, his new-found trust and love provide the ground whereon he can stand and face his anxiety. And he can also face himself. His fears have hitherto made it necessary for him to repress those aspects of his personality which he regarded as 'unworthy,' hiding them from himself no less than from others. Out of sight may be out of mind but not out of operation, and repressed drives continue to work, as psychoanalysis has so extensively demonstrated. Anxiety and insecurity about the self render awareness of those repressions impossible, and the person is delivered into the hands of a struggle, a split between the rival factions. When he can accept himself, however, he can accept all of himself; he can afford to look squarely and honestly at what previously filled him with fear and horror. Some of the demons will disappear with the dawn. Hostility and resentment are the offspring of the compulsion to conform, and when conformity no longer is essential to approval, the progeny perishes with the parents. Reparative patterns of behavior, sexual or otherwise, erected as barriers against anxiety, can be dismantled and discarded when the enemy abandons the siege. This is not to say that perfection is achieved, that problems and difficulties do not remain, but they can be endured and even in some cases solved. A tolerance and understanding of the self as well as of others replaces the old suspicion and rejection. A pretense that hostility and jealousy and sensual desire are non-existent is no longer necessary. Such feelings can be recognized and confronted therapeutically, raising the question as to their source in anxiety. One who has arrived at a measure of inner integrity can afford a self-analysis of this kind because it does not represent any basic threat to his personality. He is secure, and he is whole. The neurotic cannot raise such questions because they undermine the entire structure he has built up to defend himself. Emotional sincerity, what the Bible calls 'truth in the inward parts,' is impossible for him in the face of his constant need to hide his real feelings and mask them with counterfeit substitutes. The psychoanalyst discovers almost daily that a patient can endure the pain of an unpleasant insight into himself only on the hard-won ground of security, be it ever so small.

The points of contact between Christianity and psychoanalysis in this connection are as numerous and significant as those of conflict. Both are essentially anti-moralistic, seeking the transformation of the personality rather than the mere suppression of symptoms. Both describe in considerable detail the distortions of human existence under the pressures of anxiety and estrangement, displaying a realistic pessimism. They also share a measure of optimism about man's essence, finding untapped reservoirs of creativity and community which flow forth spontaneously once the dam of fearfulness has been breached. This is the source of the antinomianism of Pauline Christianity and of psychoanalytic permissiveness, a conviction that anti-social, immoral behavior is the result of estrangement. Once that rent is healed so that a man learns what it means to live in love, his neurotic or sinful activities will wither away because they are no longer necessary. Paul saw the Law as superceded by the new convenant relationship with God established by Christ, in which love for God and neighbor becomes the dominating motive force, so Augustine could say, 'Love God and do as you please.' Similarly, the psychoanalyst allows his patient to select his own goals in life because he believes that neurotic behavior vanishes in the wake of neurotic anxiety, releasing the latent forces of love and community. This is not to say that in either case complacency and abandonment of all efforts at self-improvement become the rule. There is always the awareness that a gap exists between what a man is and what he wants to be, but the gap is no longer the decisive element. What is important is that he is accepted and loved as he is. So long as his own perfection, moral or otherwise, is seen as the pre-condition of his acceptance, he is doomed to frustration, since 'none is good save God.' When he knows that he is loved in spite of his failures and shortcomings, he can deal with his flaws in freedom.

Both psychoanalysis and Christianity work toward the creation of emotional sincerity and inner integrity in human beings, casting out the demons of anxiety and estrangement through the power of acceptance and love. Conflicts arise over the role of religious faith in this enterprise. Many analysts are still living on their heritage from Freud, regarding all religion as illusion, the projection of one's childhood need for an omnipotent father into the cosmos, and there is much in popular Christianity which supports such a belief. Promises of an easy peace of mind flow from pulpits like a flood. God is the guarantor of happiness and success to those who believe in him, protecting the faithful from all danger. Even death is glossed over with easy words of immortality. But the transformation of Christianity into a success story is a caricature of a faith whose central symbol is the Cross. No one who takes Biblical religion seriously is under any illusion that his belief acts as a shield against the perils of existence. The man of faith is not different in any respect from anyone else in the world in what happens to him externally. He is subject to exactly the same slings and arrows as any other man. Bacteria or bullets are not deflected by divine intervention. The only differentiation between faith and unbelief lies in the interpretation placed upon events. The Christian sees the hand of God in all creation, meets God and responds to his demands in every human encounter. He is profoundly convinced of the ultimate meaningfulness of life and accepts Christ as the supreme revelation of the character of that meaning, which is to say that he believes that God is love. But he stands daily before a cross and knows that the divine love is a suffering love, a suffering which he may be called upon to share. He is not delivered by his faith from his existential anxiety, but he is enabled to go on in spite of it. Whether his belief in the purposefulness of the world is illusory is a question which cannot be settled by psychological analysis, nor will it be resolved by polemics on either side of the issue. Theologians and psychoanalysts agree in condemning unhealthy religious faith which is masochistic or overly dependent, but the nature of a healthy faith is a subject for further exploration, requiring time and patience. The parallels between Christianity and psychoanalysis are being probed and the conflicts discussed in increasingly fruitful ways. Much of the past controversy has been the result of misunderstanding and misinformation on both sides. Analysts have sometimes been unaware that the best of Christianity makes a clear distinction between religion and magic, eschewing any attempt to manipulate the divine for one's own protection or profit. Clergymen and Christian laymen have frequently been under the misapprehension that psychoanalysts deliver their patients from any sense of responsibility and encourage them to engage in sexual irregularities. Fortunately, there is an increasing enlightenment on both sides, and it is to be hoped that it will continue to grow.

The implications of the Christian doctrine of redemption for an interpretation of sex are fairly obvious. In so far as anxiety and estrangement are dispelled by love and trust, the resulting inner integrity renders possible genuine community, human relationships based upon mutual respect and mature love. Self-respect and respect for others are the two sides of one coin. Integrity precludes allowing one's self to be used as an It instead of a Thou and bars the way to such a use of another person. Maturity means that men and women become more than objects to be exploited for one's own purposes. The Christian sees his neighbor as a brother, a child of God to be regarded and treated with responsible love. He will not pretend that purely erotic attraction is anything more than that, nor will he feel especially guilty about the fact that he finds himself so attracted. Freud was correct in his contention that there are sexual undertones in many Platonic relationships. It is perfectly normal to enjoy a mild erotic stimulation from such activities as dancing, the reading of novels, or watching movies or plays, or swimming at the beach where the two sexes mingle in scanty attire. Even a quiet evening's conversation between a man and a woman physically attractive to each other can serve as a kind of erotic play. There are many occasions when sexual attraction and sexual stimulation are involved without consummation. Sometimes coitus does result from such stimulation and for that reason some individuals are suspicious of situations which contain temptation, but that sort of attitude betrays a negative attitude toward sexuality itself. So long as sexual arousal is not an end in itself, as in pornography, there is nothing evil or sinful in the fact of mutual attraction. When the persons involved are responsible and mature, recognizing the limits to such a relationship, the kind of erotic stimulation provided by social contact can be a source of pleasure which is genuine and innocent. To be sure, there are dangers involved, but no area of life is without perils. The denial of the presence of sexual attraction on the dance floor, the beach, or at the theater is far more dangerous than open admission and free enjoyment. In the final analysis, the only effective barrier to immature and irresponsible sexual behavior is inner integrity. Taboos and inhibitions which are external are destined inevitably to fail. The person of maturity has learned to live in accordance with the reality principle. He does not find himself compelled to act upon every passing impulse, for he has more enduring goals in life than mere immediate gratification. He will neither condemn himself for feeling sexually attracted nor pretend that he has no such feelings. No severe struggle will be involved in suppressing them, because he is more concerned with his total integrity than with the momentary satisfaction of sexual desire. He has too much respect for himself and for others to use persons as objects, as means to an end instead of ends in themselves.

The difficulty with all moralism is, as David Roberts has pointed out,[8]

. . . it assumes that man can live up to any ideal or law that is obligatory upon him. He fulfils what he ought to do by making the principles of reason and conscience triumph over the irrational and sensuous elements in his make-up. . . . This sort of organization of the self . . . represents a continual condition of internal division and strife. The moralistic individual has not made fully 'his own' the ideals which he strives to promote, and they fail to satisfy important needs and capacities. The more he has to force himself by conscientious effort, the more something in him is obviously resisting. The attempt to become virtuous

8. David E. Roberts, *Psychotherapy and a Christian View of Man,* Charles Scribner's Sons, New York, 1950, p. 96f.

against one's 'wants' instead of by transforming them is foredoomed to failure, and the history of moralism illustrates the failure.

Both Jesus and Paul recognized and broke with the moralistic ethics of Pharisaism, substituting the ethics of the law of love. The Christian doctrine of redemption joins forces with the psycho-analytic understanding of human behavior in a common refusal to focus attention on outer behavior, which is purely symptomatic, and in a steady insistence that inner motivation is decisive. Only a transformation of the orientation and attitudes will be effective. 'Except a man be born again.'

This raises the whole question of the status of monogamy in a Christian culture. Is monogamous marriage an order of creation, a dictum of natural law, to be imposed by God or the Christian society upon all men, or is it a matter of Christian liberty, an estate voluntarily embraced by men of inner integrity who know the meaning of mature love? The essence of all Christian ethics is opposed to external legalism, measuring every human relationship by the touchstone of love, a love which is genuine and mature, marked by emotional sincerity and social responsibility. Certainly such a criterion points strongly in the direction of monogamy, but there is some question whether its status as an absolute is justifiable. Luther refused to make it the *sine qua non* of Christian sexual relations. From the point of view of emotional sincerity and inner integrity, it is conceivable that one man should love several women in such a fashion that sexual relations between them would be consistent with mutual affection and respect, and a similar relationship between one woman and several men seems equally feasible. There are many societies where the demands of social responsibility are adequately met by polygamous or polyandrous families, and it is not beyond the realm of possibility that changing social conditions in western culture may require some shift in marital customs. If a situation should arise in which the best interests of personal growth and development could be served more fully by non-monogamous marriages, if, for example, a very large number of men should be killed in a war, leaving thousands of women doomed to spinsterhood, should monogamy remain, the Christian ought to be prepared to meet the issue creatively.

An analogy might be drawn here between marital custom on the one hand and political and economic institutions on the other. Western man is convinced that democracy is the best type of political instrument for conserving the values he cherishes, and that the free enterprise system is best designed to allow personal liberty, individual worth, and initiative to flourish. But it is increasingly recognized that such freedom of enterprise is a luxury which many nations of the world can no longer afford, and the attempt to impose American patterns on these nations is both futile and foolish. They are not to be judged or condemned because history has forced them to adopt another sort of economic organization of their common life. Rather they are to be helped to evolve the best solution to their problems within the framework of their society. To insist that they follow the United States or even the West as a whole, is arrogant imperialism. Similar considerations apply to marital mores. Christendom has traditionally regarded monogamy as the institution best suited to preserve personal values, the atmosphere most conducive to the rearing of healthy and happy children, but this need not imply any condescension toward other cultures with different sexual and marital customs. Questions can be raised about certain types of polygamy, for example, harems, whether they are calculated to foster personal affection and mutual respect. But the plumbline of judgment is love, which is genuinely mature and socially responsible, not monogamy as such, which is no more an absolute than democracy or the free enterprise system. This is not to say that polygamy can be justified under present circumstances in the Christian West on the grounds that a man loves more than one woman, for such a practice would be socially irresponsible, but the possibility must not be denied that some other culture or some future era may successfully combine personal love and social responsibility in a non-monogamous relationship.

When monogamous fidelity is maintained on the basis of external standards, without mutual love and inner integrity, it can be the most fettering and freedom-destroying relationship possible between a man and a woman, a dangerous situation breeding resentment and hatred. On the other hand, monogamy can be the most emancipating of relationships when it is willingly and gladly assumed out of a love which is so satisfying that it has no desire for other sexual outlets. Mild erotic attraction to other persons may co-exist with a genuinely monogamous love, but its consummation would be shallow and cheap beside the deep and enriching coitus which is enjoyed by those who have become one flesh. This is the difference between the ethics of love and those of moralism. The latter focuses all attention on external behavior, demanding rigid conformity to a given norm, without regard to inner motivation. Scrupulous fidelity is demanded and praised even though it covers a reservoir of resentment and adulterous desires. The ethics of love, on the other hand, sees all behavior as symptomatic of the personality as a whole and centers its concern on inner transformation of attitude, rather than outer conformity of act. Love liberates the person from the bondage of his own anxiety and hostility. Moralism adds still more shackles. This was the essential insight of the Apostle Paul, and it was because of that understanding that he waged so energetic a struggle against the Law on behalf of the Gospel.

In summary, it may be said that the doctrine of Creation leads to a positive affirmation of the material world, the human body and all of its parts and functions as the creations of God. Sex is a divine gift, the doorway into community. The doctrine of original sin, however, engenders an awareness of the fact that all men suffer from anxiety and estrangement, separated from God and neighbor and divided within themselves. They develop, perforce, 'reparative' strategies, patterns of behavior which are designed to allay anxiety. This is the significance of all sexual aberrations, whether they are actual perversions or merely the use of sex as a selfish means of exploitation and gratification. Toward all such behavior a moralistic or negative attitude will result only in further anxiety and estrangement, which will in turn reinforce the necessity for reparative activity. The doctrine of redemption is underlined by the psychoanalytic conviction that a therapeutic or redemptive approach to all human beings is essential. Only inner transformation, the replacing of anxiety by trust, of estrangement by community, of conflict by integrity, of repression by emotional sincerity, will in the long run prove of any real avail. Expressed in religious terms, such a transformation occurs in the man who loves God with heart and soul and mind and strength and his neighbor as himself, who is delivered from his anxiety and estrangement by the God who speaks to him the word of forgiveness and acceptance in Christ. It can also be described psychologically as a state of integrated goals, self-acceptance, and relatedness to others, but it is the reality which is important rather than the language used to portray it. Theological orthodoxy is decidedly secondary in significance to existential wholeness, even where the latter may be skeptical or agnostic toward traditional religious language and forms. The Christian can recognize the presence of grace and its healing power and need not be nervous about the fact that others cannot. The psychoanalyst is able to mediate trust and love only because both he and his patient find themselves in a structure of reality where such forces are available. The essential thing is that those forces should be used, not that all men should agree on the names by which they are called. The psychoanalyst seeks to lead his patient into the experience that his theory describes, not into mere intellectual assent to Freudian propositions. The analyst's indifference to the patient's acquaintance with technical terminology should point some moral for the theologian, who is sometimes overanxious about orthodoxy at the expense of actual religious experience. In so far as anxiety and estrangement are genuinely replaced by trust and love, sex ceases to be an instrument of exploitation and becomes a sacrament, the outward expression of an inner union, the fulfillment of one flesh. Inner integrity keeps company with social responsibility, with the acknowledgement of society's legitimate interest in sexual relations, based on the desire to introduce children into life under optimum conditions. But Christianity must refuse to judge sexual morality solely in external terms, centering its concern rather on motivation and meaning, seeking to help those who go astray, not to punish them.

Sex Education

The relationship between organic, constitutional predisposition and the influence of the culture and the environment on sexual behavior is by no means clear. Scientists differ with one another rather sharply in this latest version of the heredity versus environment battle. Kinsey, for example, regards a rather high proportion of sexual 'perversions' as inevitable, as independent of any education or training, because he believes that they are phylogenetically produced. All forms of sexual behavior become for him normal and natural because they are 'being done.' Horney and Rado, on the other hand, although they reach their conclusions by different routes, regard sexual perversions as culturally or environmentally produced, and they believe that the proper educational atmosphere can reduce sexual deviants to a minimum. Kardiner admits that a small number of perverts may be biologically predisposed, but the vast majority he sees as the victims of anxiety created by social pressures. He finds every society forced to adopt some means of preventing irresponsible procreation, a possibility known only to humans, where sexual maturity precedes social maturity by several years, unlike the animals where the two are simultaneous. Western civilization has barred the way to premature parenthood with roadblocks of anxiety and guilt about sex, a device which has on the whole been successful but bought with the price of perversions, reparative patterns designed to allay the anxiety and appease the guilt. If some other method of social control were utilized, the fears would disappear and with them the accompanying deviations. Kardiner cannot agree with Kinsey that toleration and acceptance are the only possible attitudes toward sexual perversion. A change in cultural mores would for the most part dissipate the activities which now require tolerance.

When the doctors differ who shall decide? This whole problem is an area for scientific research, for patient investigation and research. It is not to be settled by fiat, either theological or psychological, but one or two comments can be made from a Christian perspective. The Roman Catholics seem to be right in their opposition to mass sex education, on two counts. In the first place, the real curiosity of children and adolescents is directed at first-hand experience rather than mere factual information. Courses and books about sex are pale substitutes for the living reality itself. And second, most of the difficulties in sexual adjustment spring from emotional attitudes rather than from ignorance or misinformation. One can know all about the facts of life in considerable detail and still be anxious about sex in such a way that reparative patterns develop. On the other hand, a person may not discover where babies come from until late adolescence and still not forfeit his chances for a reasonably good sexual adjustment in life. This is not to say that sex education is not desirable and helpful, but those who believe that it is a panacea are naïve. It is the emotional atmosphere which surrounds the imparting of sexual information which is fundamental, and even parents who convey to their children a positive and healthy attitude may not be able to forestall the corrosive influence of teachers or playmates. In general, however, sexual difficulties in later life are the result of much more than a negative attitude toward sex alone. They almost always prove to be built upon the foundations of anxious and insecure feelings about life as a whole, called forth as a response to a rejecting and critical environment. The ideal situation is the combination of three factors: the basic support of acceptance and affection for the child as a total person, honest answers to his questions as he asks them, and a positive attitude toward the sexual organs and functions. Of course, children must learn a certain modesty of behavior and restraint of language, but both those ends can be attained without creating shame about nudity or guilt about functions of the body.

Parental attitudes toward masturbation are especially important in this connection, and the term masturbation is used here in its wider context of any form of manipulation of the genitals for pleasure. Most children engage in it at an early age, and the parental response is of considerable consequence. If it is taken for granted that the child should explore and experiment with all parts of his body, he accepts his sexual organs as casually as his fingers and toes. Continued and habitual masturbation which is compulsive indicates an inner disturbance, the need for reassurance. Scolding and threatening will only complicate the difficulty. Patient attempts to discover the source of the problem and to deal with that instead of its symptoms will prove the only adequate approach. Masturbation is no more serious than thumb-sucking or nail-biting and should be regarded in exactly that light, as a stage through which all children pass. It is scarcely necessary any more to point out that masturbation can do no physical or psychological damage. Where no restrictions are placed upon children, as in many primitive tribes where even early attempts at coitus are not tabooed, both girls and boys masturbate regularly until marriage without developing either weakened bodies or feeble minds. The sole danger of masturbation lies in the feelings of guilt attached to it. The Christian acceptance of the body has an important place in the training of the young. Children should be taught to value and appreciate their bodies, that sensual pleasure is one of God's gifts to his creatures, not a snare set to trap them.

The Role of Women

Since the question of woman's role in life has been a subject of extensive consideration in both Christian and psychoanalytic interpretations of sex, a special word needs to be said on that score. The differences between the two sexes are probably greater than mere physiology. Freud seems to have been correct in his contention that anatomy is destiny, that women's biological construction has psychological consequences. But many preconceived notions about what those consequences are, about the role required by female biology, are obviously the products of cultural conditioning, of a society where male arrogance has been a dominant factor for centuries. The only thing that seems clear and incontrovertible is the fact that women must bear the offspring. But the bearing and the rearing of children are not so inextricably associated as it was once assumed. The so-called maternal instinct seems to be largely the development of tender feelings toward the objects of attention and care. Fathers who feed, bathe, and dress their children find that their love is not so different from their wives', and there are women who genuinely dislike children and prefer not to have anything to do with them.

Rado's differentiation of the two sexes into push and pull is biologically grounded, but whether psychological analogues are implied is not clear. There are wide variations in feminine function from culture to culture, as Margaret Mead has shown in her *Male and Female*. The better part of wisdom would seem to call for a complete freedom for women to enter whatever realm in life they choose, without, of course, abolishing the special safeguards or working standards set up for the protection of women in industry, in so far as those represent genuine safeguards and not covert barriers to free competition with men. Freed from the restraining ties of masculine domination and the over-compensatory mechanisms evoked by that domination, woman may find her place in life. Meanwhile Christianity must keep in mind two Biblical words: 'In Christ there is neither male nor female' and 'There are diversities of gifts but the same Spirit.' The one obviously requires absolute equality, while the other recognizes that there are different functions to be performed within a harmonious whole. What the diversities of gifts are, whether certain tasks are better performed by women, whether it is purely a question of individual temperament regardless of sex differentiation, is by no means apparent. There are no reserved domains for either sex, apart from procreative roles, where substitution is impossible. An open society, where women are entirely free to seek their own fulfillment may produce new light on the problem. It is interesting to note that many modern young women, having won the right to vote and to hold almost any job, are content to be wives and mothers, a complacency which arouses the scorn of their more militant mothers and grandmothers. But psychologically everyone resents imposed restraints and cheerfully accepts tasks freely assumed.

Conclusion

One final word needs to be said about sin and neurosis. The two terms have been used more or less synonymously in the preceding pages, regarding them both as rooted in anxiety. Sexual perversions and deviations have been described as reparative patterns of behavior, to be approached therapeutically and redemptively. But what of the man whose sex life is 'normal,' who has a positive attitude toward sexuality, who confines his interests and activities to heterosexual relations which are socially responsible and acceptable? Is he, then, 'without sin'? Even the psychoanalyst would answer such a question in the negative, for there is no such thing as perfection in human life. The only man without problems is one who is dead! A state of grace or of health, depending on the standpoint, is characterized not by the absence of problems but by the ability to deal with them as they arise. The character structure is not rigid and the behavior is not compulsive, but flexibility and freedom do not imply infallibility. Errors of judgment and mistaken motives are inevitable. All men are anxious, even those who love God and have been psychoanalyzed. Anxiety is a part of the human situation. This is why the New Testament portraits of Jesus, show even him as beset by anxiety about his mission, about his impending death. Kierkegaard pointed out that freedom always involves anxiety. Without anxiety there is no humanity; there are only robots or animals. In so far as a man is anxious, he will be tempted to withdraw into himself, to be hostile and suspicious of those around him, and to act reparatively, seeking to allay his anxiety. Neither the experience of redemption nor a successfully completed analysis means that a man is free from all anxiety. St. Paul spoke of dying daily unto the old man and of rising daily to newness of life in Christ.

The indestructibility of anxiety and hostility renders perfection impossible and humility essential. A kind of guilt about mistakes and shortcomings can be creative when it is illumined by the spirit of Reinhold Niebuhr's well-known prayer: 'Lord grant me the patience to accept what cannot be changed, the courage to change what must be changed, and the wisdom to know the one from the other.' Even the psychoanalyst recognizes the value of a sense of guilt that is realistic and constructive, which results in action to change what must and can be changed. In fact the absence of any feelings of remorse is the symptom of a very serious illness. Psychoanalysis sees as destructive only that guilt which is false, which weeps over what cannot be changed, which does not lead to positive action but wallows in self-torture and self-negation. The Christian can only agree that such guilt is neurotic and distorted.

The man of faith looks upon his own state as one which both can and cannot be changed. He cannot change the fact that he is always to some degree anxious, estranged from God and his neighbor and divided within himself. Yet there is a sense in which he accepts responsibility for his situation. He knows that anxiety is an inescapable aspect of humanity, but he also knows that he is more anxious and self-centered than he needs to be. He can rearrange his symptoms, altering the particular ways in which his basic anxiety and estrangement affect his behavior, overcoming individual manifestations of anxiety and selfishness. But he can never entirely escape his impulses to use and to exploit others for his own purposes, and he remains always an adulterer, in Jesus' terms, finding himself frequently looking upon a woman to lust after her in his heart, desiring her as a body, a means to the end of his self-gratification. Awareness of the failure to live in love and in trust begets humility, the recognition that one is never perfect, never entirely free of anxiety and self-concern. He lives in a state of tension between what he is (his existence) and what he longs to be (his essence). He has a sense of guilt but he also knows that he lives under grace, that his salvation does not depend upon his perfection. He knows himself to be a sinner but a sinner forgiven and accepted by God as he is. The knowledge of grace delivers him from self-hatred and the moralistic strivings after perfection to which that gives rise. He can accept himself at the same time that he is anxious about himself, knowing how to be abased and how to abound. He faces his shortcomings and failures realistically; yet he can say with St. Paul, 'By the grace of God I am what I am.'

When the Christian is true to his essential faith he gratefully receives the joys of the flesh from the hands of God, regarding sex as a divine gift, making it possible for men and women to express their love for one another by becoming literally one flesh. He turns away from any feelings of guilt or shame about the body or any of its organs and functions and seeks to communicate the full measure of the doctrine of creation to his children. He cultivates growth both in them and in himself toward inner integrity and emotional sincerity, based upon trust in and love for God and neighbor. He will love himself as he loves others, and will, so far as in him lieth, resist the temptation to exploit or to use his fellow creatures for his own selfish gratification. Sex will stand for him as a means of expressing his love in a mature and responsible way, producing children as the perfect symbol of the unity that exists between himself and his mate. He will not condemn those who deviate from 'normal' paths but will seek to help and to heal them, knowing that their behavior is only symptomatic of a deeper disturbance. He will not become perfect; his trust will falter and his faith will fail. He will lust in his heart, but he will not despair. He will rather seek to keep his mind and heart filled with the knowledge and love of God and will run with patience the race that is set before him, looking unto Jesus, the author and finisher of his faith.

INDEX

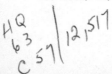